The Windows Guide Book

Copyright © Gill Gerhardi, Vic Gerhardi & Andy Berry 1991

ISBN 07457 0041 1

Published by:

Kuma Computers Ltd
12 Horseshoe Park
Pangbourne
Berks
RG8 7JW

Tel 0734 844335
Fax 0734 844339

This book and the programs within are supplied in the belief that the contents are correct and that they operate as specified, but the authors and Kuma Computers Ltd shall not be liable in any circumstances whatsoever for any direct or indirect loss or damage to property incurred or suffered by the customer or any other person as a result of any fault or defect in the information contained herein.

ALL RIGHTS RESERVED

No part of this publication may be reproduced, stored in a retrieval system or transmitted in any form or by any means, electronic, mechanical, photocopying, scanning, recording or otherwise without the prior written permission of the author and the publisher.

Printed in Great Britain by The Bath Press, Avon

Other Computing Titles From Kuma:

Desk Top Publishing IBM PC & Compatible Micros
Desktop Publishing Sourcebook - Fonts & Clip Art for the PC by Jami Lynne Borman	07457 0030 6
PageMaker 4.0 for Windows by William B. Sanders	07457 0031 4
ZBasic Quick Reference Guide for PC & Mac by John Sumner	07457 0140 X
Desk Top Publishing with Timeworks by Terry Freedman	07457 0147 7
The DR DOS 6 Quick Start Guide by John Sumner	07457 0038 1

Apple Macintosh
Desktop Publishing Sourcebook - Fonts & Clip Art for the Mac by Jami Lynne Borman	07457 0050 0
ZBasic Quick Reference Guide for PC & Mac by John Sumner	07457 0140 X
The Quark Book by Rod Lawton & Isaac Davis	07457 0052 7

Psion Organiser
Psion Organiser Deciphered by Gill Gerhardi, Vic Gerhardi & Andy Berry	07457 0139 6
Using & Programming the Psion Organiser by Mike Shaw	07457 0134 5
File Handling on the Psion Organiser by Mike Shaw	07457 0135 3
Machine Code Programming on the Psion Organiser 2nd Ed. by Bill Aitken	07457 0138 8
Psion Organiser Communications Handbook by Gill & Vic Gerhardi & Andy Berry	07457 0154 X

Psion Series 3
First Steps in Programming the Psion Series 3 by Mike Shaw	07457 0145 0
Introduction to Using the Psion Series 3 by Rod Lawton	07457 0146 9

Atari ST
Atari ST Explored 2nd Ed. by John Braga & Malcolm McMahon	07457 0141 8
Program Design Techniques for the Atari ST by Paul Overaa	07457 0029 2
Programming by Example - ST Basic by Dr. G. McMaster	07457 0143 4
A Practical Guide to Calamus Desktop Publishing by Terry Freedman	07457 0159 0
Desktop Publishing with Timeworks by Terry Freedman	07457 0147 7

Cambridge Z88
Z88 Magic by Gill Gerhardi, Vic Gerhardi & Andy Berry	07457 0137 X

Games Consoles
Sega Megadrive Secrets by Rusel deMaria	07457 0037 3

Commodore Amiga
Program Design Techniques for the Amiga by Paul Overaa	07457 0032 2
Intuition A Practical Programmers Guide by Mike Nelson	07457 0143 4
The Little Red Workbench Book by Mark Smiddy	07457 0048 9

Sharp IQ 7000 & 8000
Using Basic on the Sharp IQ by John Sumner	07457 0034 9

Contents

Introduction	1
Welcome	1
About This Guide Book	1
Who Is This Guide For?	2
How To Use This Guide	3
Keystrokes	3
Tips	3
What You Need Before You Start?	3
Installing Windows	5
Equipped And Ready To Roll	5
Rules Of The Road	5
Why Are The Rules Important?	6
Different Types Of Memory	6
Computer Worlds Are Unstable	6
What's In A Reset?	7
Is Rule 2 Just Being Over Cautious?	8
Beware Complacency	8
Your Invitation	9
PART 1 Preparation	10
Chapter 1 - Surveying The Landscape	11
What Is Windows?	11
The Benefits Of Using Windows	13
The Graphics	13
It's Easy To Use	13
You Only Need To Set Your Printer Up Once	13
Windows Is In Control	14
No 'Modes' To Get Tangled In	14
Displaying More Than One Thing At A Time	14
Multitasking	14
Transfer Information between Files Easily	15
An Application is a Program	15
The Downside Of Windows	15
Extra Kit	16
Hold Your horses	18
Chapter 2 - Learning The Lingo	19
Introduction	19
Windows And MS-DOS	19
Things That You Can Only Do In MS-DOS	19
Major MS-DOS Principles Used By Windows	20
Files	20
Naming Files	20
Filename Extensions	20
Filename Extensions Used By Windows	21
Directories	21

Contents

A Computerised Tree?	22
Path Names	23
Disk Drive Names	24
An Example Of A Path Name	24
Two Files With The Same Name?	25
Wildcards	25
Chapter 3 - First Encounters	**28**
Introduction	28
Mousing Around	28
Mouse Versus Keyboard	28
An Upside Down Mouse	28
Run Out Of Rope For Your Mouse?	29
Buttons	29
Clicking And Dragging	29
Taming Your Mouse	32
All About A Window	32
Things You Can Do With A Window	32
The Grey Buttons	33
Moving Windows With The Title Bar	33
Altering The Size Of A Window	34
Minimised Windows	34
The Menu Bar	35
More To Follow	35
Selecting Options	35
'Greyed Out' Options	35
Keyboard Shortcuts	36
Direct Commands Via The Keyboard	36
Switch options	36
To Close A Menu	36
Scroll Bars	36
Breaking Down A Scroll Bar	37
Moving around With Scroll Bars	37
To Move From Window To Window	38
Letting Windows Arrange Your Windows	39
Tiling Windows	39
Cascading Windows	39
Windows Within Windows	39
Inside A Window	40
Dealing With Dialogue Boxes	41
The CANCEL Button	41
What's Inside A Dialogue box?	42
Making Choices From Boxes Within Boxes	42
Lists Of Choices	42
Hidden Lists	43
Choosing More Than One Item From A List	43
One Choice Only	43
More Than One Choice	43
Selection Sliders	43

Contents

Dialogue Boxes Are Not Always Friendly	44
Using Fonts	44
What You Need To Know About Fonts	45
Attributes of Fonts	45
WYSIWYG?	45
Let's Follow A Font...	46
Bitmapped Fonts	47
How To Find Fonts	48
Which Type Of Font?	48
Yet More Fonts...	48
Using Fonts With A New Printer	49
Getting Help	50
The User Guide	50
The On-Line Help System	50
Inside The Help Window	51
Cross References	51
Different Types Of Cross References	51
The Help Window Menu	52
Copying	52
Printing	52
Making Notes In Help Files	52
Bookmarks	52
Part 2 - The Controllers	53
Chapter 4 - The Program Manager	54
What Does the Program Manager Do?	54
Running programs	55
To Open A Window And Run A Program	55
Adding and Taking Programs/Files off PM	56
Adding More Programs To Program Manager	56
Adding A Program With New	56
Adding A Program With Setup	58
Storing Files With PM	59
The Delete Option	60
How Programs And Files Will Be Displayed On PM	60
Using the Properties Option	61
Changing The Way Programs Look	62
Changing The Description	62
Changing The Icon	62
Group Windows	63
Creating And Deleting Group Windows	63
Creating A Group	63
Deleting Groups	63
Changing The Contents Of Groups	63
Copying Icons	64
Auto Arrange	64
Minimise On Use	65
Arranging Group Windows	65

The Window Menu	65
Arrange Icon Option	65
Selecting A Group	65
Saving The Changes	66
The Task List	67
The Grey Buttons	68
Chapter 5 The File Manager	**69**
Introduction	69
File Manager's Window	69
The Status Bar	70
Minimise On Use	70
Constructing Your Tree	70
Selecting The Right Disk	70
The Sapling	71
The Tree Display	72
Directory Windows	72
Leaping From Bough To Bough	72
Going Down	73
Going Up	73
Climbing Aids	73
Making Your Tree Grow	73
Pruning	74
Working With Files	74
Selecting The Files You Want To Work With	74
Selecting And Working With One File	74
Open	75
Print	75
Move And Copy	75
Delete	75
Rename	76
Change Attributes	76
Read Only	77
Archive	77
Hidden	77
System	77
Selecting More Than One File	78
Selecting A list	78
Scattered Files	79
The Keyboard Selection Mode	79
Select All And Deselect All	79
Using Wildcards As Selection Aids	80
What Can You Do With A Selected Group Of Files?	81
Associate	82
No Selection Needed	82
Run	82
Search	82
Looking At Your Trees And Branches	83
Displaying Directory Windows	83

Contents

Replace On Open	83
Organising Your Files	83
Different Ways Of Displaying Files	84
Putting Files in Order	84
Sorting By Name	84
Sorting By File Type	84
Sorting By Size	84
Sort By Date	85
Juggling	85
Confirmation	85
Confirm On Delete	86
Confirm On Subtree Delete	86
Confirm On Replace	86
Confirm On Mouse Operation	86
Working With Floppy Disks	86
Copy Disk	87
Label Disk	88
Format Disk	88
Make System Disk	89
Saving The Changes	89
Chapter 6 - The Print Manager	**90**
Why Have A Print Manager?	90
Queues, Queues And More Queues	90
Using The Print Manager	91
Print Manager Menus	92
Priority Options	92
Flash Options	92
Network Option	92
Leaving The Print Manager	93
The View Menu Options	93
When Not To Use Print Manager	93
Chapter 7 - Control Panel	**94**
Introduction	94
The Control Panel And WIN.INI	94
Control Panel Settings	95
Group 1	95
International	95
The Country Setting	95
Language	96
Keyboard	96
Measurement	96
List Separator	96
The Four Format Options	97
Date Format	97
Short Date Format	97
Long Date Format	97
Time Format	98
Currency Format	98

Contents

Number Format	98
The Date/Time Settings	99
Group 2	99
The Sound Setting	99
The Keyboard Setting	99
Mouse Settings	100
Mouse Tracking Speed	100
Double Click Rate	100
Swapping Left/Right Buttons	100
Group 3	101
Ports	101
Printers	102
Selecting An Installed Printer	102
Altering A Printer's Configuration	102
From Configuration To Setup	103
Adding A New Printer	104
What Printer?	104
Ready To Install?	104
Configuring A Newly Installed Printer	105
Re-installing A Removed Printer	105
Fonts	105
The Fonts Dialogue Box	106
What's Wrong With Non-Windows Applications?	107
The 386 And Sergeant-Major To The Rescue	107
Putting It All Together...	108
Group 4	109
The Colour Setting	109
A Ready-Made Scheme?	109
Colour Palette	110
Defining Customised Colours	110
Working with Rainbows	110
Working With The Red /Green/Blue Boxes	110
Adding A Customised Colour	111
When Changing Your Colour Scheme....	112
The Desktop Setting	112
Pattern, Wallpaper And Sizing Grid	112
Wallpaper	112
The Sizing Grid	113
Fine Tuning Your Windows	113
Icon Spacing	113
Border Width	113
The Cursor Blink Rate	114
Part 3 - Your Kit	115
Chapter 8 - Paintbrush	116
Before You Start	116
Image Size	116
The Picture May Not Look The Same When It's Printed	117
Which Palette?	117

VI

Contents

The Colour Selection Box	118
Applying The Changes	118
Ways Of Seeing Your Picture	118
Zooming In	118
Pixel View	119
Menu Options	119
Tools	119
Colours	119
Zoom Out	119
Image View	119
Editing Your Picture With Cut And Paste	120
Colours	120
The Screen View	120
The Undo Option	121
The Tools	121
The Cutout Tools	121
The Pick Menu	122
The Airbrush	122
The Text Tool	122
The Font Menu	123
The Style Menu	123
The Size Menu	124
The Erasers	125
The Colour Eraser	126
The Eraser	126
The Roller	126
The Brush	127
The Line Tools	128
The Curve	128
The Shape Tools	129
Customising Your Palette	129
The Paintbrush File Menu	130
The New Option	130
The Open Option	130
The Save Option	131
The Save As Option	131
Choosing The Right Colour Option	132
The Page Setup Option	133
The Print Option	133
The Printer Setup Option	135
The Exit Option	135
Chapter 9 - Write	137
General Features Of A Word Processor	137
How Is Write Different?	138
Necessary Extra Kit	139
Write Files	139
Opening Files	139
File Formats	139

Contents

Saving Write Files	140
Saving Files In Different Formats	140
Make Backups	141
When Is A .BKP A .BAK Extension	141
Extensions For Back-Up Copies In Different Formats	142
Print	142
Printer Setup	143
Page Size	143
Repaginate	143
Page Break Markers	143
Automatic Page Break	144
Page Breaks You Put In Yourself	144
One Of The Things We Love To Hate	144
Editing Text	145
No Change Case Command	146
The Undo Option	147
Undo Typing	147
Undo Editing	147
Undo Formatting	147
Undoing What You Have Undone	148
Cut, Copy And Paste	148
Inserting Paintbrush Files Into Write Files	148
Colours?	148
Positioning Pasted Pictures	149
Selecting Pictures	149
Moving Pictures	150
Altering Your Picture's Size	150
Looking For Something?	151
Find	151
What Can You Look For?	151
General Guidelines	151
The Invisibles	152
Wildcards Again!	152
Whole Word Box	153
Match Upper/Lower Case Box	153
Repeat Last Find	153
Change	154
Go To Page	154
Conjuring Up Odd Characters	154
How To Change Fonts	155
The Fonts Dialogue Box	156
The Fonts Section	156
The Sizing Section	156
Attributes Section	157
Using Different Fonts/Attributes In The Same File	157
Laying Out Your Text	158
The Ruler	158
Aligning Text	158

Contents

The Left Option	159
The Right Option	159
The Centred Option	159
The Justified Option	160
The Line Spacing Options	160
Indents	160
Headers And Footers	161
Tabs	162
Setting Tabs	162
Working With Tabs	163
The Page Layout Option	163
Chapter 10 - The Clipboard	164
Copying, Cutting And Pasting	164
A Tour Of Clipboard's Menus	165
The File And Edit Menus	165
The Display Menu	166
Transferring Data Between Applications	166
The Print Screen Key	167
Chapter 11 Notepad	169
Notepad - The Basics	169
Files You Can Change With Notepad	169
Notepad And Write	169
Notepad Files	170
A Tour Of Notepad	170
A Do-it-Yourself Change Option	171
Page Setup	171
No Large Files Here	173
The Big Four Files	173
Syd - The System Configuration Editor	174
Chapter 12 - Cardfile	175
Understanding Cardfile	175
What Is A Database?	175
What To Store On Cards	176
Organising Your Database	176
Keywords	176
Fields	176
Planning Your Database	177
Looking At Your Database	177
Starting Cardfile	177
Viewing Cards	178
Searching Through Cards	178
Changing Index Lines And The Information Area	178
Adding Pictures To Cards	179
Printing Cards	179
Page Setup	180
Merging Card Files	180
Autodialling	180
Preparing To Use Autodial	180

IX

Autodialling A Number	181
Chapter 13 - The Clock And The Calendar	182
The Clock	182
A Minimised Clock All The Time?	182
The Calendar	183
Calendar - The Basics	183
A Tour Round The Menus	185
Travelling In Time	186
Chapter 14 - The Calculator	187
What You'll Learn	187
Calculator Basics	188
Using The C, CE And Back Buttons	188
The Memory	188
Using The Standard Calculator	189
Using The Scientific Calculator	189
What's Operator Precedence?	189
Loads Of Brackets	190
The Scientific Functions	191
The 'Programmer's' Functions	192
The Statistics Box	195
What Is The Statistics Box?	195
Opening The Statistics Box	195
Controlling The Statistics Box	195
Copying Numbers To The Statistics Box	196
Right, Now For Some Lies...	197
Putting It Together...	197
Other Uses For The Statistics Box	198
The Clipboard And The Calculator	198
Chapter 15 - The Terminal	200
No Computer Should Be An Island	200
Who's Out There?	200
The Downside	201
Transferring Files	201
Before You Start...	202
Settings	203
Phone Number	203
Terminal Emulation	204
Terminal Preferences	204
Function Keys	204
Text Transfers	204
Binary Transfers	205
Communications	205
Modem Commands	205
Saving The Settings	206
Getting On-Line	206
Welcome To The Wonderful World Of Talking Computers	207
Using On-line Services	207
Transferring Files	208

Contents

	Compressing Files	208
	Sending Just Part Of A File	209
	Oh, It's Not Working	209
	Nothing Works At All	210
	How To Test The Communication Link	210
	What Is A BOB?	211
	Alternatives To BOBs	211
	What Does A BOB Do?	211
	Your Testing Strategy	212
	Step 1 - Checking that your computer is working	212
	2 - Testing Compatibility	213
	3 - Setting the Speed and Flow Control Method	215
	It Nearly Works	216
Chapter 16 - The Recorder		218
	What Does Recky Do?	218
	Some Jobs Recky Could Do...	218
	Getting The Most Out Of Recky	219
	What Is Recky Recording?	219
	What's A 'Macro' Doing On A Micro?	220
	Macros Within Files	221
	What's Nesting?	221
	Merging Files Of Macros	222
	Telling Recky What To Record	222
	Running Macros From The Program Manager	223
	Shortcut Key Codes	224
	Creating A Rolling Demo	224
	The Problem Page	225
	Recky Hates The Mouse	225
	Recky Doesn't Like Movement	225
	Recky Gets Confused By Overlapping Windows	225
Part 4		226
The Back Pack		226
	Installing Windows	227
	Do I Need To Install Windows?	227
	Preparing To Install Windows	228
	Can My Computer Run Windows?	228
	Backing-Up And Checking Your Hard Disk	229
	Creating An Emergency Restart Disk	229
	Installing Windows	229
	Using Setup To Install Windows	230
	First Installation Screen	231
	Second Installation Screen	232
	Third Installation Screen	232
	Fourth Installation Screen	234
	Fifth Installation Screen	234
	Sixth Installation Screen	235
	Seventh Installation Screen	236

Contents

A Diversion Into MS-DOS Land	236
CONFIG.SYS And AUTOEXEC.BAT - Your Options	237
Leaving Setup In Control Of Autoexec And Config	237
Reviewing Autoexec And Config	237
Creating Copies Of Autoexec And Config	238
Eighth Installation Screen	239
Ninth Installation Screen	240
Tenth Installation Screen	240
Eleventh Installation Screen	240
Running Windows For The First Time	241
Running Setup Once Windows Is Installed	241
Installing A New Version Of Windows	242
Windows Setup Explained	243
Changing Basic Hardware	243
Adding New Applications To Windows' Repertoire	244
Housekeeping For Windows	245
Backing-Up Your Hard Disk	246
Checking Your Hard Disk	247
Creating An Emergency Restart Disk	248
Preparing For Disasters	249
What's The Partition Table?	249
What Is CMOS RAM?	250
What's In The BIOS?	250
The CMOS RAM Battery	252
Running Non-Windows Programs	252
What Are PIF Files?	253
Basic PIF Editor Options	254
PIF Editor In Standard Mode	254
PIF Editor In 386 Enhanced Mode	255
Choosing PIF Settings	256
The Window Control Menu For A Non-Windows Application	257
Using The Clipboard With Non-Windows Applications	257
Chapter 18 - The First Aid Box	258
Running Windows If WIN Doesn't Work	258
Windows Modes	259
No Life In Your Mouse	260
No Display?	260
Unrecoverable Application Errors	261
After A UAE...	262
Crash Recovery	263
Recognising A Crash	263
After A Crash...	264
Disaster Recovery	265
Disaster Recovery - Initial Steps	265
Disaster Recovery - Before You Panic	266
Cures For Windows Traveller's Diseases	267
Out-of-Memory Disorder	268
Shortness Of System Resources	269

XII

Contents

Out-of-Disk Space Sickness	269
Contents of \WINDOWS Directory	271
Contents of \WINDOWS\SYSTEM Directory	271
Slowness Syndrome	272
The Truth About Improving Windows Performance	272
Cures for Slowness Syndrome	272

Introduction

Welcome

You are about to embark on a fabulous journey. There are many of you waiting to start and some who have come by this guide book late in their journey. Whichever you are, this guide will be useful. Most of you will travel alone, like Buddhist monks, rarely meeting a fellow traveller who you can swap tales with.

The world you are about to enter is generally - you will be happy to hear - a friendly one. The natives welcome travellers with open arms. But we will warn you now, there is a dark side that seems to relish giving lone travellers a hard time. You will need to be on your guard.

Your mission is to learn about this world. You will need to observe its processes, map its terrain, become fluent in its language and understand its customs. You must be ready to report on what you have found out. Your knowledge could be vital to yourself, and others later.

This will also be a great character building exercise because the going will not always be easy. There are ridges of snow clad mountains to traverse and fast flowing rivers to cross. You will be given some equipment to take with you but this will mainly help you with your information gathering task. You will have to rely on the land for everything else.

Through it all we will be there at your side. Giving you advice, interpreting when things get difficult and offering solace when things go wrong. Above all, we shall share in your triumphs.

About This Guide Book

Yes, this is another book on Windows 3.0! As you've probably already seen, this is no ordinary Windows book. It is no ordinary computer book either, for that matter. Most computer books are written by the boffins who design, program and 'live' computers. Computers are so much a part of their lives that they talk a different language to most mortals. Their books can only be understood by the initiated few. This book will enable an outsider to become a member of that merry band even if you're a novice.

One of us authors might be categorised as a boffin but the other two certainly are not. This balance has enabled us to do two things. Firstly, to tackle some of the more technical topics that

Introduction

need to be covered for a thorough understanding of Windows. Secondly, we have been able to write this book in everyday language that should be understandable even if you have no prior experience of computers.

We've done a detailed survey and covered all the ground ahead of you. We are not sending you into uncharted territory, we have gone before you to the furtherest reaches of Windows world.

If you are computer literate, the Windows package is so different in the way it allows you to work with your PC that it might be easier to forget what you know and start again. You do not need to worry: Windows is different but it's certainly easy. Sometimes, so easy that it appears to be difficult!

Who Is This Guide For?

Who can join the trail? Anyone who wants to learn about the magic of Windows. Whether you are just starting out, have already travelled some miles alone but now need a helping hand, or you have come up against an impenetrable obstacle that has brought your journeying to a halt, this guide will help.

How To Use This Guide

Firstly we strongly recommend that you use this guide in conjunction with the official guide. Unlike most travellers into the world of computers, the official guide book gives you a very good idea of the terrain that you will be travelling through and the customs and temperament of the natives. There are gaps in what it tells you and it is sometimes biased towards the good features in the landscape and omits to tell you about the bad side. It is still far better than some other manuals that we have had to grapple with.

The official guide omits to tell you that there are Ghouls and Gremlins waiting in the shadows to drag unsuspecting travellers into the oblivion of the mire. If you are prepared, and ever vigilant, you have the power to overcome most of the damage that such evil-doers can cause. If they catch you unawares, however, they can do a lot of damage. We aim to give you the knowledge that will engender that vigilance.

We must warn you now, and will be doing so frequently throughout the time we are your companions, that the land can be deceiving. Whilst the going is easy - and it often will be once you have found your rhythm - you will be lulled into a false sense of security. When you are least expecting it the Gremlins will strike. SO BE ON YOUR GUARD.

Keystrokes

Any key sequences or commands that you have to type are printed in a different font between square brackets. A '+' between them mean that you have to press both or occasionally all the keys together. We have used the keynames as they appear on the keyboard.

Tips

Throughout this guide there will be Tips that are separated from the main text. The information they contain, although relevant to the text above and below them, is also useful in other sections of the book. Their titles are indexed and there is a separate Table of Contents for Tips. So you will be able to use them for quick reference.

What You Need Before You Start?

The world that you are about to enter is a magical one. You can go on this journey without leaving your own world but you will need some equipment before the journey can commence.

Introduction

The equipment is your means of access to the world without you having to set foot there. It will consist of:

a big square box
a monitor
a keyboard and possibly
>a mouse
>a printer

There are a host of other possibilities for additional equipment which may prove helpful on your journey.

The box, which may make a humming noise, is the means by which you can maintain contact with this new world.

The monitor is your eyes. It behaves like a viewing screen but it is totally under your control. You can choose what you want to see and where, with the keyboard or your staff (mouse), and it will appear on the screen.

Your staff is the most magical piece of equipment in your possession. It gives you direct contact to the world beyond the screen as it crosses the boundary between your world and Windows. The keyboard gives you contact too, but in a less direct way. When you rest your hand on the top part of your staff (the mouse) and move it gently, the bottom tip will move in the viewing screen. You must hold the mouse the right way round with the wire pointing away from you, otherwise the tip will move in the opposite direction to the mouse. The tip is normally the shape of a pointer or arrow but can change shape depending on where it is in Windows world. While it is an arrow you can use it to show where you

Introduction

want to go and what you want to do. More magical still, you can pick things up with it and move them about.

That is enough chatter, it's time to get down to details!

To get the very best adventure out of Windows you need to run it on an IBM PC compatible 486 computer with all the trimmings: colour monitor, hard and floppy disk drive, oodles of memory and other accessories that are compatible with Windows. If you have a lesser system than that (who hasn't) you are not excluded from the adventure. Windows can work on slightly slower 386's or 386SX's and also has two other levels that you can use to run it on even slower models.

Whatever hardware you have got, you will need to run MS-DOS Operating System version 3.1 or higher before you install Windows.

Installing Windows

The Window installation program will do most of the work for you but, to do its job properly, it will need some information from you. Some of the options will profoundly affect the ways Windows works with your computer so it is worth spending some time getting it right. If you need help, or want to check that you got it right when you set it up previously, turn to The Tool Box chapter.

Equipped And Ready To Roll

The world that you are about to enter is a very beautiful one. It is full of breathtaking views that portray a new dimension of the computer world. But it is also prone to cataclysmic disasters that come out of the blue. To weather these, as well as the Gremlin attacks, you will need to follow the 'rules of the road'.

Rules Of The Road

You needn't groan, there aren't many! Since you have just joined the ranks of nomads, you need to be familiar with the rules that they live by. Such people don't take kindly to authority. The few rules they do obey they've made up themselves, for their own and fellow travellers' safety. So you can be sure that these rules are vitally important:

RULE 1   **Always save the file you are working on frequently.**

Introduction

RULE 2   You must keep back-up copies on floppy disk of everything on your computer that is important to you.

Why Are The Rules Important?

To understand why obeying these rules is so important you need to understand something of the nature of computers. If you already know the reasons you can skip the next section. Don't think, however, that you can get away with ignoring the rules. Knowing why you should obey them, but not following them, will not save you from the catastrophes that lie in wait for law-breakers.

Different Types Of Memory

Inside your computer you have 'RAM' which is short for Random Access Memory. This is where all the programs are run from and where all their associated files are stored while you are working with them. RAM is very fast at getting information, storing it and finding it again. Its main disadvantage is that it only retains the information while it is being supplied with power. Every time you turn your computer off, its memory is wiped clean. That is why you have got a disk drive.

Disk drives record the electronic pulses - that are the basic unit that any computer works with - in the same way as an audio cassette player records sound waves. They have the added advantage of being able to move to any track quickly so perhaps a disk is more like a record or compact disk. Disks allow you to retain copies of work you have in RAM before you turn the computer off. You can over-record an old copy with an updated one or delete work that you no longer want to keep.

Computer Worlds Are Unstable

We have already issued dire warnings about Gremlins and catastrophes and this is the reason. Computers are machines and so we expect them to be very predictable. In theory, computers are the same as simple machines that, short of mechanical breakdown, will perform a specific function at the touch of a button. That doesn't always happen with computers. Why? One reason is their tremendous complexity which means that they sometimes simply tie themselves in knots. The knot tying exercise is even more likely to happen if the user tells the computer to do something out of sequence. Windows will allow you to do almost anything in any order!

Another reason for a computer's instability is that they can only be as good as the people who design, build and write the programs that run them. Engineers and programmers are as human

Introduction

and unstable as we all are, so there is no reason to suppose that computers won't be unstable too. Maybe we have less to fear about the computers of the future than science fiction has led as to believe!

So what form can this instability take? The worst is a 'lockup' or 'crash' where your computer is totally out of control. It will either not let you communicate via the keyboard or mouse or it will appear to have a mind of its own and carry out instructions not given by you. The only way out is to do a 'reset' to regain control.

There are three ways of doing a reset:

If you can still communicate with your computer via the keyboard, you can press [Ctrl + Alt + Del]

If touching the keys doesn't have any effect you will have to resort to the RESET button. That is normally on your computer itself, not the keyboard.

If the problem involves your mouse as well, the two options above may not put it right. The mouse has a tiny microprocessor inside. This will not be reset until you turn the power off and then on again.

Tip: How To Leave Windows Using The Keyboard

If something goes wrong with your mouse but you don't want to do a reset, you will need to use the keyboard to save everything first, then leave Windows in the normal way.

Pressing [Alt F S] will normally save what you are doing. [Ctrl + Esc] will put you into the Task List. [Down Arrow] until the Program Manager is highlighted then [Enter] will put you into the Program Manager. [Alt Spacebar C] will select exit and one final [Enter] should be enough to exit Windows but you may have to press Enter again if you haven't saved the files in any other window.

What's In A Reset?

A reset is pretty brutal. It will tell your computer to stop everything, without closing Windows down. All files you were working on in RAM will be lost. After checking to see that the hard disk is still intact, you will have to run Windows again and open any copies of the files that you

Introduction

made before you did the reset. If you have no back-up copies you will literally have to start again. If, however, you can fall back on the saved versions of the files on hard disk you should only have a bit of catching up to do. Although that very much depends on how long before the crash you last saved your working files. This is why RULE 1 is important.

Please note If you have to do a reset please go to THE Tool BOX Chapter before carrying on.

Is Rule 2 Just Being Over Cautious?

You need to keep copies of all files on floppy disk (RULE 2) because:-

Firstly   you cannot always recover all your files from your hard disk after a crash. Most files saved on hard disk should still be there. If the hard disk was being 'accessed', that is, if a file was being copied from RAM to the hard disk or vice versa, there is a small risk of losing that particular file from the hard disk.

Secondly   Something may go mechanically wrong with either the computer or the hard disk and you could lose everything.

Ideally you would copy the whole hard disk to floppy disks, but that is not terribly realistic. Unless you are lucky enough to have a tape drive that you can leave unattended to do it all for you. But please keep multiple copies - at least one on hard disk and one on floppy disk - of anything important.

Beware Complacency

The biggest Gremlin is called Complacency. While you are using your computer without any problems the need for back-ups doesn't arise. So it is almost inevitable that you will break both rules. It will only be when things go wrong that you will remember them and curse yourself for a fool.

What happens after complacency's first massive attack is a worse stain on each of our characters. After ignoring the warnings and coping with the consequences, common sense should dictate that we obey the rules from then on. But do we? Well, initially we do. We all put up the defences very vigorously and become extremely law abiding for a short time. Then after a while, short sightedness sets in because nothing goes wrong and we relax our vigilance yet again.

It is inevitable that Complacency strikes again and we go through the whole tortured process of trying to recover our losses again! You can be sure that Complacency is always watching you. If your defences are up, he very often won't bother to come after you at all. But he will be ready to strike at the worst possible moment, when your defences are down AND when you stand to lose a great deal of important information.

Of course, if he gets his timing wrong and attacks when you are prepared it will not affect you at all. All you have to do, once you have regained control, is to load your back-up files and simply carry on.

Every traveller has to learn the hard way. We did, so we don't see why you shouldn't have to as well! If you obey the rules from the start you will save yourself much anguish, heartache and (probably most importantly) work. So beware Complacency!

Your Invitation

You are about to embark on a fabulous magical journey. Like all good adventures you will experience good times as well as bad. Wandering aimlessly through this world would be fun but we suspect that most of you will be wanting to gain something out of this journey. Whether it is knowledge for its own sake that you are seeking, or ways of using this new world to help you in your everyday lives, we cannot determine. But you will be able to use any information that you gain and the equipment you have been supplied with after your journey is over.

Whatever your motivation we will endeavour to act as your guide. We'll point out the pitfalls and mires as well as sharing with you the glories of this bright new world. Sling your knapsack over your shoulder, gird your loins - or whatever the female equivalent is - and head into the wind. Accept our invitation and join us on a great adventure...

PART 1 Preparation

No self-respecting explorer would venture on an expedition without having done extensive preparation first. You, need to glean every bit of information you can about the world you are about to enter. Let's pause, just briefly we promise, and survey the land that we are about to journey through. We will also be covering the history of computers and the language of Windows.

Chapter 1 - Surveying The Landscape

Before you dive in at the deep end it might be a good idea to do some homework. At the very least, we need to find out what Windows is and how it fits into the global scheme of things.

What Is Windows?

There are many grand sounding words that are used to describe Windows. Words like 'environment' and 'interface' are tossed around with gay abandon by the boffins. They always seem to include 'graphical' somewhere too, often stuck on the front of these other words. Now they obviously understand what they are talking about, but do you honestly know what a 'graphical environment' is? The non-boffin on the team certainly didn't when we started writing, indeed we might have ended up writing about power saving computers curing the greenhouse effect for all they knew!

When you think about what the individual words mean it does slowly begin to make sense. So, Sit down and make yourself comfortable, we are going to tell you a story...

A long long time ago, when computers had not been around for long, the only people who had any idea of how to use them were the mad scientists who had invented them. Computers were great big things that filled rooms much bigger than churches. They had buzzers and beeps and flashing lights on them. They certainly looked very impressive but they could only do very repetitive arithmetic.

Since then, and remember it is only about forty years ago that the story started, computers have gone from the size of a warehouse to ones small enough to fit into the palm of your hand. As the size went down, memory capacity went up in an opposite curve. Increased memory size meant that although they could still only calculate fairly simple arithmetic, they could work much faster and store more information. This enabled them to work with bigger programs. The most important thing that happened, however, was that they went down in price. These developments made them more accessible to larger numbers of people.

Concurrent to that process, the programmers and others on the software side came to realise that they too had to come out of their ivory towers. Instead of writing individual packages for individual clients, they started to write for the mass market.

Chapter 1 Surveying The Landscape

One of the main things that had got in the way of programmers writing for the mass market was the lack of recognised standards. With myriads of manufacturers all producing their own hardware, software had to be written to run on just one model. They had to write their programs from scratch. Before they could start programming the computer to do the task they had in mind they had to program it to receive, store and retrieve information.

Then two things happened. First someone wrote a DOS or 'disk operating system'. In its fully refined state, DOS provides the means to make the computer work. It defines certain commands and procedures that allow you to type text or programs in, change them, store them all in an organised way and then retrieve them again.

Secondly IBM brought out their PC range. This rapidly became a recognised hardware standard. Very soon after its arrival other makes of computer and their accessories were either IBM PC compatible or they weren't. IBM, of course, had a DOS written for their PC.

With all that accomplished for them, software designers were free to leave all the boring bits to the DOS package and get on with writing more weird and wonderful things for your PC to do.

Here endeth the history lesson! How does all this effect you? Well, when you first get your PC you can't do anything with it until you have loaded in a DOS. Once you have an operating system on board you can tell your PC what you want it to do as long as the task is fairly basic. With just DOS on board your computer is still more of a programmer's tool than something Joe Bloggs from number 33 could use. Most of us would need to buy programs that:

    A. works with the DOS.
       And
    B. perform the task you want your PC to do.

Before we can actually do anything with our new PC.

DOS programs have become a bit like two way life support systems. Both PCs and the programs written for them would be useless to most people if DOS were to be hijacked. But many programs written for the PC work in very different ways, even though they all work with the same DOS. So, for example, you may have three different programs that are all involved in editing text in some form. Perhaps a word processor, a diary and a communication package. You probably have three lots of different commands to learn to edit text.

The creators of Windows have taken a leaf out of DOS's book because Windows too is a life support system. Only it has a triple role compared to DOS's double one. Windows provides us users with a link to the DOS, the PC and the programs you use.

Any programs that use Windows have the way they are displayed on the screen and the way the user works with them determined by Windows. So that's where the 'environment' comes into it. Windows and DOS together provide a working environment for all the other programs.

As far as us users are concerned, Windows is a godsend. You needn't be a programmer to make things happen on your PC - it is all much more approachable.

The Benefits Of Using Windows

The Graphics

Part of this approachability is due to the graphics. Little pictures, called 'icons', have been used as well as words to represent major options that you have available. It is much friendlier because you can pick things up and move them around yourself, you aren't dependent on the computer working from typed commands. The graphics make it feel as though you are dealing with something tangible, not just a computer program.

Windows is not just one program - as you will see when you look at the Windows directory in the File Manager - but a mass of something like eighty different programs and their associated files all working together. You will work closely with eighteen of those. Each of the main programs have their own graphic representation in the Program Manager, your first port of call when you enter Windows.

It's Easy To Use

Once you have been introduced to the way Windows works, and how you can work with it, you will be surprised at how easy it is to use. The same basic commands are used universally throughout all the programs. You only have to learn them once.

You Only Need To Set Your Printer Up Once

You only need to set your printer up once. Normally each individual program that uses the printer has its own way of communicating with it. With Windows, all programs share the same printer set-up procedures.

Chapter 1 Surveying The Landscape

Windows Is In Control

Windows controls everything for you, down to the level of not even giving you options that you can't use at that particular time. It normally won't let you do anything silly. If you select an option that has significant consequences Windows will ask you to confirm that you know what you are doing.

No 'Modes' To Get Tangled In

Another big advantage is that Windows is 'modeless'. With a conventional program you ask it to carry out a specific task and it goes into a different section with a different display. You then have to get out of that 'mode' again before you can do anything else. With Windows everything is done via 'pop up' or 'pop down' lists of options; you never leave the file you are working on.

If, for example, you want to search for a word in Write, just select the Search menu and then Find. You will be given a smaller window superimposed on top of the file you are working on to tell it what to look for. The display will show what you are looking for. Throughout the operation you stay in the file; you don't have to worry about 'getting out' of anywhere when you want to carry on editing.

Displaying More Than One Thing At A Time

Because you are able to divide your screen into 'windows' you can display more than one program at a time. In fact you can display as many as you like. Or you can have multiple copies of one program open with a different piece of work in each. You can only actually be working in one window because our brains can only do one thing at a time, unless you are a chess Grand Master! The piece of work that you are working with will be in a highlighted window. The ability to be able to switch between different documents, to check details or jot down notes for example, is incredibly useful.

Multitasking

Although we might be only able to do one thing at a time your computer appears to do more. Strictly speaking it too can only do one thing at a time. However, it can work a thousand times faster than us, so it can appear to be doing more. It is actually doing one thing for twenty milliseconds (that is a tiny fraction of a second) and then moving to something else for twenty milliseconds. It is so quick that it appears to be working on everything at the same time. It is a bit like an animation that is built up from still pictures to give a moving image.

Chapter 1 Surveying The Landscape

Multitasking means that you can be printing via the Print Manager while you are receiving data from the telephone via the Terminal program. You could also be editing a file in Write at the same time.

A task in this land is something big enough to be performed by a program not something small that you could do yourself.

Transfer Information between Files Easily

Using the Clipboard you can transfer information between files very easily. You can even move parts of files (or whole files) into different applications.

==
An Application is a Program
==

You can Cut or Copy the section of the file you want to move to the Clipboard. Then you can Paste it into a totally different Write file, for example.

But the Clipboard is even more useful than that. You can draw a graph in Paintbrush and then Paste it into a document in Write. Or you can compose a document in Write and then copy it to Terminal to be transmitted down the telephone line to America.

Whenever you need to move a block of information around, even to move it within the file that you are currently working in, the Clipboard is ready to accept it.

The Downside Of Windows

We have already warned you that there is a downside to this journey and that not everything is going to be plain sailing. There are many general factors that we have found, both in Windows itself and the accessories that go with it, that make the package less easy to use. These are listed below. It must be stressed that these are only our opinions. Opinions are affected by personal preference, expectations and by the equipment that you are using. You will probably not agree with some of our grumbles but may find some bigger ones of your own that we haven't mentioned.

Speed - Windows and its accessories are slow, particularly if you are unlucky enough to be running them on a slower machine.

Chapter 1 Surveying The Landscape

Reliability - No computer system is one hundred percent reliable but one running Windows is even less reliable than some. If you start multitasking or running non-Windows software under Windows' control, reliability goes down even further.

A whole new concept - There is a great deal to learn initially before you can start using Windows. You need to learn it all, even if you only want to use the word processor.

You need a great deal of memory - Windows is extremely greedy with memory. It needs at least one but ideally four megabytes of RAM as well as about five megabytes of disk space to run. That's why you must have a hard disk.

Too Flexible - We never thought that we would ever complain that a computer system was too flexible but this one definitely is! There are so many different ways of doing things that even after you have learnt all the commands, you can still do something by mistake and not have a clue what you did. Double clicking the mouse is a good example because that invariably does something totally different to a single click. This can be very confusing and a little disturbing while you are finding your way around. We should add, however, that the consequences of such flexibility are never disastrous, they just turn the beginners amongst us into complete nervous wrecks!

Most of the bad things about Windows are due to its 'all powerful' nature. It is trying to make the user's life easier. To do that it has to know what is happening everywhere in the system, which slows it down a great deal. The flexibility of Windows will be an asset to the experienced user, it is just difficult when you are starting out.

Extra Kit

On entering Windows you were given some accessories to help you keep a record of what you find out about this new world. Looking at the variety and number of these devices, you are expected to be quite busy, not only recording what you find, but also interacting with other travellers. Below is a brief introduction, the details will come later.

You have a clock which is like a wall clock except that you can change it from an analogue to a digital display at the flick of a switch. If it is running on a different time zone to yours, you change it from the main Control Panel, not from within the clock itself.

You have a calendar that will double as an appointments diary - who knows how many meetings you are going to need to organise along the way? You can ask for a reminder alarm either at the time you have an appointment or up to ten minutes beforehand. There is also room for three

Chapter 1 Surveying The Landscape

lines of notes each day. If you have got some spare time it might be a good idea to type in [BEWARE COMPLACENCY] or [I MUST DO MY BACK-UPS] at the bottom of every page!

You have been supplied with a notepad for rough work. This will only let you type and store text. You can edit the text and search for a specific word within it. You can move blocks of text either around that notepad or between the Notepad and other applications. You can also date stamp each entry so that you can keep a log of what you have done, seen, or heard during the day.

Write is your word processor. As with most word processors you can type text, edit it and move it around. Once you are satisfied with it (and before for back-up purposes) you can save it to a file or print it on your printer. Word processors are the ideal tool whatever you are writing, whether it is a letter home or your Annual Report. Write, however, is no ordinary word processor because you can determine the size and typeface of characters that are displayed and printed. Also, because Windows has a painting program, you can move small pictures, graphs or diagrams from there into whatever you are working on in Write. You could even design your own postcard home if you wanted to!

You have also been given a card index system to keep names and addresses safe. It is called Cardfile and is much more useful than the traditional box of cards. It keeps the cards in alphabetical order for you, and will magic the card that you ask for to the top of the pile in less than the twinkling of an eye.

There is a calculator in your pack. In fact there are two calculators; a standard one and a scientific one. You will be able to put these to work adding up your expenses, assuming you need a total for the fairy godmother who is paying for your adventure!

Paintbrush is your artist's tool box. You have more tools than most artists would dream of, plus a palette of colour that would turn most green with envy. You can of course mix your own colours too. So, whether it is a map to show where you have travelled or a bar chart to show how your future productivity will improve with Windows, Paintbrush is there to help.

You have also been supplied with a means of communicating with other computers in the outside world. The Terminal in your pack will be able to send and receive messages or files from computers anywhere in our world. Providing they have their own communications program. Both computers will need a Modem to link them to the telephone network. As well as sending and receiving messages you will also have access to vast amounts of information that is stored in the centralised computers at on-line service companies.

You also have a very small but friendly robot called, very unimaginatively, Recorder. With his

Chapter 1 Surveying The Landscape

help you can automate repetitive tasks. If you show Recky the recorder what you want him to do step by step just once he will then repeat the task whenever you want him to.

Hold Your horses

We know you are all itching to get started but before you load all this kit and let the wagons roll, you need to understand the basics of the language used in Windows world. So the next Chapter will be your introductory lesson in Windows linguistics.

Chapter 2 - Learning The Lingo

Introduction

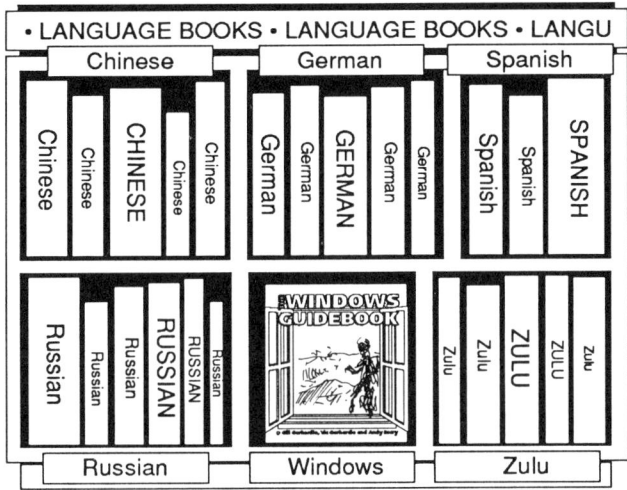

Chapter Two is for those of you who are either new to computers or want a refresher course. We will cover the basics of what you need to know about the MS-DOS operating system before you can effectively use Windows.

Windows And MS-DOS

Despite the Windows disguise you are still using an MS-DOS computer and there will be times when you will need to use MS-DOS rather than Windows. You need to understand the main principles that MS-DOS uses to organise data on your disk.

Things That You Can Only Do In MS-DOS

There are certain activities that you can only do from MS DOS.

Chapter 2 Learning the Lingo

The main one is being able to check your hard disk for open files after a crash. The MS-DOS program that will do that is called CHKDSK. Although it is possible to enter MS-DOS from the DOS Prompt option in Program Manager, you must leave Windows before trying to run CHKDSK. See the Tool Box chapter for details on checking your disk.

Other MS-DOS programs like Backup can be run from within Windows.

Major MS-DOS Principles Used By Windows

There are many MS-DOS concepts and terms that Windows uses. Many are now generic throughout the computer world - these are mainly used to describe the way MS-DOS organises the data on your disk.

Starting at the smallest unit of collected information:

Files

You use files to store your work on disk. Unlike the files you store in filing cabinets, however, these files normally only contain one piece of work.

Naming Files

There are strict rules about filenames. They can have up to eight letters, numbers or a combination of both. They can be typed in upper or lower case but will normally appear in upper case on the display. There are a few names (listed on Page 122 of the official User Guide) that have already been assigned to files or devices so these are out of bounds to you. Otherwise you can call your files any name you like but we suggest that you tailor each name to the file it belongs to. You will then know instantly what the file contains by looking at its name.

Although the books say you can use some punctuation marks within filenames we recommend that you don't. There are so many that you cannot use - listed on Page 122 of the Official Guide - that it's not worth trying to remember the few that you can.

Filename Extensions

The filename you choose can be followed by an extension of a full stop (which is why you cannot use a full stop anywhere else in a filename) plus three other characters. Extensions are usually used to denote what type of file it is. For example: .LTR for letters or .PRS for press

Chapter 2 Learning the Lingo

releases. If you don't put an extension on your filename Windows will add one automatically to show which program the file is 'associated' or works with. See table below.

Filename Extensions Used By Windows

Type Of File	Extension
Programs	.COM .EXE
Help	.HLP
Program Manager Groups	.GRP
Temporary	.TMP
Clipboard	.CLP
Write	
File	.WRI
Backup	.BKP
Microsoft Word	.DOC
Other Backup	.BAK
Paintbrush	
Bitmap	.BMP
Colours	.PAL
PC-Paintbrush format	.PCX
Microsoft Paint format	.MSP
Terminal Setup	.TRM
Notepad	.TXT
Cardfile	.CRD
Calendar	.CAL
Recorder	.REC
Pif Editor	.PIF

Use this table if you want to look for a specific type of file or if you want to check what sort of file you are dealing with. Remember that these extensions are only used if you do not put your own extension on the end of filenames.

Please note that although the same rules apply for naming both files and directories only files normally have an extension.

Directories

A directory will hold a group of files that you want to keep together. In terms of filing cabinets,

Chapter 2 Learning the Lingo

it's a bit like a drawer or section of a drawer. You can have directories within directories (called sub-directories or sub-trees).

Someone just starting out on this journey could create a directory called JOURNEY. Then they could put all files that hold information about the first week in a sub-directory called WEEK1. Different types of files can be stored in the same directory, so maps and drawings could be stored there as well as text files. In this filing system, at the end of the journey, there would be as many sub-directories in **JOURNEY** as the number of weeks you have travelled.

Alternatively you could do what the text books say and create directories called LETTERS and ACCOUNTS to collect letter or account files together. We reckon that is a bit pointless since you can use 'wildcards' to help you group files with similar names. "But, hey man it's a free world!" You can organise you files any way that pleases you. See the section on Wildcards later in this chapter for more information.

Directories make it much easier to find where each file is stored. They also allow you to call two or three different files by the same name. Don't worry if that sounds like Double Dutch, you need to know about full filenames or 'path names and 'trees' .

A Computerised Tree?

You will have to become an electronic forester and lumberjack during your journey!

Chapter 2 Learning the Lingo

A computerised tree describes the entire data storage structure on a disk. Once you start working with any computer, the number of files and directories will begin to grow. There are likely to be lots of files branching from each directory and sub-directory. Someone, back in the mists of time, decided that if you drew the structure out it looked like a tree. The only problem with this idea is that these trees are always drawn upside down. The 'root' directory (the one that is always there) is at the top and the branches are coming out of the bottom. We did warn you that this was a very strange world didn't we?

Path Names

You will need to know how to recognise the paths on your journey, not only paths that you yourself should follow, but also paths that your data can travel down safely. If you send information off into the misty blue yonder without careful thought, you could either lose the file or it could even wipe out another more valuable one.

Each file has a name and a position in the tree. The path name follows the route through the tree that your computer needs to take to get to that file. The path name describes that route in a written form. It consists of the disk drive name followed by any directory and sub-directory names that are between the root directory and the file. Each section of the name has to be separated by a '\'.

Chapter 2 Learning the Lingo

Disk Drive Names

Disk drives are known by a single letter followed by a colon. Although there are no officially recognised standards 'a:' and 'b:' are generally floppy disk drives, while 'c:' and possibly 'd:' are hard disk drives. Drives 'f:' to 'z:' are normally any additional drives that you have access to if your computer is linked to others in a network. Remember that if you are on a network, a drive doesn't have to be a whole disk. It can be just a directory or sub-directory on a disk on another computer. It can be known by a different name to the actual disk that it is occupying.

Tip: How To Find Out Which Drive Is Which

If you are unsure what drives you have got or which drives are which, you can check in the File Manager that is behind the filing cabinet symbol in the Program Manager. Once inside, the little pictures (icons) of disk drives along the top will show you what you have available.

If you have two floppy drives, you may not be sure which is which. Select the a: icon either by putting the mouse's arrow over it or by pressing Tab and Left Arrow if you are using the keyboard. Then you need to either double click the mouse or press Enter. A light will come on, on the front of one of your disk drives, as your computer tries to read a disk. It will not select the drive unless there is a disk in it, but you will know that the drive that lit up is the one your computer regards as 'a:'.

Tip: Creating A RAM Disk May Rename Some Of Your Drives

If you create a RAM disk (a section of memory in which you can store files for quicker access) it will automatically be given the next letter after your hard disk drive. Any other drives that were after your hard disk will be renamed to the next letter up the alphabet. So if you had drive 'a:' as a floppy drive, 'c:' and 'd:' as hard drives and 'e:' as another floppy drive, 'e:' will become the RAM disk. The other floppy drive will then be known as 'f:'.

An Example Of A Path Name

Let's say you have a map drawn with Paintbrush of a river that you followed in the second week of your journey which you save in a file called RIVER. Windows will add the .BMP extension to it automatically. You store it in your MAPS sub-directory located in your WEEK2 sub-directory. As we've seen, WEEK2 is a branch of your main JOURNEY directory. Drawn as part of the tree, it would look like this:

Chapter 2 Learning the Lingo

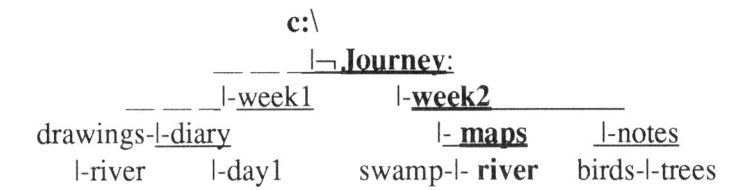

```
                         c:\
          __ __   |¬ Journey:
          __ __ __|-week1       |-week2
drawings-|-diary               |- maps      |-notes
    |-river      |-day1    swamp-|- river   birds-|-trees
```

The full pathname would be:

[C:\JOURNEY\WEEK2\MAPS\RIVER.BMP].

Two Files With The Same Name?

Looking at the tree above we have got two files called RIVER. If you try to save two files with the same name into the same branch of the tree then the new file just overwrites the one that is already saved on the disk. If it is on a different branch of the tree (in a different directory or sub-directory) it will have a different path name and there will not be a clash.

You can also have sub-directories with the same name too, provided that they come from different directories. In the example above, we could have had a sub-directory called MAPS in WEEK1 as well as in WEEK2. That will place the two sub-directories on totally different branches of the tree.

Windows is such an intelligent system that you will rarely have to type the full path name yourself. When you are opening or saving a file you just select the directory and sub-directory names from the list in the 'dialog box' (we will explain those in the next chapter). As you select one directory or sub-directory name from each level in turn, the path will be built up for you. Once it knows the path Windows (and MS-DOS too) will send the file to the right branch. It is difficult to get it wrong because Windows will give you the directories and sub-directories to select in the order that they appear in the path.

Hopefully, you now know everything you need to know to keep to the straight and narrow and to make your files follow the right path too!

Wildcards

Wildcards are some of the white magic of this world. They are special characters that can act as substitutes for one or more characters in a filename that you either don't know or don't want to worry about.

Chapter 2 Learning the Lingo

The two wildcards that you can use with filenames are '*' and '?'. If you put a '?' in a filename, Windows will look for filenames that match all the other letters exactly but won't care what that particular character is. So if you selected File Open and typed in **?END.ME** you will be given a list of all matching files that Windows found in the selected directory. Such a list could include files called:

>   MEND.ME
>   LEND.ME
>   SEND.ME
>   BEND.ME
>   REND.ME
>   TEND.ME
>   PEND.ME

You can include more than one ? in a file name if you need to. For example **?E?D.ME** would find you all the files listed above plus a whole lot more like:

>   MEAD.ME
>   READ.ME
>   REID.ME
>   HERD.ME
>   WELD.ME

The * wildcard is even more powerful. You use it to substitute any number of letters. The most common time you will see it is when you select Open from the File menu of an application. In the filename box you will see '*.' followed by the application's extension. So if you are opening a file in the Notepad you will see *.TXT already in the filename box. That is telling your computer to find any files with a .TXT extension in the selected directory.

You can use * to represent any number of letters. For example, B*.CLP would find all Clipboard files beginning with B. Remember, when using wildcards, that the extension is separate from the filename. You need to include either the full extension or a wildcard to replace it. If you just put * for the filename, Windows will find you all files without an extension. To find all files regardless of name or extension you must put [*.*].

You can use combinations of both wildcards in the same filename. This is useful if you can't remember the exact spelling or what extension you used. For example, you might know that the filename begins with EST and had one letter that you don't know, followed by RE. You could type EST?RE.* and Windows should come up with the correct file - providing you have selected the right directory for it to look in.

Chapter 2 Learning the Lingo

Tip: Not Sure Where A File Is In The Tree?

If you are not sure which directory a file is stored in, you may need to use wildcards with the File Manager's Search command. Search doesn't need to know about the path. If you type the filename or, as much of the filename as you know, with wildcards for the rest, Search will find all the files that match and give you their full path names.

You should now understand the language you will need to use when storing information in Windows. You can find out the nuts and bolts of saving information to disk and then getting it back by turning to the chapter on the File Manager. But first it might be a good idea to get to grips with the real nuts and bolts that hold Windows together.

Chapter 3 - First Encounters

Introduction

You can start walking now but please take it easy. There is a lot of ground to cover but if you go too fast you'll fall and break your neck at the first sign of difficult terrain. If you do fall, and your injuries go beyond the scope of our first aid kit, we will not be able to carry you to safety. So you could very easily end up as breakfast for the Gremlins. Gremlins much prefer young travellers who have just set out and they are always on the look-out for a juicy meal.

Right, let's move. The immediate countryside is gently sloping grassland. Easy walking country this, so take your time and enjoy the sun on your face and the breeze in your hair. Everything will be vaguely familiar, yet different to what you have known before.

Mousing Around

Hold on a moment, we are not going to get very far while you don't know how to use your staff or keyboard properly. We had better tell you about that first...

Mouse Versus Keyboard

You have two options for working with this new world. Although we use the mouse, there is nothing to stop you following the same sequences with the keys. The keyboard alternatives are well documented in the official guide, although we have included some here. We have found a knowledge of some keystrokes has been useful even though we mostly use the mouse.

An Upside Down Mouse

An upside down mouse is no good to anybody! A mouse on its back cannot run anywhere. While one pointing the wrong way will make the arrow go in the opposite direction to the way you are moving the mouse.

You need to use your mouse with the buttons uppermost and the wire coming out of the side pointing away from you. The mouse should then behave itself, making the movement of the

Chapter 3 First Encounters

arrow mimic the movements you make with the mouse.

Run Out Of Rope For Your Mouse?

If you play with your mouse, running the arrow around your screen you may find that you can't get it to reach the furthest corner.

Why do I always think I can go anywhere I like?

You can cure that by picking the mouse up - the arrow will stay in the same place - and putting it back down somewhere else. You should then be able to carry on, moving it in the direction you need it to go. The arrow will carry on as though nothing has happened.

Buttons

Normally only one of the two or three buttons along the top of the mouse will work but some applications like Paintbrush need two. You will be able to select which button you want to use as the main one from the Mouse Settings in the Control Panel.

Clicking And Dragging

Pressing the mouse button is called 'clicking the mouse'. Clicking was probably used because it sounds much shorter and sharper than the more leisurely 'press'. You cannot prolong a click

Chapter 3 First Encounters

otherwise it becomes something else.

The mouse does different things depending on whether the tip on the screen is an arrow or an I bar.

Tip: Two `Cursors'?

===
Definition: A cursor is the point that sometimes flashes on and off on the screen. It marks where you are and shows where any command will be carried out.
===

Windows doesn't often use a conventional cursor. If you are using the mouse, the arrow is your cursor, which you can move freely around the screen. If you are using the keyboard you can jump from one option on to the next. You know where you are because whatever you have selected will be highlighte.

The mouse's tip turns from an arrow into an I bar in applications that work with text. These applications also have a second cursor which is officially called the insertion point. The insertion point takes on the role of the cursor while the I bar helps it move quickly around the file and select text.

While the Mouse moves an arrow around the screen:

> A Click will select something.
>
> A Hold - one click that you hold down - will make the mouse carry on the operation you have asked it to do, continuously. For example, if you hold the little arrows on a scroll bar down with the mouse, you will move through a text file or dialogue box quickly, one line at a time.
>
> A Drag - a hold where you move the mouse as well - will select and move whatever you have selected. Whatever the arrow is pointing at (providing that it can move) will be moved with the mouse and dropped at the point where the arrow is when you let the mouse button go.
>
> A Double Click - two clicks in quick succession - will open the selected application. If you double click over a section of the screen where there are no windows you will call up the Task list. Double clicking has other miscellaneous functions in specific situations. We will

point these out as we come to them.

Shift + Click - will select more than one thing. For example, to select a list of files, move the arrow to one end of the list and click the mouse. Then, move the arrow to the other end and press Shift whilst clicking the mouse. The selected files will be highlighted on the screen.

When the mouse moves the I bar around the screen:

A Click will;

- A. move the insertion point to that point.
- B. remove any highlights from previously selected text.

A Drag will select a block of text. It will highlight text from the point you start to drag, in the direction that you are dragging the mouse, until you release the mouse button. You can change direction and speed.

A Double Click will select - highlight - either one space or continuous text between two spaces (a word).

Shift + Click will act as the second marker point - with a single click marking the first - to give you a quick way of highlighting the block of text between the two.

NOTE. If you want to select an area that is bigger than the screen, you must move to the second marker point with the Scroll Bars, not the arrow keys or the mouse. Otherwise the cursor that you left to mark the other end will move with you.

Tip: To Edit A Highlighted Area Of Text

Any highlighted text whether it is in a file or a dialog box can be edited in the same way.

Once you have an area of text highlighted you can:
Delete it with a single press of the Delete key or the Backspace key.

Delete and replace it by typing what you want there instead. The first character you type will delete the entire block, before inserting the new text into the file.

Chapter 3 First Encounters

To cancel the highlight, press any of the four Arrow keys or click the mouse button.

Taming Your Mouse

To change your mouse's behaviour you will need to go into Mouse Settings in the Control Panel. You can change the tracking speed, which determines how fast the arrow travels across the screen. The double click rate (the amount of time that can elapse between the two clicks) can also be changed.

All About A Window

Things You Can Do With A Window

1. You can start a program running by opening a window. To do this, double click the mouse on an icon in the Program Manager. You can also open a window from the File Manager but we will explain that later.

2. You can change a window's size and move it about your viewing screen.

3. You can have as many windows open on the screen as you like. They can overlap one another or even cover others up completely.

4. You will only have one 'active' window to work with but you can make any window active.

5. You can move between windows easily.

6. You can shrink (minimise) a Window back to an icon but keep the program running ready to use again.

7. You can make one window fill the whole screen - that is, maximise it.

8. You can close them.

Chapter 3 First Encounters

The controls to do most of these things are in the top border of each window. The topmost border holds the Title Bar and three grey buttons.

The Grey Buttons

The button on the left is the Window Control button. If you click over it with the mouse or press [Alt Spacebar] the Window Control menu `pops down'. If you are using a keyboard, all the window controls that you need are in this menu. You needn't bother about the other buttons.

===
Definition
A menu contains a list of options or commands. If you select an option, Windows will carry it out for you. It may, however, ask for more information first.
===

If you are using the mouse, you only need to know about three of the options on the Window Control menu. These are:

> Restore - allows you to return the window's size to what it was before you minimised or maximised it.

> Close - will close that window and stop the application that was running in it.

And

> Switch To - calls up the Task List, but more of that later.

The two buttons on the top right hand side of the window are the minimise and maximise buttons if you are using the mouse. When a window is maximised the second (maximise) button turns into a Restore button.

If you double click the Window Control button you will close the window. You will be given the opportunity to save your file if you have done some work since you last saved it.

Moving Windows With The Title Bar

To move a window: click your mouse with the arrow on the title bar and drag the window. An outline of the window will move with the mouse's arrow. The window will obediently move to

33

Chapter 3 First Encounters

the point where the outline was when you let the mouse button go.

If you double click the mouse on the title bar it will maximise the window.

Altering The Size Of A Window

If you move the arrow to the extreme outer edge of a window, it will turn into a smaller double headed arrow. If you then drag the mouse, the outline of that edge will move with the mouse. That side of the window will finish at the point where you 'drop' it and the window will reform its contents to fit the new size.

If you move the arrow to the corner of the outer edge, it turns into a double headed arrow that points in a diagonal direction. This diagonal arrow can move the two sides of the window that meet there, at the same time.

Minimised Windows

If you know that you want easy access to a program but don't need it open all the time, you can minimise it. This will turn it into a mere shadow of its former self because Windows will turn it back into an icon.

Any window that has been shrunk to an icon will be put along the bottom of the screen. If you are using the mouse you can drag these icons anywhere. If you are using the keyboard you can select the move option on the windows control menu and then move it with the arrow keys.

Tip: Lost Icons

If you have lost an icon it is probably `hiding' behind the last window you minimised.

This normally occurs when you have restored a minimised window and then minimise a second window before minimising the first one again.

There are two conflicting things at work here. Firstly, Windows places the icons of minimised windows along the bottom of your screen from left to right. It will put each icon as far left as it can. But, secondly, Windows remembers where an icon was and puts it back in the same place when you minimise the window again.

A clash between the two doesn't often happen. When it does, if the icon underneath is slightly bigger or has a longer description it is easy to see where it has gone. It's only if the smaller icon is underneath that you might lose it.

When you want to work on the file or program that's still running behind the icon, either double click the mouse over it or select it from the Task List.

The Menu Bar

The area below the Title bar is the Menu bar. This shows all the options available for the application that you are running. They are grouped together under different headings. To see what options you have got, just point the arrow at one heading and click the mouse. The selected menu will 'pop down' beneath its heading. If you are using the keyboard pressing Alt and Enter will reveal the menu on the left. To select one of the other menus with the keyboard, you can move around the menu bar (after pressing Alt) with the Left/Right Arrow keys.

More To Follow

Any menu option that has three dots after it will 'open' a dialog box when it is selected. When you select one of these options, Windows needs more information from you.

Selecting Options

To select an option, click the mouse over it or move down to it with the Down Arrow key and then select it with Enter.

'Greyed Out' Options

Any option in a menu that is 'greyed out' is not available to you at that time. There is always a legitimate reason for this and Windows will give you the option back when it is valid for you to have it.

It sometimes feels that Windows is being awkward. The problem is that once an option is greyed out there is normally nothing that you can do to get it back. You have to wait for Windows to let you have it. This can be very frustrating if you do not understand why it is greyed out in the first place.

Keyboard Shortcuts

You may have noticed that most menu options have one letter underlined. These are keyboard selection shortcuts. For example, if you want to turn the Ruler On or Off in Write with the keyboard, pressing Alt D will make the Document menu pop down and [R] will make the Ruler appear. This is usually quicker than multiple presses of the Arrow keys.

Direct Commands Via The Keyboard

Alongside some menu options that you are likely to use frequently there are 'direct keyboard commands' like F4 and ALT+BKSP. These will carry out menu options even if you are not in a menu. ALT+BKSP is shorthand for "Press the Alt key first and hold it down, while pressing the Backspace key".

Switch options

Although most menu options do something the instant they are selected, a few don't appear to do anything. These are switch options. If you select them once, a tick will appear in front of them and they will be turned on. For example, if you select Auto Arrange from the Program Manager's Option menu, from then on your program icons will be rearranged each time you alter the size of a window within the Program Manager. If you select these switch options a second time the tick will disappear and the switch is turned off. Some menus have more than one of these options grouped together; you can select as many as you need.

To Close A Menu

To make the menu disappear either select another menu or click the mouse with the arrow somewhere in the main body of the window. That is, click the mouse button within the window that you are working in but not near the menu or window controls. Using the keyboard, you can press Alt a second time.

Scroll Bars

Scroll bars appear down the right hand side and across the bottom of a window or in a box within a dialog box that has more in it than can be displayed in the space available.

Scroll bars can only be used with a mouse. If you are using the keyboard you will have to use the Arrow keys and Page Up/Page down keys to move around inside a window.

Breaking Down A Scroll Bar

A scroll bar has three different elements. There are two arrow buttons, the scroll button, and the track that stretches between the arrows.

The track represents your file or the total contents of a window. The position of the scroll button shows where the section shown in the window is in the file. So if your file fills four windows and the up/down scroll button is half way down the track, you should be near the top of the third windowful of text. The position of the scroll button is only approximately related to your position in the file.

Tip: If A File Appears To Be Empty...

If a file looks empty that you know should contain information, check the position of the Scroll buttons BEFORE you panic! Quite often the left/right Scroll button will be away from the left-hand corner of the track. Or the up/down Scroll button might be right at the bottom of the track. Either way, you may be looking at a section of the window that doesn't contain anything. If you move the scroll buttons back to the beginning of the tracks your file will be revealed in all its glory.

Moving around With Scroll Bars

There are three ways of using the scroll bars to move around. You can use the mouse button to press:

1. The arrow buttons. These allow you to move around the file slowly, line by line, or across the screen approximately two and a half characters at a time.

2. The track on either side of the scroll button. These will move you through the file faster, a screenful at a time.

   If you hold the mouse button down on either the arrow buttons or the track you can move continuously.

Or

Chapter 3 First Encounters

3   You can drag the scroll button to the position in the track where you want to be in the file. This is very fast.

To Move From Window To Window

If you can see any of the window that you want to move to, just put the arrow over it and click the mouse. The window that you have selected will become the 'active' window and overlay the one you were working in before.

To reopen a window you have minimised, put the arrow over the icon and either double click the mouse over it, or click it once and select Restore from the window's control menu which pops up.

To move between open (and minimised) windows with the keyboard; press Alt + Tab. Each time you press Tab, while holding Alt, you will highlight a different window. When you release Alt the highlighted window will become the active window. If the highlighted window is minimised it will automatically be restored when you release the Alt key.

If you can't see the window you want to move to, select the application you want to work with from the Task List. You can either double click the mouse over an empty area on your screen or select the Switch To option from any window's control menu.

Tip: Spend Time Arranging Your Screen

We have found that it is worth spending time sorting out what applications you are going to need and where to put them on the viewing screen before you start work.

Applications like the Clock and Clipboard can be made smaller and put in the corner; you can then still see their contents but they don't take up much space. If you don't mind it being very small, the minimised Clock will still show you the time.

Applications that you don't need to see all the time can be minimised. You can arrange their icons anywhere you have got empty screen. Alternatively you can leave them at their normal size, arranging them so that you can see a little of their windows poking out from underneath the window that you are working with.

All this may take a few minutes when you start work but it will reap dividends later. A little organisation at the beginning will make it quicker and easier for you to move between applications rather than using the Task List as the go-between.

Once you have established a layout that you are likely to use a great deal you can program the Recorder (Recky) to do it all for you on a two key command or even completely automatically. Now that is truly magical!

Letting Windows Arrange Your Windows

Windows has two ways of arranging your windows automatically. They are called Tile and Cascade. Both will disregard any sizing or positioning of your windows and impose its own.

Tiling Windows

Tiling will divide the screen up equally between all open windows that are not minimised. It will leave space at the bottom of the screen for the icons of minimised windows.

Cascading Windows

Cascading will again make all open windows the same size but it will overlay them in a pile, one on top of the other. All you will be able to see is the title bar and left-hand border of each window underneath the top one. It will position the bottom window in the top left hand corner of the screen with all the others on top progressing diagonally downwards. The window on top of the pile will be the active one.

If you select another window out of the cascade, that one will be put on top of the pile. It will stay in its position in the cascade, however, breaking up the nice orderly pattern. This can make it more difficult to see, and select, other windows that are open.

Windows Within Windows

Some applications have smaller windows within their main one. You can move around, minimise, maximise and close them in the same way as you can the parent windows. Examples include the Program Manager that stores different groups of applications in different windows and the File Manager that gives each directory or sub directory a window to itself.

There are subtle differences between these windows and their parent windows:

Chapter 3 First Encounters

1. An inner window can never be opened by itself.

2. When they are maximised they only grow to the size of their parent window not the entire screen.

3. They do not have a menu bar.

4. They can't be moved outside the parent window.

Tip: Don't Hide An Inner Window's Title Bar

You can move these inner windows in the same way as you can move the parent windows. Be careful as it is possible to move a window so that its title bar is concealed almost totally by the parent windows menu bar. If that happens, it is very difficult to control that window with the mouse. You should, with a little mouse dexterity, still be able to use the window controls. If not, you may have to resort to using the keyboard commands.

Tip: Don't Get Confused Between The Grey Buttons

If an inner window is maximised it is very easy to confuse the parent's Window Control Button with the inner window's. This is because the two title bars merge (the inner Window title is displayed in brackets) and the inner window's control buttons are put on either end of the parent window's menu bar. This puts them just below the parent's Window Control buttons. You could find yourself carrying out a command on the wrong window.

Inside A Window

There is a continual conversation between you and Windows. Whenever you ask it to do something, Windows will normally either tell you what it is doing, ask you for confirmation, or come back to you for the extra information it needs to carry out the task. Windows communicates with you via messages, which appear in smaller windows of their own, normally overlaying the window you are working in. The official guide calls these 'Dialog' or 'Message' boxes but we will combine them all together under the heading of Dialogue boxes - spelt the English way!

Dealing With Dialogue Boxes

If you see a dialogue box on the screen you normally have to deal with it before you can carry on with what you were doing.

If it is just an information message, pressing the OK button with the mouse (or the Enter key) to acknowledge it, will be enough to send it on its way.

If it is a confirmation message you normally have a choice of two or three buttons. These will have something like OK and CANCEL or YES, NO and CANCEL on them.

For a message that says 'please give me more information' you will need to type in what Windows needs to know. Windows will, however, try to make a calculated guess at what you might want. It will either display the initial values that its creators gave it at the beginning of time, or it will leave the values that you have used in a previous file. The first option will be highlighted ready for you to edit. You can move down to any other options that you need to change with the mouse or the Tab key. Once you have changed all you need to change, select OK or press Enter and Windows will carry out the task.

The CANCEL Button

If you select the CANCEL button in a dialogue box you will leave the box and return to your file with no values being changed, whether you have altered any or not. Any changes you make will only be actioned if you select the OK button. If another dialogue box opens inside the first one, pressing CANCEL in the outer one will not undo changes you made to the settings in the inner one.

Tip: If You Open A Dialogue Box By Mistake

Most boxes that are asking for a response from you have a CANCEL button as an escape route. However, there are a few boxes, such as Find and Change in Write, that don't.

Dialogue boxes have a Dialogue Box Control button that is very similar to the Window Control button. You can either double click this button to make the dialogue box disappear or you can click it once and then select the Close option from the menu.

Alternatively, you can always press the Esc key.

Chapter 3 First Encounters

Tip: Don't Get Trigger Happy With The OK Buttons

Once you get to know Windows dialogue boxes, the message ones become a bit of a nuisance. Like flies that plague you in hot weather you start swatting them automatically. Unless you are concentrating it is easy to press one OK too many.

If you do this in the File Manager it can have dire consequences. One of us pressed one too many OK's and started erasing the hard disk on our computer, which was not a pretty sight!

One defence against this sort of thing happening in the File Manager is to make sure that all the available options are selected in the Confirmation dialogue box. This box is found in the Options menu. This gives you a chance to change your mind even if you do something rash.

It isn't the total answer because if you really have got trigger happy this will just give you another OK button to press. You could still do something dire, yet again Vigilance should be your watchword.

What's Inside A Dialogue box?

Windows has several ways of providing you with the choices available for each option in a dialogue box. With a few options you will have to type the choice yourself but there are several other ways of selecting options.

Making Choices From Boxes Within Boxes

Some options are put into smaller option boxes inside a dialogue box in Russian Doll style, while some are just grouped together. There are many different ways of selecting choices from within dialogue boxes.

Lists Of Choices

Some inner boxes have a whole list of possible choices for one option. Such a box will often have a scroll bar. You can move to the box with the mouse or Tab key. To select what you want from the list, you can move through it using the scroll bar and then select the option you want with the mouse. If you are using the keyboard, the Arrow keys will move you to the choice you want while the spacebar will select it.

Hidden Lists

There might also be a hidden list that you can 'pull down' by clicking the button just to the right of a small option box. Once you have pulled the list down you can make your choice in the same way as for a visible list. Using the keyboard, you press Alt + Down Arrow to reveal the list.

Choosing More Than One Item From A List

Sometimes you can choose more than one item from a list. For example, in Windows Setup you can choose all the applications you want to be able to use with Windows. You are able to select any number of these from the list and Windows will add them to those that the Program Manager knows about. If you make a mistake and select one that you don't want, selecting it again will deselect it.

These multi-choice boxes are very rare and there is no indication that they are any different from the normal lists that only give you one choice. It is just a matter of trial and error to find out which is which.

One Choice Only

If there are a group of options with circles in front of them (with the centre of one filled in) these are option buttons. You can move the filled centre (it sounds like we are choosing chocolates doesn't it) to any of the circles and that will select the option next to it. You can definitely only have one of these selected so you can't be greedy!

More Than One Choice

You can select more than one item from a list if they have little square boxes in front of them. If you select one, a cross will be put in the square to show that the option has been selected. You can select an option by clicking the mouse when the arrow is over it. If you are using the keyboard, you can move over the square with the Tab key and then select it with the Spacebar. You can deselect options that already have a cross in the square in the same way.

Selection Sliders

Any dialogue box that has to do with speed will have what looks like a scroll bar across the centre of the box. The position of the button on the track will determine the speed of whatever it controls. You can treat these just like scroll bars. If you are using the mouse you can press the button on the track to move quickly to any point. Pressing the little Arrows at either end of the track will move the selection button a small amount at a time. If you are using the keyboard, you can move the selection button along the track with the Up/Down Arrows.

Dialogue Boxes Are Not Always Friendly

One of the biggest Gremlins will appear before you in a dialogue box. It is called Unrecoverable Application Error and you have our permission to quake when you see it. It eats applications, or rather the copy of the application that you are working on, for lunch and has the associated file for dessert. You can never be certain what has caused him to spring up but his appearance will have drastic consequences. He will literally stop you in your tracks and close down the application that you are working on. There will be no opportunity to buy time, save the file, or leave the application in an orderly fashion. Any work that doesn't have a back-up copy will be lost.

After he has paid you a visit you would be well advised to close down Windows before trying to carry on. Until you give Windows a fresh start Unrecoverable Application Error has a habit of calling again.

Using Fonts

You are likely to hear Fonts mentioned when you are working with text. You may also hear "WYSIWYG" (pronounced whizzy-wig). But then again, you may not! We will tell you about it anyway, just in case...

A font describes the characteristics of a particular set of character shapes - so that 'a' belongs to a different font than 'a' or 'a'.

Life was pretty boring in pre-desktop publishing days when you were restricted to just one font. But those days are gone for good. It is very difficult to imagine what this book would be like without the different sizes and shapes of letters used in the chapter titles, section headings and so on.

What You Need To Know About Fonts

In theory, you don't have to know very much about fonts, other than how to select them. You do that by opening a dialogue box in any application that supports them. For example, in Write, you select Fonts from the Character menu. To work with fonts, you need to understand what attributes are and what a "point" is.

Attributes of Fonts

Attributes are simply properties of letters like underline, superscript and boldness that exist independently of the shapes of the letters. For example, you can underline any font: "<u>a</u>", "<u>a</u>" or "<u>a</u>".

Tip: What Is A Point?

There are seventy-two points in an inch, and the point size relates to the height (rather than the width) of a character.

WYSIWYG?

WYSIWYG stands for 'what you see is what you get' and that's just what you're supposed to find. If you select a particular font, and then print it, the font as printed on the paper should be exactly the same as you saw on the screen.

Oh, what most Windows users would give if it was really like that! The reality is rather different because the quality of screen display and printout depends on: what printer you're using, what font you've selected and even what font size you're trying to use.

All this is not entirely Windows fault. It is partly caused by:

- The extreme sensitivity of the human eye to the shape of letters.
- The different resolutions of your display screen and your printer.

- A need to restrict the amount of disk space that the font files occupy.

Nonetheless, Windows 'could do better' and some other products (including Adobe's Type

Chapter 3 First Encounters

Manager and Bitstream's Facelift) to say nothing of Microsoft's own TrueType technology, , do a considerably better job than Windows 3.0.

Let's Follow A Font...

To understand what's going on, we'll follow a font from your brain to the finished sheet of paper:

1. You're writing a newsletter and decide that you need large, easy-to-read letters for the main headline.

2. You select the Character menu in Write, open the Font dialogue box and find, much to your delight, a font called 'Modern'. to recognise that this is similar to 'Helvetica' - it can't be called that for copyright reasons.

3. You select 24 point (remember, that's one third of an inch high) and type your headline; 'Windows Wanderer'.

4. Wow, look's good, doesn't it...

5. Now, print it out. Hey, it's almost WYSIWYG!

It worked because you used an 'outline' font. These are stored as mathematical descriptions of the letter shapes and are also known as 'vector' outlines - vectors are short, straight lines. They can be displayed and printed at any size by simply multiplying each number in the description by a number representing the desired size.

Now, let's assume you have a dot-matrix printer and, rather than Modern, you fancy a more formal newsletter. You decide to use TmsRmn that you recognise as the Times look-alike.

You select 24 point Tms Rmn from the Fonts dialogue box and type the headline. You expect to see a good-looking headline but you're disappointed. The headline looks like it's been nibbled by mice who have square teeth - which is not really what you wanted. So you think 'ah well, it will be all right when I print it' but, no, it's the same shape. Even worse, it appears to be printed in a different size than it looked on your screen.

Chapter 3 First Encounters

Bitmapped Fonts

The shapes of the letters in Tms Rmn are not stored as outlines that can be easily scaled, unlike those for Modern. Each shape is a 'bitmap' - a picture of the shape made up from rectangles. Each rectangle is either 'on' (which will print as black) or 'off' (which will print as transparent).

There are two separate types of fonts (we'll see later how to tell which font uses which method) because they are used differently. For example, you would normally use Modern for headlines and Tms Rmn for 'body copy'.

The eye is very sensitive to the shapes of letters, particularly at small font sizes such as those used in body copy. If you simply scale down a large font size to a smaller size, you can instantly see that it doesn't look correct. The best solution is to handcraft each shape individually so that each size retains the attributes which make a particular font what it is. If you were to examine the shape of each letter individually, you'll find that they all have subtle features.

All the information, for each letter, number, punctuation mark and foreign language character in each font, must be stored on your hard disk. To contain the amount of storage used, Microsoft compromised; they only provided a limited number of sizes in each font. They recognised that users might still want to generate other sizes so they allowed these to be generated by pixel replication. We know that probably sounds slightly obscene, so we'll hurry along with our story and explain it.

Imagine the picture of the letter "a" in 8 point Tms Rmn. To generate 24 point text for our headline, we can just repeat each pixel three times in each direction. This will only approximate the shape and won't take into account the subtle differences we just mentioned - but it will work. Unfortunately, whereas you can't see individual pixels, you can see the 3-by-3 blocks that this yields - hence our mouse bitten headline.

Out of curiosity, you try 25 point. You now see that the mice are obviously much smaller (the text appears smoother) but the letters are much bigger than the 24 point headline. If you print your headline, it now produces a much better approximation to what you saw on screen.

This is because Windows thinks there is an actual font defined at 25 point and so you see the font in all its un-replicated glory. There's actually no font defined for 25 point, but there is one for 24 point, and Windows is using that one instead. As we'll see later, Windows sometimes gets its arithmetic wrong.

47

Chapter 3 First Encounters

How To Find Fonts

To see what fonts Windows has available, you run the Control Panel application and double-click on the Fonts icon. A dialogue box opens, listing the fonts.

Which Type Of Font?

Next to each name in the Control Panel Fonts list is either 'All res' that indicates an outline font or a series of numbers that indicates what sizes are available for bitmap fonts.

Yet More Fonts...

If, by now, you think that two types of fonts are enough then we've got news for you. If you use a laser printer or a high-quality dot-matrix one, it won't be long before you'll meet another type: 'printer fonts'.

As their name suggests, these are fonts that are inside the printer (the jargon term is 'resident'). Your computer can activate these by sending special commands to the printer. In a typical dot-matrix printer, there may be three resident fonts, in a good laser printer about five and in a Postscript one up to thirty-five. What sizes you can print using these fonts is determined by the printer, not by Windows.

Windows just about understands about printer fonts. You'll see why that sentence includes 'just about' as we explain some of the problems that you may encounter.

Let's follow a font again:

1. You find out that your NEC P2 printer has an attractive font called 'Fast Focus' that you want to use for footnotes in Windows Wanderer.

2. If you've installed the correct printer driver when you initially installed Windows, or when you added the printer, you'll find that this font appears in the Fonts dialogue box.

3. When you type a footnote, you notice that Windows seems to know about the font because it displays a representation of the shape of the letters as they will be printed.

4. You now forget that it's a printer font and try to reduce its size. There's nothing to

prevent you doing this, Windows accepts the new size. But, when you print the footnote, it still appears to be in the original size.

As we've said, Windows just about understands resident fonts. If you have a laser printer, you may find that it works the other way round. The standard Windows fonts can be selected in the Fonts dialogue box and displayed, but not printed.

As a further complexity, printer resident fonts are of three varieties. They can be supplied with and be integral to the basic printer. They can be supplied in some form of cartridge. They can be 'downloaded' from your computer to the internal memory of the printer - these are called 'soft fonts'.

Using Fonts With A New Printer

Don't forget, when you buy a new printer, you should use the Printer section of the Control Panel to add it to the printer list. Windows then knows it is available. This will normally load a set of font files onto your disk so that Windows can display the resident fonts. If you ordered any font cartridges or soft fonts, the relevant disk files supplied with these should also be installed.

Assuming you have the correct printer driver installed, the Control Panel Printer Setup dialogue box will allow you to tell Windows how you have configured your printer. You can:

- Tell Windows which font cartridges are installed in the printer.

- Select the resolution for graphics images and fonts generated by Windows.

- Select the orientation of the printout (that is, whether the print is to be across the paper or lengthways down the paper).

Each type of printer has its own particular group of settings to control its unique features. You may need to look at the manual supplied with the printer to understand all the terminology used. One common problem with HP Laserjet printers is that they only seem to use their resident fonts and the Windows outline fonts.

Chapter 3 First Encounters

Getting Help

The User Guide

There are two official sources of help that come with your Windows package. You are given a copy of the User's Manual (or the Official Guide as we call it) but you also have a Help menu for each application. The manual is good on detailed step by step instructions, if you are prepared to work through a whole section in a methodical way. It is not so good as a quick reference.

The manual assumes that the user knows where to get information about a host of other hefty topics. Topics like Communications and MS-DOS have been largely ignored because of the sheer weight of material needed to cover Windows. For someone just starting out in computers that gap in knowledge can be an impenetrable barrier.

In its favour, the User Guide has a large index and a comprehensive table of contents. There is a useful mini table of contents at the beginning of each section. To be able to get the full benefit of these, however, you need to know most of the special terminology that Windows uses. Otherwise you will not know what to look for.

The On-Line Help System

Every application has a Help system all to itself. These are more useful than the Manual for quick reference and are easier to find your way around too. They are ideal for looking up things like keyboard alternatives and details of menu options that are available for that application.

You can enter the help system by pressing the F1 key on the top row of your keyboard or you can select Help from the menu bar. If you enter via F1 you will always be put into the Help Index for the application running in your active window. If you enter by the Help option you have a choice as to where you want to start. If you select the 'Using Help' option you will get help on using Help.

Tip: Shift + F1

If you are running more advanced Windows programs you can move the cursor to something within a window and press [Shift + F1]. The help system will then give you specific help. This facility is not available with the programs that you get with the basic Windows package.

However you get into the help system (if you are using Help for the first time we suggest you start with Using Help from the Help menu) the Help Window will be the active window.

Inside The Help Window

The Help window is the same as any other window in the way you can maximise and minimise it, move it and change its size. There is one difference - you can only ever have one Help window open. If you select another option from the Help menu or you press F1 when you already have a Help window open, the new option will replace whatever is in the Help window.

Inside, the window is slightly different to others because you have five big buttons to enable you to move around the Help file easily. You are not restricted to whatever option you selected before entering the window. One of the five buttons operates a Search function, which allows you to type in what you are looking for. This is not an 'intelligent' search as it will only find what you have asked for if you have used the correct terms.

Cross References

The Index and many other sections have cross references (in green if you have a colour monitor) that are underlined. If you select one of these they will provide you with more information. If you are using a mouse, the arrow turns into a helping hand. You can use the Tab and Enter keys to select the cross references from the keyboard. You must move down the file with the Arrows keys or the Page Up/Down keys because the Tab key will not move off the information currently displayed.

Different Types Of Cross References

There are two types of cross reference. One has a solid underline, which will move you to the relevant section of Help and display a full window of information.

The other type has a dotted underline and will give you a short definition of the underlined term. The definition will pop-up over the top of your window. You select these in the same way as the others but the definition will only stay on the screen while you are holding down the mouse button or Enter key. The minute you let go, the definition will disappear. You can find all these terms grouped together in the Glossary option on the Help menu in the Program Manager.

Chapter 3 First Encounters

The Help Window Menu

From this menu you can open other application's Help files. You also have a direct link to the Using Help file.

There are several other things you can do with whatever topic you have got in the window:

Copying

You can copy it to the Clipboard. From there it can be Pasted to any application. The copy you paste will not look as pretty as it did on the Help Window because you lose all tabs, fonts, lines and underlines and just get the basic text.

Printing

You can print the topic if you've got a printer. The Help files are just distillations of the User Guide so we can't imagine why you would want to print them, but you can anyway!

Making Notes In Help Files

You can make your own notes on any aspect of a Help topic with the annotate option. Your notes will be 'paper clipped' to the top of the current Help topic. You can see what you have written later by selecting the paper-clip symbol. Your notes are saved automatically for you.

Bookmarks

You can also put in bookmarks to mark places that you need to look at a lot. To add a bookmark, get the 'page' containing the information you want marked in the window. Then select Bookmark, and give the mark a name. The name will then appear on the Bookmark menu. Whenever you want to go to that section of Help, you just need to select the name from the menu.

You can have as many bookmarks as you need but unlike the paper variety you cannot move them around. If you do not want a section marked any more, you have to delete the mark.

Part 2 - The Controllers

This section of the book looks at the Gods of your new World. These are the three Managers, plus the Task List. They all work alongside the Control Panel. Since you need to work with these intimately during your journey we have covered these in some detail. If you are just starting out you will not come across them all at once but you will need to know about the Program Manager and Task List straightaway. You will need to make the acquaintance of the File Manager shortly after that, with the Print Manager following close on his heels - if you have a Printer, that is.

Chapter 4 - The Program Manager

What Does the Program Manager Do?

The Program Manager is at the centre of the Windows world. He is the controller who allows you in to Windows and gives you access to both the world itself and the equipment that you have been given. He is omnipresent. He is there from the moment you run Windows to the moment you close it down. If you try to close him down, he will close your doorway into the Windows world too.

Tip: If You Lose The Program Manager

If you lose the Program Manager through one of the dreaded Unrecoverable Application Errors you can still carry on working with the programs that are already open. You will not be able to open any more, nor will you be able to leave Windows in the normal way.

To leave Windows without having to do a potentially damaging Reset, close all open windows (including minimised ones) either by selecting Close from their Window Control menus or by pressing [Alt + F4]. Once they are all closed Windows will close down automatically.

The Program Manager allows you to see many different views of the new world. With his help you can choose what you want to look at and put it into a window. You can also choose the equipment you want to use to record what you are looking at. Whatever you want to do in Windows, you will need to collect your tools and materials from the Program Manager.

Program Manager looks after the programs that Windows knows about. The links for the programs that you selected during the set-up procedure are already in place. The programs will be stored in one of Program Manager's inner windows . You can always add more when the need arises.

Although you need him around you do not need to have PM's (which is what we affectionately know him as) window fully open throughout your time in Windows. You can always minimise it when you are not working with him.

Chapter 4 The Program Manager

You will normally use PM either when you want to use a program or when you enter or leave Windows. His other job is to allow you to organise the programs you want to run within Windows in a meaningful way.

As with all applications in Windows you will need to use the menus to do most things in PM. The menu options are loosely divided between:

Running programs

Taking programs or files into and out of PM control

Changing the way programs look in PM's window

Creating and deleting Group windows

Changing the contents of PM's Group windows

Arranging Group Windows

Arranging the contents of a Group window.

Running programs

To Open A Window And Run A Program

To run a program, you can either:

1. Use your mouse to double click over the icon that represents the program.

    If you press Shift while double clicking the mouse you can run the program in a minimised window

2. Use the keyboard to select the icon that will open a window.

3. If the program you want to run is not represented by an icon in Program Manager's window, you can select Run from the File menu and type the program name. If the program is in a directory on the `path' using just the program's name (with it's extension) will be sufficient. If not, you will need to type in the full path name.

After you've opened an application's window, you need to use the Open option from the File menu if you want to work on a previously saved file. You will be able to select the file from the Open dialogue box (see Selecting Files/Path names From Dialogue Boxes later in this chapter).

You can also Open a file, if that has been added to the Program Manager's window, in exactly the same way as running a program. The only difference is that when you open a file, the associated program is run automatically. But more of that later.

Adding and Taking Programs/Files off PM

Most programs that are compatible with Windows will install themselves automatically. If they do, they will add themselves to PM just by you putting the program disk into a disk drive and typing a simple command that will be in the program's manual. There are a few programs that don't help you very much, however, so you will have to install those yourself.

Adding More Programs To Program Manager

If you have an awkward program, there are two ways that you can install it yourself and then let PM know about it. You can either use the set-up procedure (from Windows Setup that is available through PM) or you can use the New option on PM's File menu.

Both have advantages and disadvantages: New is useful if you are installing one or two programs. It is fast, but you have to know where the file is (the full path name) and type a 'description' (the name you want put underneath the icon). Setup is slow, partly because it takes time to search the disk, but it will do everything for you.

Adding A Program With New

To add a new program to the Program Manager select New from Program Manager's File menu and then OK if 'Program item' is selected in the New dialogue box. You will then be asked for the description and the pathname (the command line).

The description can be anything that will help you recognise the program. Or you can leave it blank - Windows will then put the program name there for you.

The command line needs the program's name, either just its filename and extension or its full path name if it's not on the 'path'. If you need the full path name and are not sure what it is - or find it easier to select it from a list rather than typing it - select Browse. This will give you the standard filename selection dialogue box.

Tip: Selecting Files And Path Names From Dialogue Boxes

Whenever you need to type in a filename or a pathname you can select it from a list supplied by Windows. With the PM's New option it does not appear unless you ask for it. If you are saving or opening a file in most applications the dialogue box appears automatically.

The filename selection box has four main areas apart from the Dialogue Box controls and the grey OK and CANCEL buttons, which we covered in Chapter Three.

At the top there is the filename box. You can type the filename here, or a combination of wildcards and an extension. Wildcards will narrow down the range of files that you will be given to choose from.

Displayed underneath will be 'directory' with a space for the pathname. Windows will have built up the bits of the path that it suspects you want. The drive name and starting directory will be already displayed. You'll probably find that the starting point will be c:\WINDOWS but it will depend on the application's preference settings.

Below these are two larger inner boxes. The left hand one is for files and the right hand one is for directories.

The Files box will show you all the files which match whatever is in the filenames box and are stored in the directory you have selected. Before you have selected a directory it will show you any files that Windows has found in the directory named in the 'directory' space.

The directory box will show the sub-directories that branch off from the initial directory. It will also show the (..) which is the way up the tree, plus the disk drive names in case the file you are looking for is on another disk to the one selected.

To select a file:

1 Check that the wildcard and extension that Windows has given you are correct. If not, change the wildcard or extension.

   If the file you want is in the initial directory and you have got the extension right, the file should already be in the left hand box. If not, you will need to select the correct directory.

Chapter 4 The Program Manager

2   Select a directory.

Double click the mouse over the directory name or move to the right hand box with Tab and highlight the directory you want with the Arrow keys. Press Spacebar to select it.

If the file you want is higher up the tree than the initial directory select (..). Selecting (..) will take you up the tree one level at a time, back towards the root directory.

If it is in a sub-directory lower down, select that one or the one between it and the initial directory. For example, if the full path name for the file you want is:

c:\WINDOWS\JOURNEY\WEEK2\MAPS\RIVER.BMP

You would need to select each sub directory in turn; **JOURNEY**, then **WEEK1** and lastly **MAPS**. We've assumed Windows is the initial directory that is already selected.

When you select a directory, with a single click or move over it with the Arrow keys, it will be highlighted and put into the filename box. The selected directory will not move down to the directory space until you either double click the mouse or press Spacebar.

You should finish with the full path name in the directory space and a selection of files from the final sub-directory (**MAPS** in the above example) to choose from.

3   You can then select the file.

4   If you haven't found the file, start at number 1 again!

Windows will always try to find the program for you. It will put '*.exe' into the filename box when you ask it to run a program. As some programs have a '.com' extension, you may have to alter the extension before it will find the program you are looking for.

Adding A Program With Setup

Select Windows Setup from PM by double clicking the mouse or pressing Enter when it is highlighted. You then need to select the Set Up Applications options from it's Options menu. Windows will then carry out a search of the selected disk(s). It will be looking for all programs that it knows it can run.

Chapter 4 The Program Manager

When the search is complete a new dialogue box will appear with two smaller boxes inside it. The left hand box will contain all the programs it has found while the right hand box will receive the programs that you select. You install them in Windows by pressing the ADD button. The REMOVE button will take any program from the right hand box back to the left hand one if you have selected one by mistake. Remove doesn't de-install a program from Windows.

Once you have completed the set-up, you have given the program over to PM's safe keeping.

Storing Files With PM

You can do something even more powerful with PM - you can give him actual files to look after, as well as programs.

If you use several files a great deal, you can have immediate access to them when you enter Windows. You then don't have to run the program and then open the file that you want to work with.

As always with Windows there is a long winded way that you can add files to PM with the keyboard and a short cut way using the mouse. Your Staff really does show how magical it is here!

The shortcut way of adding a file to PM is to open a window for both the File Manager and the Program Manager. The directory that contains the file you want to lodge with PM must be open in File Manager. The two windows need to be visible on the viewing screen, so you may have to cut one or both of them down to size. Once the file has been selected, simply drag the file across to PM (an icon for the file will take the place of the arrow on the screen) and drop it in the 'Group' window where you want it to go.

To add a file to PM with the keyboard, if the program associated with it is in the Path, follow the same procedure as you would if you were adding a program. Just replace the program's with the file's pathname in the Command Line box. If the program associated with the file is not on the path you will need to put the program's pathname first followed by a space, with the full pathname for the file after that. For example to put your river map under PM's tender care you would need to type:

[c:\WINDOWS\PBRUSH.EXE] then a space, followed by
[c\WINDOWS\JOURNEY\WEEK2\MAPS\RIVER.BMP].

In this case you will not be able to use Browse to find the file's name for you. Browse would put

Chapter 4 The Program Manager

the program name in correctly, but when you add the filename it will replace the program name with the filename. This is not much good because you need both.

You could, however, use Browse to build the name up for you so that you can check that you have got it right. You will need to press the CANCEL button instead of the OK button when you can see the file in the Files box. Then type the file's pathname yourself.

If you have no idea where the file is in the tree you can use the Search option on File Manager's File menu to find it.

Tip: Opening A File Or Running a Program Without PM

You can open a file or run a program from the File Manager. Simply select the program or file and double click the mouse or select Open or Run from the File menu if you are using the keyboard. If you are opening a file the associated program will be run as well.

You can run a non-Windows program that is not in Program Manager's care by selecting the DOS Prompt icon from PM and using DOS commands to run it.

The Delete Option

Delete takes the programs or files out of PM's control but it does not delete them from the disk. Once a program is deleted from PM you will not be able to run it directly from there.

How Programs And Files Will Be Displayed On PM

Whichever way you add a program or file to PM Windows will give the program an icon. If you want to use a different one, your choices are fairly limited unless you acquire additional software.

The description under the icon will depend on what you do. If you have used the mouse the file name will be underneath the icon, although you can change it after you have added it to PM by selecting Properties. If you added the file via the keyboard whatever you type into the description box will appear underneath the icon. If you leave the description box empty the program name will be put there for you.

Using the Properties Option

You use the Properties dialogue box when you add a new program to PM. You can also select the Properties option at any time when you want to change the way programs and files are displayed in PM. Whoever said "A Leopard cannot change his spots" was wrong in this context. Rather like actors, files and programs lodging with PM can - with your help - dip into the Properties box and completely change their appearance.

You will rarely need to change the Command line entry. The only time you might need to change it would be after rearranging your filing system and moving your files to different branches of your directory tree. If PM can't find the file at the location you have given him he will not be able to open it.

HEALTH WARNING! Don't, whatever you do, try to rearrange the programs that came as part of the Windows package. They are all interlinked and you are very likely to finish with your very own Windows scrap heap instead of a nice bright world.

Changing The Way Programs Look

Changing The Description

You can change the description for any selected program or file if it will make more sense to you with a different name. For example, Reversi (to us) is really the same as Othello so we have put that into Reversi's description. You may also need to change descriptions if you move several files onto PM with the mouse that are associated with the same program. If you do not change the description immediately you add each file you will not be able to tell which file is which.

Changing The Icon

You can also change the icons used to represent the programs and files on PM.

Each Windows application has been given one or more icons that are embedded in its program file. When you select the Change Icon button in the Properties box the Select Icon box will appear. If you want a different icon, pressing the View Next button will show what other icons have been included with the program.

In general the major controlling programs like PM, Control Panel and File Manager do have a choice while the humbler accessories like Paintbrush and Write don't. If none of the icons included with a program take your fancy, you can borrow one from another program. To do that, type the name of the program that has the icon you want to use. Then select one of the icons that program has available. For example you could have the Paintbrush icon representing a Recorder file by typing [PBRUSH.EXE] in place of [RECORDER.EXE].

Non-Windows programs do not normally have an icon with them so PM's program (PROGMAN.EXE) has a selection of very basic ones for you to choose from - it will automatically give it the DOS icon to start with. You can always type another program name into the Filename box and use any of the other icons available. You can also use the selection of icons in the PROGMAN.EXE file for any other program or file.

If you want to be more adventurous and modify existing icons or create ones of your own, you will need an Icon Editor. You do not get one with Windows but they are in the 'public domain' so they are very cheap. The best place to get public domain software is down the telephone line. You will need to use Terminal and a modem to 'log on' to an electronic Bulletin Board and 'download' the programs from there onto your disk. For more information, turn to the chapter about the Terminal.

Chapter 4 The Program Manager

If you change the icon for a program or file, that change only applies inside PM. When you minimise the Window it turns back into its original icon.

Group Windows

PM initially displays four inner windows. These divide the programs PM is looking after into meaningful groups and surprise surprise, they are called group windows! You can move between these easily. With the mouse you just click on the window, whilst with the keyboard you can either press [Ctrl + Tab] or you can select the window you want from PM's Window menu. You can minimise or maximise a group. See Chapter Three for a reminder of what the differences are between inner windows and their parents.

Creating And Deleting Group Windows

Creating A Group

To create a new group window, select Program Group from the New option on PM's File menu and type the name you want displayed in the new group's title bar into the Description box. You will not need to type in a filename because Windows will put one in for you automatically.

Deleting Groups

The Delete option will also delete a group window. If you select a minimised group window and then the Delete option, that window and its icon will be deleted. You will not be given a chance to see what programs and files are going to be deleted.

You will not be able to delete an open group window if it has any icons in it because whenever you select a window you also select an icon as well. You can only select the group window and delete it if it is empty.

Changing The Contents Of Groups

If you want to rearrange the programs held by PM you can move the icons into different group windows. Using the keyboard, you can use the Move option on PM's File menu. If you're using a mouse, you simply select the icon of the program that you want to move and drag it to where you want it.

Copying Icons

If you want to display only one group window at a time and keep the other group windows minimised, you may want some programs to be available from wherever you are. You could decide, for example, that you need a copy of File Manager in each window. Or if you have a window for each project that you are currently working on, you may need a copy of Write, File Manager and Clipboard in each project's Group.

To copy an icon between groups either use the Copy option on the File menu or drag the icon with the mouse while holding down the Ctrl key at the same time.

NOTE: If you do not mind where the icon is positioned in the group window that you are going to move or copy it to, you can leave the destination window minimised. It will still accept the icon.

Auto Arrange

Auto Arrange and Minimise On Use on the Options menu are both switch options and so are either on or off.

Auto Arrange will automatically arrange the icons in a selected group window after you have changed the size of the window. The gap between icons will be determined by the icon spacing option in the Desktop setting in the Control Panel. PM will not do anything if you have just

Chapter 4 The Program Manager

added icons or taken them out of a window. See the section on the Arrange Icon option below.

Minimise On Use

Minimise On Use will automatically minimise PM after you have opened the program you want to work with. This is only useful if you are never going to want to open more than one window at a time. If you do want to open more than one window and you've got this turned on, you will need to restore PM's window as often as you have other windows to open.

Arranging Group Windows

The Window Menu

Tile and Cascade will resize and rearrange any open group windows into the same patterns as these options organise the parent windows into. See the section on 'Letting Window Arrange Your Windows ' in Chapter Three for more details.

Arrange Icon Option

The Arrange Icons option will regiment the icons in your selected group window, whenever you want.

To change the gap between icons in all windows you will need to go into the Desktop Setting option in the Control Panel. Icon spacing is measured in pixels. To make a noticeable difference you will need to alter the gaps between the icons by at least ten pixels. A pixel is too small for one or two to make a difference.

Selecting A Group

To select a group with the mouse is easy; just move the arrow into the window you want to work with and click the mouse's button.

To select a group with the keyboard you will need to use the Window menu. This has a list of your group windows. Get the one you want highlighted and press Enter. If you select a group window that is minimised it will be restored automatically. There is a slight problem here, however, because sometimes a group window can appear to get 'lost'.

If you are like us and like things neat and tidy, you might like to put all the icons that you use

Chapter 4 The Program Manager

most in one group window and make PM's window just big enough for that one and the minimised icons of all the others.

When you restore a group window that is bigger than PM's window it may not appear in the window. Scroll Bars will appear down the sides of PM's window. The restored group window is there somewhere, you just can't see it.

It can be very confusing when this happens because you can be left with a window full of inactive groups and no active window in sight. We totally flipped when it happened to us, overlooked the scroll bars and ended up resorting to Tile as the only way we could get the group back!

To avoid this, leave Windows and Save the Changes if you have made radical changes to the size and make-up of PM's window. That should help him keep track of where you want group windows put.

Saving The Changes

There is not a Save option on any of the menus in PM. The only way you can save any changes that you have made is to select the Save Changes box in the Exit Windows dialogue box - which is the last thing you see when you are leaving Windows. Windows will load the arrangement of Group Windows and the icons within them that you have Saved into PM every time you enter Windows. If you have made some major changes to PM it is a good idea to leave Windows straight afterwards to Save them. That way you shouldn't lose them if something goes wrong.

The Task List

The Task List, like PM, is available always. It will give you a list of all the programs you are running. It acts like a magic gateway giving you immediate access to any window (whether it is open or minimised) and the program or file inside. You can enter or leave any window this way. You can request the Task List's presence by double clicking the mouse button when the arrow is anywhere on the bare surface of the 'desktop' - any area of the viewing screen not occupied by a window. You can also use the Switch To option on the Window Control menu on any window to make the Task List window appear on your viewing screen.

You cannot leave the Task List running in a non-active window. Once you have used it to drop in to another window the Task List will disappear. Similarly if you call it up and then don't use it, it will disappear in a puff of smoke!

Inside the Task List window you will have all the applications that you are running, with the filenames alongside. There is no menu bar here, just the Window Controls menu on it and that only has a miserly two options. All the options you have are spread between a multitude of grey buttons.

Chapter 4 The Program Manager

The Grey Buttons

The SWITCH TO button allows you to switch to another window with the keyboard, after you have selected it with the Arrow keys. To operate the gateway with the mouse simply select the application that you want to work with and then double click the mouse button.

The END TASK button should carry a HEALTH WARNING. There is a dangerous piece of black magic lurking behind this button so don't use it unless there is absolutely no alternative. If you press it, it will stop the selected program dead in its tracks with awesome possibilities. It could leave temporary files that don't belong anywhere, files open that data will fall out of, procedures started but not finished and generally mayhem everywhere. Any one of these could cause a crash. But worse still, you could also lose the whole file that you were working on.

The CANCEL button will send the Task List on its way without doing anything if you select it by mistake.

The CASCADE And TILE Buttons will rearrange your open windows.

The ARRANGE ICONS Button will put any wayward minimised icons back along the bottom of the viewing screen. This is useful if you like your icons along the bottom of the screen but if you have other ideas for your icons it isn't terribly helpful!

The spacing between the icons will be determined by the Icon Spacing box in the Desktop Setting on the Control Panel if you use this button.

Chapter 5 - The File Manager

Introduction

The File Manager looks after all the files and programs that you are using. From now on we will just talk about files but please read 'files' to include programs as well.

The File Manager enables you to construct and move around the trees that hold your files, work with individual files and work with disks. If you are unfamiliar with electronic trees turn to your botanical guide! As you probably won't have one of those you'll have to make do with the section on Trees in 'Learning The Lingo'.

When you enter the File Manager you will see the tree display showing the tree that is on your hard disk. You can see a tree on a floppy disk by selecting the relevant drive. You can move up and down the tree and see what files you have got stored in what branches. You can also create new branches and cut out the dead wood of old ones.

Once you move to a branch, the files you have stored there will be in a window. Each directory is given its own inner window Once you have selected one or more files from a 'directory window' you can carry out a range of operations on them. From opening a window so that you can see what information a single file contains, through to deleting a group of them so that they are no longer on the disk.

You can Format floppy disks so that they are ready for you to work with. File Manager also enables you to Copy the entire contents of one disk to another and give them an internal name (volume label). You can even make a system disk but we will explain that when we get there.

There are very close links between the File Manager and the terms and concepts used in MS-DOS. So if your knowledge of MS-DOS is scratchy and you haven't followed this journey fully, you will not be able to drop in here and get all the answers. If you try, you will just finish up getting yourself incredibly lost. We will be referring to 'Learning The Lingo' anyway, because that has all the details, but you will need to read it first to be able to use File Manager effectively.

File Manager's Window

File Manager's window has all the normal things that a window has but there are a couple of extra controls on the Options menu.

The Status Bar

There is an optional element that is unique to File Manager's window. The Status bar is on the bottom border of the window. Its information will change depending whether you are looking at the tree display or at files in a directory window.

When the tree display is selected, the Status Bar will tell you how much space you have free on the selected disk. You need to keep an eye on how much free space you have because it has a habit of disappearing quickly. When you run short of space you will find that you cannot carry on doing what you want. If you find yourself in that situation, turn to the First Aid Kit.

When you have selected a directory window the Status Bar will tell you how much space the selected files occupy. This is useful as a rough guide if you are copying files to a floppy disk that only has limited space. But you may find that you can't use all the free bytes you are supposed to have available. Disk space is divided into blocks or clusters. Your files are stored in groups of clusters. If you have three-quarters of a cluster empty after your file has been saved it will remain empty. If the Status Bar tells you that there are 5000 bytes free and the selected files only add up to 4500 bytes you could still not be able to get all the files onto the disk.

Minimise On Use

Minimise on Use is an option that affects File Manager's window globally. This is the same as the Minimise on Use option in the Program Manager and will minimise the File Manager's window every time you open a file from there. You can look at directory windows and move files around but as soon as you open a file the window will be minimised automatically.

Constructing Your Tree

Selecting The Right Disk

A tree is tied to a disk, so if you:

    A. Have the wrong disk selected in File Manager

    Or

Chapter 5 The File Manager

B. Have the wrong disk in the disk drive

You'll be barking up the wrong tree! Sorry, we couldn't resist that.

If you have got the wrong drive selected you will need to select the one you want. You do this by moving the arrow over the required drive and double clicking the mouse. If you are using the keyboard, you need to press Tab, then Left or Right Arrow (until the dotted outline is over the one you want) and then press Enter.

If you have got the wrong floppy disk there is not a great deal we can do to help! It is important to label all your disks clearly, in pencil, so that the label can change as the contents change.

WARNING Never write on a five and a quarter inch floppy disk's label in ball point pen once the label is on the disk. You could damage the magnetic disk inside.

Tip: Selecting Different Trees

If you are moving around your forest, looking at several different disks do not take the disk out until you have selected another disk drive. The controllers in this world seem to like to have a last private look at a tree before they move on. You can only take the previous tree's disk out of the drive after you have selected another drive and there is another tree on the screen.

If you do try to remove the disk before selecting another drive you will get a message to say that your system cannot read the previous disk. You will not be able to do anything else until you have put the disk back into the drive.

The Sapling

You will probably notice that the sapling you see when you first enter File Manager is even stranger, as trees go, than we said it would be. Not only is it upside down with it's root at the top and branches at the bottom but it's a fraction one-sided too! Added to that, they grow down rather than out. We don't reckon this forest is a safe place to be when the wind starts blowing!

When you install Windows, the File Manager's display (if you have the c drive selected) will have a little sapling already growing.

If you already have other directories then your tree will be bigger than the one we are describing below.

Chapter 5 The File Manager

The Tree Display

On the File Manager's display you will be able to see the root directory c:\ with two branches (directories) DOS and WINDOWS coming off the trunk. If you select the root directory and double click the mouse, or press Enter, the files and directories it contains will appear in an inner window.

It is easy to tell the difference between a file and a directory inside the File Manager. The icon for a directory is bigger and looks like a filing cabinet's drawer divider. The file icons are smaller. Also directory names are put in the top left-hand corner of an inner window and are displayed between square brackets.

Directory Windows

The File Manager will give each directory its own inner window. From now on we will call an inner window in the File Manager a directory window.

Leaping From Bough To Bough

Whether you were a tree climber as a child or not you will be able to move up and down your tree (monkey fashion if you like) easily and quickly!

Going Down

You have two ways of moving inside a directory. You can either select it from the tree display or from the directory window of the directory it branches off from.

To select the directory straight from the tree display, expand the branch by clicking the mouse on any directory icon with a plus sign on it or use the Expand Branch options on the Tree menu. You can expand your tree automatically with the mouse when you select the drive, by pressing the Shift key while double clicking the mouse over the drive. Once you can see the name of the directory you want, you can open a window for it by double clicking the mouse or pressing Enter with the arrow over it.

You can also move down your tree one step at a time by opening a window for each directory in the path in turn. So if you were in a leisurely mood you could Open a window for 'Journey', select 'Week2' from there, select 'Maps' from 'Week2' and so on.

Going Up

The tree display is always available, so you can move up the tree quickly by selecting it again and moving directly to the branch you want. If you want to move up slowly one branch at a time, select the [..] directory from inside each directory window in turn. This moves you up the tree one step at a time.

Climbing Aids

Use the options in the Tree menu to display the tree if you are working with the keyboard.

The bottom of the Window menu will have a list of all the directory windows you have open. You can move from branch to branch by selecting a directory from there. You will be whisked to that branch as if by magic.

Making Your Tree Grow

Building your tree is simple. You can use the Create Directory option from the File menu from the tree display or a directory window.

The name of the new directory will appear in a lower branch on the tree display. It will also be put in the directory section of the directory window above it in the tree. Wherever you select it from, a new directory window will open. It will be empty apart from[..], the route back up the tree. The new directory will now appear in the file selection dialogue boxes.

Your trees can grow as big as you like but don't let them get out of hand. It is always a good idea to delete files off your hard disk that you are not using anymore. The same is true for directories; dead branches should be cut out.

Pruning

You can delete a directory in the same way as you delete a file. If there are any files that you want to keep, you must move them to another directory before deleting the one they previously occupied. If the directory has any files in it, you must delete all the files before Windows lets you delete this directory.

If you select the Delete option you will be need to press the DELETE button in the Delete dialogue box. Windows will then go away and delete the directory or files. If you have selected Confirm on Delete from the Confirmation option in the Options menu, you will have another chance to change your mind.

Working With Files

Selecting The Files You Want To Work With

Whenever you enter a directory window one file or directory will be selected or highlighted. That probably won't be the one you need so you must first select the one(s) you want.

Any files that you select will be highlighted. The last file you select will have a dotted white outline. If you deselect any files the last one will have a dotted black outline. These outlines serve the same function as a cursor does, helping you keep track of where you are.

Selecting And Working With One File

Selecting one file is easy. If you are using the mouse, move the arrow over the file and click the mouse button. If you are using the keyboard, the Arrow keys will move the highlight until you reach the one you want.

Once selected you can carry out any of the menu options that are relevant: Open, Print, Move, Copy, Delete, Rename and Change Attributes.

Open

The Open option has the same effect as double clicking the mouse while the arrow is over the selected file. It will open a window, run the program associated with the file and load the file into the window for you to read or work on.

Tip: Opening A Window So That It Is Minimised Straightaway

If you want to have ready access to a file but don't need it in an open window straightaway, you can press Shift while double clicking the mouse button. File Manager will then open a window, run the program and load the file as it would normally. It will minimise the window before you see it open!

Print

You can send the file to the Print Manager to be printed, provided the file can be printed and you have a printer, of course.

Move And Copy

You can move or copy the file to another disk or directory. If you want to use the mouse to move the file, move the arrow over the selected file and drag it either into another directory window or to a disk icon on the tree display. If you have the Confirm on Mouse Operation option in Confirmation selected you will always be asked to confirm that you really do want to move or copy the file.

To move or copy a selected file with the keyboard, select the appropriate option from the File menu and type in the path name of the directory you want to move the file into. If you are copying the file, you will also need to type the filename that you want the copy of the file to be called.

Delete

You can delete a selected file. Be careful because you will not be able to get the file back once it is deleted. Some computers have an 'Undo Delete' command but yours isn't one of them!

Chapter 5 The File Manager

Rename

You can rename the selected file but make sure you follow the rules for filenames. Remember that the mechanism for linking or associating files with programs is the extension on the filename. You can use Rename just to change a file's extension if you need to.

An example of where that might be appropriate would be to recover a corrupted Write file. Write creates a back-up file (.BKP) if you request it to, which is the previous saved copy of the file. You will not be able to open a .BKP file, however, because it is not associated with a program. You could change it into a Write file with Rename, simply by changing the .BKP extension to .WRI.

You could achieve the same effect on all your .BKP files by using the Associate option. This will link all .BKP files with Write so that you can refer back to them whenever the need arises.

If you need to use Rename on more than one file you will have to type all the filenames. If you are changing the filenames just to change their association, using the Associate option might save you some time.

Tip: Opening A File With No Extension

If you knock out a filename's extension by mistake you will not be able to open the file in the normal way. You will just be given the 'no association for this file' dialogue box. All is not lost because there is a way round it. If you run the program you need to use to work on the file first and then Open the file.

Don't forget, when you open the file you will need to change the *.extension in the file selection dialogue box. If you change it either to a single * or to *.* your file will appear in the Files box. If you leave any extension in the filename box your extensionless file will never put in an appearance. Alternately, you could type the name of the file you want to open yourself and not rely on Windows to do all the work for you.

Change Attributes

The Change Attributes option will allow you to change the attributes of a file. They are normally set by various MS-DOS programs automatically. So you should not need to use this option very often.

The attributes act like switches that are either on or off. If you are using MS-DOS programs like

BACKUP or XCOPY these will be able to reverse the switches. So if you selected Archive to turn on the archive switch, BACKUP could come along and deselect it, which could be a bit confusing if you thought you were in sole control.

If an attribute is turned on its initial letter will be displayed in the last column of the File Details table. You can ask File Manager to display File Details from the View menu.

Read Only

The Read Only attribute on your file acts like a write protect tab does on your floppy disks. You will only be able to read the file, not add to it, change it in any way or delete it. You could use this for a finished piece of work that you do not want to be changed. If you have it selected an R will appear in the attributes column of the File Details Table.

Archive

The Archive attribute will put an A in the File Details display for any file that has been created or modified since you last backed-up your disk. Setting it will force that file to be included in the next back-up. It is only useful if you use a backing-up system, like the MS-DOS Backup command, that allows you to be selective about which files you want backed-up.

Hidden

If you have selected the Hidden Attribute the file will not be displayed when you open its directory window. This is ideal for secret files that you don't want every Tom, Dick and Harry to read. They are not very secure however, because you can reveal hidden files by selecting the Show Hidden Files box in the Include dialogue box on the View menu. You can deselect the Hidden attribute if you decide that the secret's not secret any more.

System

You only need to worry about the System attribute if you are writing Windows applications.

NOTE: Don't change the attributes of an open file. Once a file is in a window it is under the control of the program that is running, not the File Manager.

Chapter 5 The File Manager

Tip: Don't Use File Manager Options On Open Files

Any file that is not open is under the control of the File Manager. When you open a file, control passes from the File Manager to whichever program you need to run to work on the file. If you select a File Manager option, like Move or Copy for a file in a window, Windows will give you a Sharing Violation Error. Two program cannot work with the same file within Windows.

Selecting More Than One File

There are marked differences between selecting a number of files with the mouse and the keyboard. So we have clearly marked which are instructions for the mouse and which are for the keyboard.

Selecting A list

MOUSE To select a list of consecutive files with the mouse select the top or bottom one in the list in the normal way. Then move to the other end of the list of files and press Shift while clicking the mouse button.

To deselect a list, just click the mouse again with the arrow over a file, or press an Arrow key.

If you have selected a list but want to extend or shorten it, move the arrow to where you want the selection to end and press Shift + click the mouse again. This doesn't always work the way you think it should. We recommend that you spend a few minutes experimenting with a selected list to see what happens.

KEYBOARD - To select a list of files, move to one end of the list with the Arrow keys, then press Shift + the Up or Down Arrow key to select each file in turn. If you press Shift + Left/Right Arrow the arrow will move into the next column and all files between will be highlighted.

To change your mind after you have selected a list, you can press Shift + the opposite Arrow key to deselect files in the reverse order. Pressing an Arrow key on its own will deselect all files except one. Which file will still be selected will depend on which Arrow key you pressed to deselect the list and so has nothing to do with the list.

Chapter 5 The File Manager

Scattered Files

MOUSE To select files scattered all over the directory window with the mouse, move the arrow over each of the files you want to select and press Ctrl and click the mouse.

You can deselect each file by Ctrl + clicking the mouse over any that you have selected.

You can use Ctrl + click and Shift + click in the same selection sequence. For example, if the files you want to select are mainly in a big group you could select those with Shift + click. If there were several others dotted around the window that you wanted to join onto the selected group, you could select those with Ctrl + click.

To select two groups of files that are separated by a few files that you don't want; highlight all of them, including the ones you don't want, with Shift + click. Then you can deselect the odd ones that you don't want with Ctrl + click.

The Official Guide gives you another way of selecting a second group after you have selected a first but we reckon that it's too complicated. We already get confused between Shift + click and Ctrl + click, we don't need another combination as well!

KEYBOARD To select scattered files with the keyboard you need to use the Selection Mode. We know we said Windows doesn't use Modes but here is one mode that you need to know about.

The Keyboard Selection Mode

Shift + F8 will give you a flashing outline, which is sometimes difficult to see, round the file that is highlighted. You can move this flashing outline from file to file with the Arrow keys and select the ones you want with the Spacebar. To deselect a file press the Spacebar a second time with the outline around it.

Selection mode will be turned off automatically when you select an option from the menus. If you want to turn it off yourself, press Shift + F8 again.

Select All And Deselect All

There are two options on the File menu that allow you to work with the entire contents of a directory. They can be used in conjunction with other selection techniques. You could for example, highlight all files with Select All, then deselect the ones that you don't need to work

79

Chapter 5 The File Manager

with, either with the mouse or the keyboard.

Deselect All will deselect any files that you have selected, no matter whether you have selected two or twenty. So you could use it to tidy everything up when you have forgotten which key combinations you should be using!

Using Wildcards As Selection Aids

You can use Wildcards in place of part or all of a filename if you just want to select files that have part of their names or their extensions in common. For example, you could select all files in the active directory window with a .BMP extension or all files beginning with B. For more information turn to the Section on Wildcards in 'Learning The Lingo'.

CAUTION: While you are going through the selection process unexpected things could start happening if you hit a wrong key. The easiest wrong key to hit is Enter because that is right next to the right hand Shift key. If you do inadvertently press Enter, File Manager will open a file. If a window opens and the file you last selected appears, it's not too difficult to understand what has happened. But if a totally different file is opened, it can be a bit perplexing. Windows could have opened the file that the cursor just happened to be over or the very first you selected.

If an unwanted file is opened you must resist the very strong temptation to ignore it and carry on by reselecting the File Manager's window. You should close the window first.

Tip: Dealing With The Unexpected Or Unexplainable

If the unexpected happens in Windows it is all too easy to brush it under the carpet and hurry back to familiar territory. Rather like young children learning to read, who call every word they don't know 'wheelbarrow' and hurry on.

With some unexpected things, once you have got a basic understanding of how Windows and its applications work, you will be able to work out what has happened if you give it some thought. There will, however, be times that you cannot make any sense out of what is happening. As you gain more confidence in this new world you will develop antennae to pick up these. They could be the only warning you get of an impending Gremlin attack.

The safest way of dealing with the unexplainable is to close down Windows and then reenter it again. You can then open your windows, load the files you were working on and carry on. Closing Windows will force it to sort out (or forget) any twists it may have got itself into. When you restart it again you should start with a clean slate.

Chapter 5 The File Manager

You will obviously not want to have to shut Windows down every five minutes, and neither should you need to. While you are feeling your way you will not understand much of what is happening anyway. As we have said before, and will no doubt say again, your best defence against Gremlins is to have back-up copies of everything. When you have developed your antennae you may be able to stop yourself going through quite as many crashes as you had to endure at the beginning. However, even if you develop antennae that look like antlers you will not be able to foresee every crash that is coming your way! SO BACK-UP EVERYTHING IMPORTANT.

What Can You Do With A Selected Group Of Files?

All the options that are available to you when you select one file will be open to you if you select a group of files. They do not all work on all selected files at once. Most do, some that need a filename to work with can cope with more than one filename in their dialogue boxes. They do this by separating the filenames with spaces. You can Delete, Rename, Move, Copy or Change Attributes of a number of files at the same time. Change Attributes, will disregard the attributes of individual files and change them all to the ones you have selected for the group.

There are two options, Open and Associate, that cannot work with multiple files.

If you Open a group of files you will be given a dialogue box saying that there is no association for that file. That really means that Windows doesn't know which file you want to open.

Associate

Associate is one option that is on its own. It only needs to have one file selected but it will act globally on files that may or may not be amongst the selected files.

Associate links files with programs. Normally Windows will do this automatically by adding the program's extension onto the end of the filename when you Save it. But if you want to use your own extensions or you want to look at the contents of a file that has no association, you can use Associate to create the link for you.

You can see clearly which file has an association with a program and which hasn't, by looking at the file icons. Files that have an association will have lines on their icon, while those that don't will just have a bare file icon. If you give a file a link through the Associate option its icon will change to one with lines on it.

Associate is only interested in the extension of one selected file. If you ask it to associate a file with a .BKP extension with WRITE.EXE (you must use the full filename of the program you want to link the file with), all files with a .BKP extension will be associated with Write.

When you have selected more than one file, Associate will pick up the extension of the top file that you have selected and will change the association for that one.

No Selection Needed

There are two options that do not work with selected files in the same way as the ones we have talked about above.

Run

Run is another way of running programs rather than going through the Program Manager. It will not pick up the name of a selected program and put it into its dialogue box for you. You must type the program's full filename (including the extension) into the Command Line.

Search

The Search option doesn't need a selected file. It finds files that you have mislaid in your filing system. You can type the name of the file you are looking for but you don't need to worry about the path name. If you are not sure of the name, you can use wildcards. You can also use wildcards if you want to find several different files.

To find all Notepad files, for example, you would type [*.TXT]. If you only know that the file you are looking for begins with a 'BR' you could type [BR*.*]. For more information on Wildcards see 'Learning The Lingo'.

You can also use Search if you need to know the full pathname of a file.

Looking At Your Trees And Branches

There are many different ways that your trees can present themselves (these trees get more unusual by the minute!). You will find these options in the View, Options and Window menus. It is not essential that you use these but you may find them useful when you have got time to explore them.

Displaying Directory Windows

There are several ways of displaying directory windows within the File Manager. Options like Minimise, Maximise, Tile and Cascade are common to other application windows but there is one which is unique to File Manager.

Replace On Open

Replace on Open on the View menu will replace the directory window on the display with the next one you select. This is useful if you want to go through several directories. You could potentially have ten or more directories, and that number of open windows might get a bit confusing.

Organising Your Files

There are many options that alter the way your files are displayed inside their directory windows.

We think that the View menu divides into two. The first three options allow you to select the way you want files displayed in a directory window. The second group will sort your files for you.

Chapter 5 The File Manager

Include, which is in a menu compartment of its own, also sorts your files but it allows you to select the type of file that you want to display. You can choose from Directories, Programs, Documents (associated files) and Other Files (files with no association).

Different Ways Of Displaying Files

You can display files by name or by file detail. 'Name' will give you just a list of filenames sorted in whatever order you have asked for. 'File details' on the other hand will list your files in a tabular form that shows the File's name, its size, last modification date and time, and attributes.

The Other option allows you to be selective about which file details you want to show. So you could just have your files name and size, or their name, size and last modification date, if you didn't want the whole table.

Putting Files in Order

Sorting By Name

If you sort your files by name they will be arranged in alphabetical order showing either just the name or the file details you have selected.

Sorting By File Type

Sorting by type will organise your files by their extensions. So all .BKP files will be together, all .WRI files will be together and so on. Within each group they will be sorted alphabetically by name. So FLORA.WRI will appear after FAUNA.WRI but FLORA.BKP will be near the beginning of the list with the .BKP files.

The Sort By option repeats Name and Type but gives you two extra ones; Size and Last Modification Date.

Sorting By Size

Selecting Size from the Sort By option will sort your files into descending order with the biggest file at the top.

Sort By Date

The Last Modification Date option will sort your files into the order that you last worked with them. In this order the last shall be first and the first last.

But, and it is a fairly big but, the files will only be in the right date order if the time and date are set correctly in your computer. If your computer's internal clock (which holds the date as well) is wrong when you save a file, your files will never appear in the right order when sorted this way. To try to make sure that this doesn't happen you will need to check that your computer's clock is correct every so often, particularly after a crash. You can check it from the Clock and Calendar applications. If you need to set the clock use the Date/Time settings in the Control Panel.

Changing the Sort By settings will only change the way the files in the active directory window are sorted. Although selecting the Set System Default box is supposed to make the sort apply to all directory windows, it only works from the tree display.

Juggling

To change the initial settings you will need to juggle with both the display options and the sort options to get the effect you want. Windows has been set up with 'Name' selected in both sections of the View menu. This will list the filenames in alphabetical order.

Because you have got similar options in both the display section and the sorting section it looks complicated but isn't really.

Confirmation

No, this doesn't involve a Windows World religious ceremony!

We have put it in a section on its own because it doesn't go alongside the others very easily. It gives you the chance to decide what actions you want to be asked about a second time. This is to make certain that you are absolutely sure what you want to do, before Windows goes away and carries out your instructions. We recommend that you select all of them. It will give you more dialogue boxes to select OK for but it may save you from total disaster. You may find you don't need the extra safety net that these boxes give you when you know what you are doing. But we have still got all ours selected.

There are four options here: Confirm on Delete, Confirm on Subtree Delete ('Subtree' is

Chapter 5 The File Manager

'windowspeak' for directory), Confirm on Replace and Confirm on Mouse Operation.

Confirm On Delete

To delete a file, if you have not got Confirm on Delete selected, you only have to select the DELETE button from the Delete dialogue box for the file to be deleted. If you have got Confirm on Delete selected you will get a second dialogue box after you have pressed the button. This will say "Are You Sure you want to delete this file?".

Confirm On Subtree Delete

Confirm on Subtree Delete gives you a dialogue box if you are deleting a directory. Remember that deleting a directory will delete all the files that the directory contained as well as the directory itself.

Confirm On Replace

Confirm on Replace will give you a confirmation dialogue box if you are saving a file onto a branch that already has a file of the same name. If you don't have Confirm on Replace selected the file in the branch will be overwritten by the one you are saving. You will have lost the file's previous contents forever. If it was just a previous version of the file then that will not matter. If, however, you have made a mistake with the filenames and accidently called two files by the same name and tried to store them in the same directory, then it could be disastrous. It is these sorts of disasters that Confirm on Replace is designed to help you avoid.

Confirm On Mouse Operation

We think that you should always select Confirm on Mouse Operation. If you are using a mouse with File Manager it is easy to move whole directories into other directories without meaning to. If we didn't have this selected our filing system would be in a terrible state. We have had to select the NO button more often than not when the 'Are you sure you want to move this file into that directory or that drive' message appears.

Working With Floppy Disks

You need to find your way round using floppy disks to load programs and files onto your system and take files and programs off. Generally the traffic in programs will be one way. When a program has been loaded onto your hard disk you will still have the original copy on floppy disk.

So if you decide you don't want it on your hard disk any more you can delete it. The only time you might want to copy a program to floppy disk would be to create a back-up.

Files, on the other hand, will probably travel both ways. If you thought floppy disks had been superseded by the hard disk, well, that is not quite how it has turned out. The extra memory available has been gobbled up by more powerful programs. Windows could never have been written without the invention of hard disks because it needs too much disk space. After you have collected a few more programs, you will find that you won't have enough room for storing large numbers of files. So, not only will you need to keep copies of important files on floppy disk, for back-up purposes, you will also need to take old files off your hard disk. Leaving as much space as possible for the files you are using daily will become a pressing priority.

If you don't think about saving disk space (and even if you do) you will run out before long. The First Aid Kit will give you some clues of how to cope when it does strike, meanwhile here is the low-down on using disks.

The File Manager's Disk menu has six options. We will not be covering the last two options here as they deal with topics outside the realm of this book.

Copy Disk

The Copy Disk option allows you to copy the contents of one disk to another one. It will only copy whole disks. The disks that you are copying the data from and to must hold the same amount of information. So you can't put the contents of a high capacity disk onto two low capacity disks, for example.

Anyone who has copied disks on an older machine, with less memory than this generation of computer, will be pleasantly surprised. Gone are the days when you had to sit there for hours playing disk jockey because the computer could only absorb minute portions of the disk before you had to change the disks over.

To copy a disk, you select the drive you want to use and insert the disk you want the information copied to (the destination disk). File Manager will check that the disk is empty and ready to receive the contents of the other disk. You then insert the disk you want to copy (the source disk) and Windows copies the contents to your computer's internal memory or hard disk. Once that is done you will be asked to switch disks. The copy in your computer will then be copied onto the destination disk. The disk should then contain all the files that were on the other disk. Don't let the message in the dialogue box worry you when you first start - it says it is copying when it is only reading your source disk. You may, or may not, be asked to swap the disks again.

Chapter 5 The File Manager

File Manager does sometimes say it can't copy a disk. If you have used the disk before without any problem, and you haven't got the write protect tab/switch on, try it again. It should copy the disk without any trouble. So persevere, Windows might just be being 'finicky'.

If you want to copy only part of a floppy disk to another and the files are not also on your internal hard disk you will need to use the Copy option on File Manager's File menu. You will need to follow the same procedure as Windows did to copy the whole disk manually. That is, copy the files to the c: drive and then change disks and copy them back the other way.

Label Disk

The Label Disk option allows you to give your floppy disk a 'name' that is stored on the disk. It can be longer than a filename, up to eleven characters. The name you type into the dialogue box will appear on the tree display between the disk icons and the tree area, on the left hand side.

If you use this option, you will still need to put an actual label on the outside of your floppy disks. A 'real' label should stop you having to put the disk into the drive every time you want to know what files it contains.

You can also give your hard disk a volume label too. This is more useful if you are on a network, to identify which disks are which. Don't forget to tell other people if you change your hard disk's label if you are on a network.

Format Disk

You need to use the Format Disk option before using a new disk. It will erase anything that was on the disk and create a new root directory ready for you to create directories and store files. The disk will be checked to see that it is working properly. If there is anything wrong with the disk, Windows will tell you it can't format it.

If you get the Unable to Format message and are sure that:

    A. You have inserted the right sort of disk for your computer

    B. You have selected the right capacity, either high or low

    (Your disk box label should tell you whether you have brought the right type of disk and what capacity they are)

C. You haven't got the write protect tab/switch on or the Write protection switch in the Protect position.

Try to format the disk several times. If you are still unable to format it you can be fairly sure that it's faulty.

Make System Disk

If you want the disk you are formatting to be a system disk you must select this option from the dialogue box.

System disks hold the information that your computer needs to 'Boot Up'. The Make System Diskette option will copy your system files onto a floppy disk. For further details, see the Emergency Recovery Disk section in the Tool Box chapter.

Saving The Changes

There is not a File Save option in File Manager. The only way you can save any changes that you have made to any of the menu options is to select the Save Changes box in the Exit File Manager dialogue box. This will enable you to put your settings in place of the initial values that came with the system. You can save the way you want files sorted or displayed and the level of confirmation, so that they are automatically selected whenever you enter File Manager.

Here endeth your Forestry lesson. Its time to move on and make you a Master Printer as well!

Chapter 6 - The Print Manager

You may only ever see the Print Manager fleetingly as a minimised icon at the bottom of your viewing screen but to be a Master Printer you need to understand what's going on behind the scenes.

Your first real meeting with Print Manager will be when your printer jams or if you forget to load your printer with enough paper. Then, behind a dialogue box that shows a message which is normally not too helpful, you glimpse Print Manager lurking in the background.

This may suggest that Print Manager is sinister. It is the only part of Windows that seems to have a mind of its own - popping up when you don't expect it. But Print Manager is a friendly soul and can help you convert your masterpieces from the electronic world of Windows back into our world - on paper.

Why Have A Print Manager?

Remember, right at the beginning of this book, we said that Windows can 'multi-task' more than one application at a time?

Multi-tasking can cause problems for printers. Imagine that two programs are running and they both try to print at the same moment. If one's printing a short story and the other is printing your company's annual report, you may see:

> Once upon a time, Your chairman says, there was a little house that we've had a good year...

This will impress neither your shareholders nor your publisher!

Using Print Manager allows your application to carry on printing even if your printer goes off-line temporarily, say, because it's run out of paper.

Queues, Queues And More Queues

The Print Manager avoids this by introducing a 'print queue' of documents waiting to be printed. This queue is like every other queue in life; you join it as the beginning, gradually move along it and, finally, you receive whatever service you've been patiently (or not) waiting for.

Chapter 6 The Print Manager

The Print Manager writes the information that the printer needs, and that your application would have sent to the printer, to a hidden file. It then tells Print Manager to include this file in the queue.

The description above is rather too simple. Print Manager can manage more than one printer and many applications trying to access it at once.

Print Manager has some special internal magic that allows it to start a print job, if the printer is available, before the application has finished producing the file. Like a cat chasing its tall, it never overtakes itself.

Using The Print Manager

Whenever one of your applications is printing, the Print Manager is started automatically and runs as a minimised icon. Even if no print jobs are queued, you can open the Print Manager's window by double clicking the Print Manager icon.

The window that opens has four sections. There's a menu along the top, an area with three buttons, a message box and a list of print jobs.

If you have more than one printer, there is a separate print queue for each one. You can select a print queue by clicking the mouse over the printer name.

The buttons are: PAUSE, RESUME and DELETE. Some may be greyed-out if there are no jobs in the selected print queue or if you previously selected PAUSE for a printer.

PAUSE will temporarily suspend a print job. This has the same effect as if your printer runs out of paper. Print Manager doesn't always stop immediately so you may need a good deal of luck if you want to replace paper between sheets.

RESUME will be available only after you paused a print job. It resumes the job from where it left off. If your printer jams you can't tell Print Manager to reprint that page - you have to delete that job and restart the printout from the beginning. Some applications include 'From' and 'To' page numbers when you print from them - you can then print just the pages after the problem.

To delete a print job, you press the DELETE button. Print Manager asks you to confirm that you want to stop printing. If the application is still giving Print Manager data when you confirm that you want it to stop, you may see a Sharing Violation dialogue box. Just click the CANCEL button.

Chapter 6 The Print Manager

The main area of the window shows which jobs are in the print queues for each printer. The list is in the order in which they are to print, with the job now printing at the top of each list.

Print Manager Menus

There are two menus: Options and View.

The three groups of options in the Options menu control different aspects of Print Manager's operation.

Priority Options

Selecting a higher priority for Print Manager will produce printouts more quickly at the expense of slowing down your applications. A low priority means that printing will not interfere as much with your applications but slows down printing. The best setting depends on the speed of your computer, the speed of your printer and on personal preference. Experiment with different combinations and then decide which suits you.

Flash Options

The next group of options controls what Print Manager does when it wants to let you know that it needs attention. They are only relevant if the Print Manager is not the active window and the problem is not urgent. The Flash Always option always alerts you by displaying a message in a dialogue box.

The Flash if Inactive option just BEEPs (if the Sound option is on in the Control Panel) and flashes the window border or the minimised icon. You must open the Print Manager's window to see what it wants.

The Ignore if Inactive option doesn't display messages if the Print Manager window isn't active.

If the situation merits your immediate attention, like a printer being off-line, Print Manager always opens a dialogue box straightaway.

Network Option

The Network... option is only available if your computer is attached to a network. We won't say much about this, only that it allows you to control various aspects of Print Manager's use of any printers attached to other computers on the network.

Leaving The Print Manager

You can leave Print Manager by selecting the Exit option. If there are any print jobs either queued or printing, you see a dialogue box warning you that leaving Print Manager will stop all the print jobs. If you select OK, you'll have to rerun the applications, open whatever files you want to print and then select print.

The View Menu Options

We'll only mention two options in the View menu as the other options control various aspects of networked printers. Time/Date Sent is a switch that allows you to decide whether or not to display the date and time the file was sent in the print queue display. Print File Size is also a switch; you can display the sizes of print files or not.

When Not To Use Print Manager

As we've said, Print Manager is a friendly little fellow when you get to know him. So, why do the Printer options in the Control Panel have a box that allows you to by-pass him and print directly to a printer?

The answer is simple: Print files can grow quite large. Graphics images can require one or two Megabytes per page. It's not unusual to see print files of ten or twenty Megabytes even if the file you're printing is just text and only fifty Kilobytes long. Almost all printing in Windows uses graphics, so you always create huge files.

That's fine if you have plenty of disk space because Print Manager does a good job of tidying up after himself, but it can cause problems if you're short of disk space.

There's another, more subtle reason to by-pass Print Manager. He adds another layer to the process of getting a page printed. The application first writes the file and then Print Manager must read the file and drive the printer. This all makes printing a file slower.

If you have only one printer and you never start more than one print job at a time, it's worthwhile running for a couple of days with the Print Manager disabled. If you notice an improvement, fine. If not, continue using Print Manager so that you'll be ready when you get your second printer!

Chapter 7 - Control Panel

Introduction

The Control Panel enables you to have some say in the way this world presents itself to you and the way you can work with it. It is your very own Spell Book. It will enable you to adjust the equipment that you have been given so that it works in the way you want, not the way the gods have preordained.

The Control Panel And WIN.INI

All settings in the Control Panel are actually stored in your WIN.INI file. WIN.INI is Windows' initialisation file that Windows applications look at when they begin work, to pick up their settings.

It is possible to change these settings by editing WIN.INI from the Notepad, but it is safer to do it from the Control Panel. There are some settings (more advanced and not covered here) that you have to change directly from WIN.INI. Be careful if you want to change those. If you make a mistake with WIN.INI you could as good as send your whole system up in a puff of smoke! So make a back-up copy of the present version first. For more information about WIN.INI read the WININI.TXT and WININI2.TXT files that you will find in the Windows directory on your hard disk.

Each application will only check the WIN.INI file once, when they are first started with the Run or Open options. Any settings you have changed by editing WIN.INI will only affect applications that you open after you made the changes, not ones currently in a window. The Control Panel, however, has some more powerful magic all its own. Any changes you make there will take immediate effect.

Having said that, changes can only have an effect if they apply to the applications you currently have on your system. Some of the options from the Control Panel might sound very useful but they are not used by the programs in the Windows package. You will only use them if you install more complex packages like Microsoft's Excel.

Control Panel Settings

The range of Settings available from the Control Panel vary from important things like what country you are in, to mere playthings like being able to fill the unused background of your screen with pretty patterns. We have divided them into groups. The important ones we will cover first. The less important ones we will leave till last and give you the pleasure of finding out how they work yourself. Why should we do all the work?

Group 1 includes things that you should have checked at the beginning of your journey. The settings in Group 2 contain options that allow you to adjust various things like the mouse buttons and the keyboard's key repeat rate. Group 3's settings will only become important at various stages of your journey. If, for example, you install a new printer, or want to use Windows and non-Windows applications together you will need to alter the settings there. Group 4 doesn't need looking at until you either have an idle half hour or you feel like having some fun!

Group 1

The settings in Group 1 are International and Date/Time. If you synchronised your clocks before you installed Windows and selected the correct language during Setup both the International and Date/time settings should be correct, but it is as well to check.

International

There are a number of things like time, numbers and currency that vary in the way they are written from country to country. If you set the right language during the Setup procedure all the other options should be set automatically, although you can change them if you need to.

The Country Setting

If you change the Country setting the four Format options will be altered automatically. The Date, Time, Currency and Number formats will be changed to agree with the Country you have chosen, as long as you haven't changed them yourself. Once you have changed a format, Windows will assume that you want that setting to stay. So if you need a format changed when you change the country setting, you will have to alter it yourself.

Language

When you select your language in Setup it will set all the other International options to agree with it. If you change it after that, nothing else changes!

When we saw that you could select the language, we thought that it meant that Windows was a multi-lingual package and could communicate with you in the language of your choice. But we were wrong! It can only work in English. The Language Setting does very little unless you are using advanced Windows programs that can carry out language specific tasks.

If you want to change the language setting you will need to tell Windows where to find the file with the information it needs. Normally this will be on one of your original Windows disks.

Keyboard

There are a large number of different keyboard layouts that are country based. For example, the French keyboard is different to ours and the German one is different again.

You will have selected your keyboard during Setup so there should be no reason to change this Setting. The option is here if you ever need it.

Measurement

You have two choices for the type of measurement that you want your system to use. You can have English or Metric. We have not found an application that uses this option in the basic Windows package. The only one that we thought might have done was Write because that uses a Ruler and measures margins but that automatically works in inches. If you want to work in centimetres you have to select that from within Write.

List Separator

A List separator is a character that tells your computer where the end of one item in the list is. It then knows anything that follows is part of a new item. Separators are most commonly used in databases to separate different parts of the name, address and any other information you want to include in a record. The option in the Control Panel is set to a ',' which is the most common one.

As far as we are aware this is not needed for the applications that come with Windows.

The Four Format Options

The four formats each have their own CHANGE button. If you press these they will open another dialogue box that contains all the different elements that you can alter.

Date Format

There are two date formats: a long one and a short one. The Short Date format allows you to choose how you want the date displayed in a numerical form. The long one enables you to change the way it is displayed when the date is written out in full. Both options give you a choice on the order that you want to display the different elements of the date. So you can change the position of the year, month and day easily.

Short Date Format

The Short Date format allows you a choice of:

    A. A character to separate the different elements.

    B. Whether you want a zero put in when the day or month is a single digit.

    C. Displaying the year in its full or abbreviated form.

The short Date Format is used by the File Manager for the Last Modification Date. It is also used by Notepad if you ask for your file to be date stamped every time you open it.

Long Date Format

The long date format has the added option of including the day's name. You can either have it in full, 'Sunday' or in an abbreviated form 'Sun'. The day that you see is only an example, the right day will be put in when you return to the International dialogue box. Provided that your date setting is correct, of course!

Some word processors allow you to type a code into the text instead of the date and they will insert the full date automatically. Write doesn't have this facility but some of the other Windows W.P. packages probably do.

Time Format

There are three options for displaying the time. You can either select a twelve or twenty four hour clock. A different separator can go between the hours, minutes and seconds. Finally there is an option to put a zero in front of an element when it is a single digit.

The File Manager will use the time format you select in its Last Modification Time column in the File Details table.

Currency Format

In the Currency Format dialogue box you can choose what currency symbol you want to use and where you want it put in relation to the figures. You can also select how you want a negative figure displayed and what symbol you want to use. The final option is how many decimal places will be displayed for monetary values.

There are lists of different placements and forms of negative that you can choose from. For the other two options you will have to type in what you want.

Number Format

You can alter the number of digits you want displayed after the decimal point. You can even change the decimal point to something else if you need to. The separator between the hundreds and thousands can be changed to another character and you can choose whether you want a decimal to have a zero in front of the point or not.

Both Number and Currency formats will be crucial for Spreadsheet and Accountancy packages. They do not appear to be used by the basic Windows software, however.

Tip: Check What Additional Software Needs

Check to see what additional software is looking for. It may be that the programs do all their own setting up, in which case it won't matter what you have got the settings set to in WIN.INI.

If your add-on software doesn't pick up its settings from here, and it is looking for different formats or separators to the ones you have asked Windows to use, it could cause problems.

The Date/Time Settings

Use the Date/Time Setting to set your clock and calendar to the correct time and date. They will both be displayed in the format selected in the International settings described in the previous section. So here is something that uses International's formats!

You can change them simply by selecting the segment that needs changing with the mouse or Tab key and overtyping the number already there with the one you want. If you are using the mouse you can also make slight alterations by using the tiny arrow buttons at the side, after selecting the segment you want to change.

Group 2

The settings in group 2 mainly alter physical things about your system like whether you computer beeps at you and the speed that the cursor moves across the screen when you are pulling it with the mouse.

The Sound Setting

This setting allows you to make your computer "BEEEEP" at you when you ask it to do something it cannot do. If you carry on pressing the Down Arrow when you have reached the end of a file, for example, your computer will complain bitterly by beeping continuously.

It is entirely a matter of personal preference whether you want this on or off. We have got our 'beeper' turned on. It wakes us up with a jolt when we do something wrong! If you don't select it and you ask Windows to do something it cannot do, nothing will happen.

The Keyboard Setting

The Keyboard Setting allows you to change the Key Repeat Rate. When you hold a key down for more than half a second the key will be repeated at the rate you have selected. If the rate is set fairly fast you will get lots of multiple characters when you hold a key down too long. A fast repeat rate will however, allow you to move around quickly with the Arrow keys. Alternately, if you cut the repeat rate down to nothing, you will eliminate multiple characters altogether but you will only be able to move around a window at a snail's pace.

You therefore have to strike some sort of balance between the speed you want to move around the screen and the margin of error you want to allow for the accuracy of your typing.

To change the speed, move the selection button along the track. If you have forgotten how to do that go back to the section on Selection Sliders in Chapter Three. You can then type some characters into the Test box, or try holding down a key, to check that the new rate is alright before you press the OK button.

Mouse Settings

The settings available for your mouse allow you to adjust the magic of the mouse so that it will move at a different speed across the screen. You can also change the time that can elapse between two clicks. That determines whether it is a double click or two singles.

Mouse Tracking Speed

The Mouse Tracking Speed determines how fast the arrow, or whatever is on your mouse's tip, will move across the screen when you move your mouse on the mat. If you set it too fast there is a danger that it will spend more time off the screen than on! Because the arrow is white and is often moving over a white background inside a window, it's quite easy to lose it when it is on the screen. We have found the mouse easier to work with, if we slow the tracking speed right down. Although you might be able to cope with your arrow moving faster.

Double Click Rate

The double click rate lets you determine what is a double click and what is not. It specifies how little time you can leave between two clicks if you want them to be a double click. If you click the mouse twice, slower than that, Windows will treat it as two single clicks.

It is easier to execute a double click if the rate is slow. If you slow it down too much, however, you increase the risk of Windows interpreting two clicks as a double click and doing something that you didn't want done!

Swapping Left/Right Buttons

You can swap the mouse buttons round so that the one you use predominantly is the Right one instead of the Left. You have even got a TEST area to try the other button out for size. Don't do what we did, however, which was to change the buttons over and then wonder why we couldn't press the Swap Left/Right button to change them back again. We eventually managed to change them back via the keyboard. It was only after that we realised we'd been pressing the wrong mouse button!

Group 3

You'll find that the settings in Group 3 become more important as your knowledge of Windows increases and as you add additional equipment onto your computer.

Ports

Your computer can have up to four serial ports. You can connect a printer, a modem or a more specialised peripheral like a plotter to each port. Usually, you find the connectors for these ports on the back panel of your computer. If your computer has just one serial port, it may be labelled "Serial". If you have more than one, they may be identified as "COM1" to "COM4".

When you use serial communication to talk with a peripheral, you need to set various 'parameters'. You will find the settings you need in the manual for the device or you can ask your supplier.

When you select Ports from the Control Panel, a dialogue box opens that has four pictures of plugs and sockets together with buttons labelled OK, CANCEL and SETTINGS. Underneath each picture is the serial port name. Even if you have only one serial port, all four pictures appear and can be selected but any changes you make will be ignored.

To alter the parameters on a serial port you either double-click on the picture or single click and then press the SETTINGS button. Windows doesn't highlight the picture - it's up to you to remember which one you've selected although the Settings dialogue box reminds you.

The Ports Settings dialogue box has a box for the Baud Rate with a hidden list of settings ranging from 110 (very slow indeed) to 19,200 (very fast). It also has groups of buttons for the number of data bits, the parity (to provide rudimentary error checking), the number of stop bits and the flow control method (rather like traffic lights). You must match the settings of each of these to what your peripheral expects to see. For details of these settings, see the chapter on the Terminal.

There's a rather clever feature in the Ports dialogue box. If, instead of clicking over a port, you hold the mouse button down, then the arrow changes to a connector. If you "plug" that connector into another port, by dragging it, a dialogue box opens that asks you to confirm that you want to copy the settings to the port into which you've plugged it. Just press the OK button to copy all the settings or CANCEL to 'unplug' the connector.

If you connect a printer to a serial port, it will use the settings you set here. The two applications

Chapter 7 Control Panel

that use serial ports to communicate with modems, Terminal and Cardfile, do not listen to these settings. They do things their own way!

Printers

Stand by for an explosion of dialogue boxes as you wander round from here. We counted four on screen at once with a dot-matrix printer and we think we got up to five with a laser printer. If you want practice using dialogue boxes, here's your chance!

The profusion of dialogue boxes means that it's difficult to get to the Help window. If you think you'll need Help, it's a good idea to select this from the Control Panel before you select Printers. You'll then be able to select the Help window from the Task List even if it gets hidden behind some of the dialogue boxes.

Selecting An Installed Printer

As with all good stories, this one begins simply enough. If you select Printers, a dialogue box opens that lists the installed printers, the printer that will be used if you don't select another one (the so-called 'default' printer) and a few buttons. You can switch between printers from here and decide whether you want applications to use the Print Manager or to direct their output straight to the printer.

You can also make printers Active or Inactive. If you have only one printer attached to each port on your computer, pressing the ACTIVE and INACTIVE buttons are just like turning the printer on and off line. If you share ports between printers, only one printer can be active on a port. When you select another printer and press the ACTIVE button, the printer that was Active automatically changes to Inactive. If that seems Irish, try it and see for yourself.

To change the default printer, double-click the mouse button with the arrow over the printer you want to work with. Using the keyboard, you select the box with the Tab key and then select the printer with the Arrow keys. The default printer must be Active.

Altering A Printer's Configuration

After you've selected a printer from the Printers dialogue box, you can press the CONFIGURE button. Another dialogue box opens. From here, you can select the port for the printer and two 'timeouts'.

One of the options in the list of ports is FILE. If you select this, Windows writes the data that would be sent to the selected printer, to a file. You choose where to store this data, each time an application starts printing, by entering the filename into a dialogue box. Once the data is stored on a file, you can copy it to a floppy disk and give it to someone with a printer that you want to use even if they don't have Windows. With our printer, this didn't quite work, but you might be luckier.

You'll normally leave the Device Not Selected and Transmission Retry timeouts unchanged. You only need to alter them if your printer is particularly slow. If Windows reports that your printer is off-line when it's not, increase the Device Not Selected timeout. If it reports that it cannot print, when the printer is operational and on-line, then increase the Transmission Retry timeout.

There's also a REMOVE button in this dialogue box. You get a chance to change your mind if you select this by mistake but you should be careful. Removing a printer means that any configuration changes you've made will be forgotten. Also, the files that were installed with the printer are not deleted, that includes font files which take up a lot of disk space. You can, as we'll see later, re-install a removed printer. Nonetheless, it's best only to remove a printer if you're sure that you'll never use it again.

From Configuration To Setup

The SETUP button on the Printers Configure dialogue box opens another dialogue box. We hope you're following this chain of dialogue boxes so far!

You're nearly on your own from here as the dialogue boxes which start appearing from here depend on the type of printer you're setting up. Different printers need different information and these dialogue boxes may have been designed by authors who don't always follow the Windows standards.

Typically, you'll see boxes that allow you to select the resolution of graphics printing, the paper and print orientation, the source of paper, what font cartridges you've got and any options installed in the printer. Most of these dialogue boxes have HELP buttons that help you find out what the settings do.

When you first install a new printer, these settings will be loaded for you. You'll normally only need to alter these if you install a new font cartridge or want to change the orientation or paper source.

Adding A New Printer

To add a new printer, you press the ADD PRINTER button in the Printers dialogue box. The box expands to show a long list of printers that your version of Windows knows about. You can scroll through the list.

What Printer?

If you're lucky, your new printer appears in the list. If not, you may have a floppy disk with a Windows printer driver or one may be available from the printer's supplier. To use that driver, you'll need to select Unlisted Printer at the end of the list.

If a special driver is not available, you may find that your new printer can 'emulate' (that is, behave exactly like) a printer in the list. If it can, then you must check how to make it emulate the one you're going to select. This may involve setting up some switches or going through a set-up procedure on the printer.

Even if you can't find out what your new printer can emulate, it's worth trying three 'industry standards'. For a dot-matrix printer, try Epson FX-80 or IBM Proprinter. For a laser printer, try HP Laserjet. It's surprising how many printers have hidden emulations. You may find that your printouts are the wrong size but at least you'll be able to print.

Only as a desperate last option should you install the printer as Generic/Text Only. As the name implies, you'll only be able to print text in a font that your printer, not you, decides.

Ready To Install?

When you've decided which printer you want to install your new printer as, you are ready to press the INSTALL button.

If you selected a printer other than 'Unlisted Printer', Windows tries to be helpful by telling you which disk, from your original Windows disks, to place in the a: drive of your computer. This is fine if you have the original disks handy and if you originally installed Windows from the a: drive!

If you installed Windows using the alternate method described in the Tool Box chapter, you don't need to find your original disks. You can type over the a: with the name of the directory that holds all the original Windows files - this will be different from the directory that Windows itself runs from. Then press the OK button, Windows will happily install the driver just as if you had inserted the correct floppy disk.

If you've selected Unlisted Printer because you have a special driver, a dialogue box that looks like a standard File Open one appears. Merely select the correct drive, directory and file name and press OK.

We have seen drivers with separate help files that do not load automatically. If you see a Drive Not Ready message when you select Help in the Setup dialogue box, the driver you've installed is one of these rogues. You should copy any files with .HLP extension from the original disk to your Windows directory and try again.

Configuring A Newly Installed Printer

Even after you've installed a new printer, you've not quite finished. You must let Windows know how to talk to the printer by opening the Configure dialogue box. You may also have to change Windows' idea of how the printer is set-up to match the printer's actual set-up. From the Configure dialogue box, press the SETUP button. As we said earlier, you're then on your own...

Re-installing A Removed Printer

If you accidentally remove a printer, you can avoid having to reconfigure the driver. Select Unlisted Printer from the Install list and then type the name of the Windows directory in the dialogue box that appears. You'll have to look down the list for a filename that matches the printer you removed but most drivers are in files that bear a close resemblance to the printer's name.

You can do this because, as we said earlier, Windows does not delete the driver file from your disk when you remove a printer.

Fonts

The Fonts dialogue box allows you to add and remove fonts. You'll be changing the list of fonts that Windows knows how to display on screen. As we've seen earlier in the book, that may be different to the list Windows knows about when you print.

After you try adding and removing fonts, you'll probably come to the same conclusion we have: Don't do it!

The official Users Guide says that you can remove fonts to free memory - and so you can. It also says that you can add new fonts - well, you can if you have any compatible ones available. But what it doesn't mention is that you don't seem to be able to put back a standard Windows font after you've removed it.

Despite these caveats, there are legitimate reasons to add and remove fonts. The standard fonts occupy about 240 Kilobytes of precious memory so, for example, if you decide that you are never going to use the Script and Modern fonts, it makes sense to remove them. Again, you may have a foreign language font that you want to display. There's no harm in adding it but remember that it's in your computers memory all the time, whether you are writing a document that uses it or not.

If you have a third-party program that enhances Windows font handling, such as Adobe's ATM or Bitstream's Facelift, you should use their configuration program, to add or remove fonts.

The Fonts Dialogue Box

After you select the Fonts icon in the Control Panel, a dialogue box opens with three areas. There's a list of fonts with a scroll bar, three buttons labelled OK, ADD and REMOVE and a box at the bottom that shows various sizes of text in the font selected.

You will notice that there's no CANCEL button. That's because changes you make take effect immediately, you get no second chance to change your mind after you've altered something. You can close the dialogue box by using the Close option in the Window Control menu or by pressing Esc but all the changes to the font list that you've made will still be there.

You can look at examples of any installed font by clicking on the font name in the listing. If the font is marked with 'All Res' it's an outline font and can be scaled between one point and 127 points, depending on the application. Following other fonts are numbers that show the available sizes.

To add a font, you press the ADD button. A standard File Open dialogue box appears. Find the file that contains the font you want to add and press the OK button. Windows updates the font list and samples of the new font appear in the box at the bottom of the Fonts dialogue box. If Windows thinks that the font is already installed, it will tell you.

To remove a font, you press the REMOVE button. You see a dialogue box asking you to confirm and, if you press the OK button, Windows removes the font and updates the font list.

386 Enhanced

The options in the 386 Enhanced dialogue box control the operation of your computer when it's running Windows and non-Windows applications together. You can only do this if your computer has a 386 or 486 microprocessor, hence it's name.

You need to understand Multi-tasking in a little more depth than we've covered it so far. This is the stuff that make Computer Science degrees, so we suggest that you award yourself a B.cS (that's a Baby of computer Science) after you've waded through the next few sections.

What's Wrong With Non-Windows Applications?

We said that Windows supports multi-tasking. We explained that multi-tasking means that your computer is doing more than one task (in other words, running more than one program) at a time. We also mentioned that, since there's just one microprocessor in your computer, it is very busy switching from one task to the next and back...

Normally, Windows applications cooperate with one another to share your computer's resources amongst themselves.

Introduce a non-Windows application into the picture and the situation changes. Non-Windows programs have no idea that your computer is running any other programs apart from themselves. They are not sociable programs and therefore are not used to working with others. So they behave like spoiled children and grab everything in sight!

In particular, they grab the ports on your computer and the CPU or Central Processing Unit (the brain of your system) for as much time as they want, without regard for any Windows programs that may be running. That's bad news for everybody and the result could be chaos, with applications sending garbled data and your computer locking up.

The 386 And Sergeant-Major To The Rescue

In the interests of social harmony and to force the Gremlins out of Windows World, the community living within Windows, who have access to a 386, are affluent enough to employ the services of a Sergeant-Major.

That's why you can only multi-task non-Windows applications on a 386 computer. This highly trained military man is also a very accomplished diplomat. He can isolate each application so that they all imagine that they have sole use of the computer and are blissfully unaware of other applications.

The Sergeant-Major sorts out most of the lock-up problems. If an application tries to grab the processor, his job is to thwart the Gremlins by keeping everything going. He will divide your computer's time amongst all the applications and just give each one a share.

The Sergeant-Major can also detect when an application uses a port. So he can warn Windows when a non-Windows application tries to take over a port that a Windows application is already using. The Boffins say that the tasks are "in contention" for the port. The Sergeant-Major, or rather the 386 processor, has a major limitation - he can only monitor one port, not all of them.

Putting It All Together...

With this background information, we can explain all the options in the 386 Enhanced dialogue box.

The Minimum Timeslice is the minimum amount of time that each non-Windows application receives each time the Sergeant-Major decides it can run. You set this time in units of milliseconds, that's in thousandth of a second. If you increase it, applications that receive data from the outside world may miss something. If you decrease it, your computer spends more time deciding what to do and less time doing useful work.

The Scheduling options control what priority you attach to applications running in the active window (this is the foreground task) and to those running in the background (all the other open windows). You assign higher priorities if you want the tasks to receive more time. Don't set the priorities for foreground and background tasks to widely different numbers. If you select Exclusive in Foreground, you are saying that the active window receives absolute priority - so your computer will not be able to multi-task.

The Device Contention options allow you to choose one port. The port you select should be that being used by the non-Windows application. For this port, Windows can always notify you, by a dialogue box, if a contention occurs or you can choose to receive no warning at all. If a contention occurs after you select the Never Warn option, then chaos will follow. You should only select this if your non-Windows applications do not use any peripherals. If you are warned that a contention has occurred, your only course of action is to close one of the applications.

The Idle time acts like a guard time; Windows inhibits its applications from using the port until the non-Windows application has not accessed it for longer than the time specified. That stops Windows from allowing its applications to interrupt a non-Windows application which pauses briefly before it carries on. There must be a long lull before Windows gives the port to another program.

Group 4

This is where the fun begins! With the last two settings you can change what your screen looks like. Neither are essential for Windows to run correctly. These are purely for your benefit.

The Colour Setting

If, like us, you are working with Windows day in and day out over a long period of time, it makes a big difference being able to alter what you are looking at from time to time. The Colour setting will certainly alow you to do that.

When you get fed up with the variations on a theme of grey, you can select the Colour setting and change them all.

A Ready-Made Scheme?

The colour dialogue box will show you a representation of the screen with the present colour scheme. There are other ready-made colour schemes available from the pop-down Colour Scheme menu. If you select one of those, the colours in the representation will change to give you some idea what your screen will look like. If you like what you see just press OK. You will then have to wait a few seconds while Windows gets dressed!

Chapter 7 Control Panel

If you want to choose your own colour combination, select the COLOUR PALETTE button.

Colour Palette

Once you select the colour palette the Colour dialogue box doubles in size. You can select the screen element that you want to change and then the colour you want it to be. You can also select the screen element by pointing the mouse's arrow at it in the representation. When you are satisfied, select the SAVE SCHEME button and type a name (which can be any length because they are stored in a file, not as a file) for it. Press OK and your screen will be updated with the new colours. You can then return to what you were doing. If you don't want it saved just press OK. The colour scheme will still change but you will lose the scheme if you have a crash.

Defining Customised Colours

If there are still not enough colours for your artistic vein you can mix your own by choosing the DEFINE CUSTOM COLORS button. Another window will then drop over the original Colour dialogue box with a 'rainbow square' in it.

Working with Rainbows

You can select the colour you want from the rainbow square by just pointing to it with the mouse. You will also need to select the level of light or dark from the graduated strip alongside.

You may find it difficult to get pure colours from the Rainbow Square. You already have pure colours in your ready mixed palette, so it could be argued that you don't need to mix them yourself. We have found, however, that pure colours can act as a good reference point especially when you are mixing colours to use alongside ready-mixed ones. To get pure colours you may have to use one of the other means of selecting colour.

If you are selecting colours with the keyboard your task is slightly harder because you cannot use the Rainbow Square. You are confined to using either the Red, Green and Blue boxes or the Hue, Saturation and Luminance boxes to mix your colours. Both these sets of boxes are linked together. If you alter a number in the Red/Green/Blue boxes, the numbers will change in the Hue/Sat/Lum boxes as well. So you don't need to worry about both.

Working With The Red /Green/Blue Boxes

If you are using the Red Green and Blue boxes don't be surprised when they don't mix together in the same way as paints. You are dealing with coloured light, like a lighting technician in the theatre, not blocks of primary colour.

The settings in the boxes have a range from zero to two hundred and fifty five. Zero in all the boxes will make black, while all of them turned full on will give you white. As you would expect, one hundred in each will make a mid grey. Pure Red Green or Blue is two hundred and fifty five in that colour and zero in the others. While a lighter colour, say pink, needs Red set at two hundred and fifty five, and the other two set at around a hundred and twenty. For a darker colour all numbers go down. Maroon will need Red set at around one hundred and twenty, while Blue and Green will be at around thirty five.

How do you get colours other than shades of Red, Green and Blue? Purple is easy because, as with paint, it is a mixture of Blue and Red. Yellow is a different kettle of fish! Pure Yellow is Red and Green on maximum, with Blue on zero. Orange needs less Green, so Red will stay at two hundred and fifty five while Green will go down to one hundred.

However you have chosen the colour it will appear in the small left hand square underneath the rainbow square. Alongside the colour you have mixed is the closest of the sixteen base colours that all the other colours are made up from.

Windows can only work with sixteen colours. All the additional colours that you can see on your viewing screen are not really there!

Impressionist painters discovered that dots of pure colour next to one another can fool the eye into seeing a different colour altogether. Programmers have done the same with pixels of colours. The boffins christened this technique 'Dithering'. Most colours that you mix yourself and some of the ready mixed colours have a pattern or texture woven into them which is a direct effect of dithering. You can see this for yourself by painting with a dithered colour in Paintbrush and then selecting Zoom In from the View menu.

Adding A Customised Colour

The ADD COLOUR button will put the colour you have mixed in the empty squares below the ready-mixed palette in the Colour window. Once you have filled the custom palette, you will need to move across to the Colour window and select the square you want the new colour to go into before you select the ADD COLOUR button. Otherwise, Windows puts the new colour in a square it chooses, not one that you choose.

Any colours that you create and use in a colour scheme will be saved when you save the scheme. Any extra colours that you create will not be saved.

When Changing Your Colour Scheme....

Make sure that your colour scheme makes your active window stand out against the inactive ones. When you have got a number of open windows on the screen you need to be able to distinguish the active one easily. Otherwise you can totally lose which window you are in.

Dark lettering needs a fairly light coloured background otherwise you cannot read the letters. Greyed-out options also need a lighter background than the available options, otherwise they standout more prominently.

The colour you choose for the Window Frame will also divide up your menus and form the background colour for the Page number bar in Write. Page numbers are written in white lettering so you need a dark background to make them readable.

The choice is slightly more limited for some screen elements than for others. Window Text and the Menu Bar, for example, will not accept dithered colours. If you select a dithered colour, the nearest pure colour will be used.

The Desktop Setting

Pattern, Wallpaper And Sizing Grid

All these are all options that will make your screen look pretty! You will only need to use either Pattern or Wallpaper. Both alter your screen background, the area not occupied by open or minimised windows.

The Pattern option has a number of small patterns that can be spread across the entire screen making it look like material. They give the screen an even more textured look than the dithered colours. You can edit any of the ready-made patterns to make up your own by pressing the EDIT PATTERN button.

The pattern will be created with the background screen (desktop) colour and the colour you have selected for window text. So if these are the same you will not see a pattern even if you select one.

Wallpaper

Wallpaper allows you to put bigger patterns or pictures on your screen background. You have a few designs to choose from, but since they are all .BMP files you can create your own in

Paintbrush. For larger designs you would normally select Centre. Smaller designs can be repeated across the screen with the Tile option. Designs bigger than the screen will not be used.

The Sizing Grid

If you select a granularity level, from the Sizing Grid box, of greater then zero and below ten, a mesh of invisible lines pull your windows into position. The lines have 'magnetic pads' in the corners that will force the corner of a window to snap into place where grid lines meet. The higher the level of granularity the further apart those points will be. When you are moving a window it will jump from grid intersection to grid intersection like children playing Hopscotch instead of moving smoothly with the mouse. You use the grid if you want your windows to appear lined up and uniform and you don't want the bother of lining them up yourself.

Fine Tuning Your Windows

Icon Spacing

The Icon Spacing option allows you to determine how much of a gap you want between program icons or minimised windows. After you have changed this option there will be no change in the Program Manager window until you either select the Arrange Icons option from the Windows menu or have Auto Arrange selected from PM's Option menu. Don't forget that Auto Arrange only takes effect after you have altered the size of a window.

The Icon Spacing option will also affect the spacing between minimised window icons if you press the ARRANGE ICONS button in the Task List.

To change icon spacing you must alter the number in the box by at least ten otherwise you will not see the difference. Icon spacing is measured in pixels that are tiny, far too small for the eye to see.

Border Width

It is entirely up to you how wide you make your window borders. We have found that it is slightly easier to change a window's size with the mouse if the border is wider. When you change a window's size, the border is picked up by the double headed arrow. Wider borders are easier to pick up and you will not be trying to do keyhole surgery!

The Cursor Blink Rate

The 'cursor' that this controls is the insertion point and appears in text application windows like Write and Notepad. It is controlled primarily by the keyboard although it can be moved around with the mouse's arrow. It is essential the insertion point blinks (flashes on and off) otherwise you would never find it among a pageful of characters. It's entirely up to you what you set this option to. We have a habit of losing the cursor and find it more easily if it is blinking fast.

Part 3 - Your Kit

This is where we explore the additional kit you were issued with at the beginning of the journey. You will need everything that has gone before to understand what we are talking about in Part 3. We generally "Say things only once"!

Chapter 8 Paintbrush

Chapter 8 - Paintbrush

Welcome to the high-tech side of windows. Most of the kit you were issued with may seem complicated, if you haven't seen a computer before, but their displays are relatively simple. In comparison Paintbrush looks as though you are about to take off on another voyage, into space this time!

There are some very clever things you can do with Paintbrush but you don't have to start with those. You can start at whatever level you like, trying out things and learning as you go.

There are a lot more controls here than there are anywhere else. Your paint pallette is along the bottom of your window. The line thickness box is in the bottom left hand corner. Your artist's tool box is down the left hand side.

All this is on top of a full complement of menu options and the window controls as normal.

You can get much pleasure just playing with Paintbrush. Drawing with the mouse is a bit tricky at first but you will soon get the hang of it. You have also got all the ready made shapes that you can use as a starting point for some stunning abstract art!

If you are going to print your creations you will need a printer. Colour printers are expensive but that would be the ideal. But if your budget cannot run, to one a black and white printer will be much better than nothing. If you work in Paintbrush in colour, and then print it on a black and white printer, all the colours will be translated into different shades of grey.

Before You Start

The first thing you have to do, as any artist would, is to choose what size paper you want to use and which palette suits the occasion. You can select both of those from the Image Attributes option from the Options menu.

Image Size

Inside the Image Attributes dialogue box you have got three selection areas. The size is determined by the Width and Height, but the numbers you put into those boxes will be determined by what Units you select. If you are going to want to transfer the picture you create to another application or if you are planning to include text, you will be better off selecting pixels.

The Picture May Not Look The Same When It's Printed

Whatever size you choose for your picture, it may not be printed in exactly that size. Windows uses ninety six pixels to the inch but your printer will probably work in a different resolution. Which means that your picture may not look quite the same when you print it as it does on the screen. When you print your picture you will have to decide whether you want to print it at the printer's resolution or not.

Let's say, for example, that your printer prints one hundred and fifty pixels to the inch. If you select Use Printer Resolution (from the Print dialogue box) your printer will print one pixel for every one of yours. But because your picture has only got ninety six pixels to the inch and your printer uses more, you will end up with the printed picture being smaller than it was on your screen.

If you are sure that you want your picture to be printed at the size you have chosen in the Image Attributes box, don't select Use Printer Resolution. Paintbrush will then do its best to keep your picture the size you've asked for. But it can only do that by adding more pixels into the picture or taking some away. The boffins call this process `interpolating' because it is bit more than plain interpreting. Paintbrush has to try to add pixels where there aren't any in your original, and still keep it looking like your picture. Your picture may be slightly distorted by this process which is why we don't recommend you use this for a picture containing precise or detailed information.

Which Palette?

You have two choices of Palette, either Colour or Black and White. If you choose Black and White you will get black and white and twelve dithered shades of grey. Or you can keep the colour palette which has twenty six colours. If you have a computer that can deal with more than sixteen colours, the palette may be larger.

If you want to work on a different coloured background you must select it now before you start a new picture. To change the background, move the mouse's arrow to the colour you want the background to be and press the Right mouse button.

The Colour Selection Box

Immediately to the left of the colour palette there is a small rectangle enclosed in a larger rectangle. This is where your selected colours are displayed.

You can select the colour in the central rectangle, from the palette, with the left mouse button. The official Guide calls it the foreground colour. While the area outside the small rectangle is the background colour that you select with the right mouse button.

The background colour is not only used as the paper colour. The background colour will be used as the outline for any of the filled shape tools. It will form the shadow for text if you select Shadow from the Style menu and also will be put over what you've erased.

Applying The Changes

The changes you make in the Image Attributes dialogue box will not appear in the current file. You will either have to select New from the File menu or double click the mouse over the right hand Eraser tool (third row down) to get a new file where the changes you have made will be used

Ways Of Seeing Your Picture

The artists amongst you will know that there are as many ways of looking at a picture as there are people to look at it! But while you are working on a picture in Paintbrush there are only four ways that you can view it.

When you are working on a picture, you normally don't see the whole picture. It depends what size of picture you are working with. You might see the whole image if you're working with a small picture. From the Normal View you can always zoom in or out.

Zooming In

If you Zoom In, the mouse's tip will turn into a small rectangle that you can move to the area that you want to magnify. When you click either mouse button, your entire working area will be filled with just that section.

You also use the Zoom In option to return to the Normal View after you've zoomed out.

Chapter 8 Paintbrush

Pixel View

Once you've zoomed in from the Normal View, you will see a grid covering your working area. Each tiny square represents one pixel. We call this the Pixel View.

Menu Options

While you are looking at the Pixel View, what you can do is limited. Zoom Out and Undo are the only menu options available to you. Zoom Out will take you back to the Normal View. Undo will undo everything you have done while you have been zoomed in and will zoom you out automatically.

Tools

It is not easy to see what tools are available as it is with menu options because they don't `grey out'. You can only use the two tools on the fourth row of the toolbox, the brush and the roller. The brush colours one pixel per mouse click - brush shapes don't apply here. The roller will fill whole areas of pixels but you need to have an enclosed area otherwise the colour will `leak' out into other areas as well.

Colours

If you have selected one of the non-dithered colours you can use that to fill the areas of pixels you want to change. If you choose to work in one of the dithered colours, how do you know what colour to put where? You don't have to worry, just click the left mouse buttons in each pixel in turn in the area you want to change. Paintbrush will work out what colour should be where to make up the pattern for the selected colour. Now that's what we call real magic!

Zoom Out

The Zoom Out option will take you from Pixel View to Normal View and from Normal View to Image View.

Image View

The Image View reduces the picture so it can fit all on your working area. It is the only way you can see the whole picture. Use it to step back and get a better overall view of your work.

119

Chapter 8 Paintbrush

Editing Your Picture With Cut And Paste

The only options you have available from the Image View are those on the Edit menu. In Paintbrush parts of the pictures that you have cut or copied to the Clipboard are called 'cutouts'. When you Paste a cutout into your picture while in the Image View, a grided rectangle appears in the top left hand corner of your picture. You can then drag it to where you want it to go. When you click either mouse button outside the picture the cutout will replace the gridded rectangle. If you use the Paste From option to paste a cutout that you have saved as a file earlier, it works in the same way.

The only tool you can use is the Pick Tool which allows you to select an area of the picture that you want to Cut or Copy to the Clipboard. If you select the Copy To option, Paintbrush will save your cutout as a file rather than to the Clipboard.

Colours

Because the size of your picture has been reduced, Paintbrush has had to throw away some of the pixels. This might make a difference if you have used dithered colours. Dithered colours need all their pixels to keep them true. So dithered colours will sometimes be different in the Image view to the Normal one.

Tip: X And Y Co-ordinates

The Normal, Pixel and Image views have the facility to tell you exactly where you are in your picture, pixel by pixel. If you select Cursor Position from the bottom of the View menu, a small dialogue box will appear in the top border of your Paintbrush window. As you move around your picture the numbers in the box will change. This is very useful if you are doing detailed work that needs to be lined up exactly.

In the Pixel View this works slightly differently. While you are moving around the numbers don't alter. They are only updated when you press a mouse button.

The Screen View

The Screen View is another way of seeing your picture but without the distractions of everything else on the screen. You will just have the picture, no windows, no mouse's tip and no desktop!

There may be less distortion to the colours than in Image View because Paintbrush doesn't reduce the image. If the picture is bigger than the screen, Paintbrush will show you as much as it can from the left-hand corner downwards. If the picture is smaller than the screen Paintbrush will give it a White border.

There are no menu options or tools available from here use the View Picture option purely for looking! When you are ready to go back into Paintbrush, press any key or click a mouse button.

The Undo Option

Paintbrush's Undo Option will undo more than the last thing you did. It will undo everything from the last time you changed tools. It ignores changes to line size or colour. You can limit the amount you will undo by reselecting the same tool every so often, especially after you have completed a section that you are happy with.

The Tools

The Cutout Tools

The Cutout Tools are at the top of your tool box. They allow you to cut out pieces of your picture, move them to different positions, copy them or turn them back to front and inside out! You can also Cut or Copy them to the Clipboard. In fact, you can use any option from the Edit or Pick menu (which is only available when you have got a cutout defined).

The Cutout tool with the Star shape (the Scissor Tool) is used for cutting out freehand. You effectively 'draw' round whatever you want to cut out.

The other one with a rectangle shape in its icon (the Pick tool) will cut out a rectangle shape. You just put the cross (yes, the mouse's tip changes shape yet again) where you want one of the corners of the cutout to be and drag the mouse until the dotted rectangle is the right shape and size. You can then let go of the mouse button. If you let go of the mouse button too early, simply click the mouse button once, the outline will disappear and you can start again.

If you want to copy a cutout, you need to hold the Shift key down while you are dragging the mouse. The mouse should bring the cutout with it. To 'sweep' a cutout, hold the Ctrl key down while dragging.

Chapter 8 Paintbrush

Tip: Copying Cutouts

If you are copying a cutout, Save the finished design before switching to other windows. If you don't, you could lose some of the copies.

The Pick Menu

Once you have a cutout defined, the Pick menu becomes available. From there you can turn the cutout upside down (flip vertically). You can turn it back to front. You can even tilt it (that could help you draw the Leaning Tower of Pisa!). Invert (which turns each colour to its opposite) works fine in black and white but with colours you get some rather unexpected results. Lastly, you can scale the cutout to whatever proportions you like.

The Airbrush

The Airbrush sprays colours onto the working area. It will spray circles wherever you move the mouse. The line size will determine how big the spray is.

The beauty about Airbrush is that you can vary the amount of colour you spray onto your picture. The spray is operated by holding the mouse button down but you can determine the thickness of paint by how long you keep the mouse in one place.

You can produce some subtle colours by spraying continuously while moving fairly quickly over the area you are working on. Never mind that your poor old computer is having a hard time trying to work out what the colour should be!

The Text Tool

To add text to a picture, select the Text tool. You have three whole menus that give the Text tool a wide variety of options. These are Font, Style and Size.

When using the Text tool if you select a font, style or size, all the text that you have drawn since you selected the Text tool will be changed to the newly selected options.

The mouse's arrow changes to an I bar, in the working area, just to remind that you are working with text. Text will be added to your picture wherever you click the mouse. This position will become the left hand margin if you press the Enter key to begin a new line.

Chapter 8 Paintbrush

Paintbrush is a lousy text editor. The only editing facility you have is the Backspace key and that only works as you are typing. As soon as you do something else, that text becomes part of the picture. You can't edit it as text any more but you can use any of Paintbrush's other tools to change it.

The Font Menu

The fonts you have available in Paintbrush are:

- Terminal - the font used in the Terminal application that looks like that used on old VDU screens.

- Symbol - a font that just contains mathematical symbols.

- Helv - a Helvetica look-alike similar to the lettering on traffic signs.

- Courier - a font that resembles that used by IBM typewriters.

- Tms Rmn - a Times Roman look-alike as used in The Times newspaper.

- Roman - an outline font that has features that look like Times Roman.

- Script - a florid, curvaceous outline font that looks like joined-up handwriting.

- Modern - an outline font loosely based on Helvetica.

- System - the standard font used in Windows dialogue boxes.

These are the basic Windows fonts - Paintbrush doesn't know about printer fonts. The shapes of letters in those fonts described as 'outline' fonts are stored as a set of lines. The lines used to display letters in these fonts are normally just one pixel wide. Letters in other fonts defined by 'bitmaps' may have thick and thin lines, depending on the characteristics of the font.

If you remove or add any fonts using the Control Panel's Font dialogue box, the list changes. If you use additional software, such as Adobe's ATM, the list may contain additional fonts.

The Style Menu

You can use options in the style menu to change the appearance of the font you've chosen from the Font menu.

Chapter 8 Paintbrush

Normal deselects any other options. Selecting Bold makes letter shapes wider. For outline fonts, Paintbrush simulates the effect by repeating each line three times. Not all bitmap fonts have bold shapes defined for them so selecting Bold may not change the letter shapes.

Italic creates text in which all the letters are slanted about thirty degrees towards the right. For bitmapped fonts, this may cause vertical lines to appear jagged, particularly at larger sizes.

When you Underline a font, Paintbrush draws a solid horizontal line just under it. You cannot alter the position of the underline and it clashes with letters that have descenders, like "g". You can't easily underline just words and leave the space between them clear.

You can choose any combination of Bold, Italic and Underline. These can be combined with either Outline or Shadow.

You may select Outline or Shadow but not both. You should select another background colour that is different to both the foreground and the paper colour to see these effects.

Outline draws a one pixel line, in the background colour, around the shapes of the letters. Shadowed text appears to stand out from the page. Normally, you'll choose a background colour that is a darker shade of the foreground colour although an interesting effect can be obtained by using a darker foreground against a lighter background. The characters then appear to be solid and lit from below.

The Size Menu

The Size menu contains a range of text sizes between six and eighty-four. Unlike the rest of the Windows applications, these sizes do not give the size of text in Points. Instead, they are in pixels.

Tip: Text Sizes In Paintbrush Printouts

Unless you need a precise idea of what your printout is going to look like, it's easier to try a few combinations and see which is nearest to what you want. But if you do want to be precise, read on...
You need to do quite a few calculations to work out what size text will appear in a printout from Paintbrush. You'll have to consider your printer's graphic resolution, the settings of Scale and Use Printer Resolution in the File Print dialogue box and the size of the text in pixels.

If you select the Use Printer Resolution box, the formula you need to use is to multiply the size

Chapter 8 Paintbrush

in pixels by the Scale and then divide that by your printer's resolution in dots per inch. That answer will be in inches; multiplying by seventy-two gives the text size in Points.

If you don't select Use Printer Resolution, the formula is to multiply the size in pixels by the Scale and then multiply that by 0.75 to get the size in Points.

For example, let's look at an HP Laserjet with 300 dpi resolution, a Scale of 300% (which means three times original size) and a text size of 13 units. If you don't select Use Printer Resolution, the text size will be (13*3*0.75) or about 30 points. When you select Use Printer Resolution, the text shrinks to (13*3/300)*72 or about 9.4 points.

You'll see that some sizes have asterisks against them. These are the sizes for which Windows has handcrafted shapes available.

If you select a bitmapped font and then go into the Size menu, you'll notice that some sizes are greyed-out. Paintbrush can only use font sizes that are multiples of those that have asterisks. As elsewhere with Windows arithmetic, it doesn't always get it quite right. Our computer reckons, for example, that seventy is a multiple of fifteen, one of the asterisked sizes.

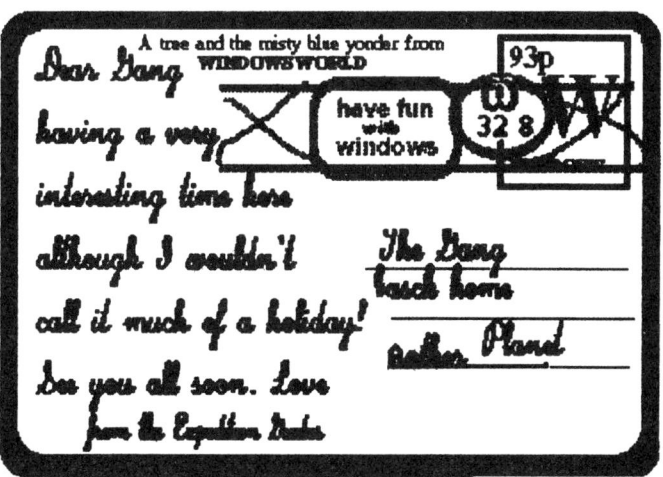

The Erasers

The Erasers are wonderful painting tools in their own right. You can use them to apply large blocks of colour because they seem to glide more easily over the working area. Even through they are square you don't have to end up with cubist shapes! You can sweep them round in bold curves or jagged edges.

The Colour Eraser

Whatever the Colour Eraser touches will be changed from the selected foreground colour to the selected background one. So if you wanted to change some royal blue in your working area to green, you would select blue with the left mouse button and green with the right button and then erase the area you want to change.

It will do more than that, because any dithered colour that includes royal blue will be changed too. Royal blue pixels will be changed to green, which will subtly change the dithered colour to another shade. You can mix shades of colour totally outside the colours in your palette this way. It may take a bit of time to work out exactly what colour you will get. Unless you keep meticulous notes you will find it difficult to remember how to reproduce any particular dithered shade. But if you like surprises, this will certainly keep you happy!

You can ask the Colour Eraser to change all the foreground coloured pixels in the window to the background colour automatically by double clicking the mouse over its icon.

The Eraser

The Eraser will put the selected background colour over everything else. If the selected background colour is the same as the background you are working on it will erase everything in its path. If the selected background colour is different to the overall background, the eraser becomes a drawing tool.

If you want to erase (or draw) in a straight line, hold the Shift key down while dragging the mouse in roughly the direction you want to go.

Double clicking the mouse over this Eraser (the right hand one) will erase everything and give you a new sheet. It is just the same as selected New from the file menu. It will use the size you have set in Image Attributes and the selected background. So if you want either of these to be different on the new sheet you must change them before you double click the Eraser.

The Roller

The roller will cover enclosed areas of your picture with colour. It will always work if you are

Chapter 8 Paintbrush

painting over non-dithered colour. If you are working with a dithered colour, the effect may not be what you expect. You'll either just alter a few pixels or change the shade of the area in subtle ways. The roller will also work in exactly the same way in the Pixel View, allowing you to fill whole areas of your picture.

If you don't put paint from the Roller into an area enclosed by either a different colour paint or the borders of your picture, the paint will leak out and fill much larger areas of the picture than you intended.

If you put the Roller on a thick line, it will `fill' the line.

The Brush

You have forty eight different brushes in your box, which should be enough for anyone! How do we get such a large number?

Double click the mouse over the Brush icon and you will see that you have six different shapes of brush to choose from. You can have each of those shapes in the eight different line thicknesses.

If you want help to paint a straight line, hold the Shift key down while you drag the mouse roughly in the direction you want the line to go. You can only do horizontal and vertical lines

127

Chapter 8 Paintbrush

like this. If you want your straight line to go at an angle you will have to use the Line tool immediately below the brush in your tool box.

When a brush is in your working area the mouse will be the selected brush shape. The Brush will be in the opposite colour to the one you are working with so its impossible to see whether you have made a brush stroke or not until you move the brush away.

The Line Tools

With both the Line and Curved Line tool the mouse's tip is a cross.

Both of these draw a `rough' line while you are dragging the mouse. Paintbrush doesn't put the line into the thickness and colour that you have chosen until you have defined where you want it to go.

The Curve

The Curve tool allows you to define where the beginning and end of a curve is going to be by drawing a straight line between the two points in rough. You can then put the mouse on either side and drag it into the curve you want. It will still be in rough when you stop dragging in into shape because this tool is really designed to put two curves into the one line. The line will only be put in properly when you click the mouse button a second time.

To produce two curves, you can drag once on one side of the line, move the cross and then drag the mouse again. You'll see some sort of curve with two bends if you have clicked on both sides of the line. You'll change the curve you've already got if you've dragged somewhere on the same side.

If you only want to have one curve and you click the mouse button anywhere (even if you click it on the line) your curve will be changed. What you have to do is move the mouse to another point around the curve, press the mouse button and drag the mouse back to the line. The curve will be distorted when you start the drag. When the mouse gets back to the line your curve will be almost the same as it was before.

You can also create some wonderful irregular shapes by putting the end point in the same place as the beginning point. You can then drag the mouse and stretch it as far as it will go, which will just give you a tapered line. Then move round to one side and stretch it again. This will `open out' the shape. We reckon this is much more fun than using the ready made Shape tools.

Chapter 8 Paintbrush

The Shape Tools

These fill up the rest of your tool box. There are four different shapes with two tools for each. Each shape can be a hollow shape or a filled one. The thickness of a shape's outline will be the selected line width. The hollow shape is just an outline in the foreground colour, whilst the filled shape will have a solid filling in the foreground colour and an outline in the background. You can make both foreground and background colours the same, but (different the overall background) to get a bigger solid shape.

The mouse tip is a cross shape when you are using all the shape tools. First, position the cross where you want the shape to start and then drag the mouse away from there. You will get a rough outline that you can drag to where you want the final shape to go. You can move it about as much as you like while you are holding the mouse button down. When you release the mouse the shape will be put in for real.

If you make a filled shape too small you won't see the filling, only a bit of the outline. If you are using the same background colour for the shape as you are for the main background you won't see anything.

The Polygon tools allow you to construct a multi-sided object out of straight lines. The first side of the polygon must be drawn by dragging the cross. You can then either drag or click to the next point. To `close' the polygon, to make sure that the last side joins with the first, double click over the last point. This is useful as you then know that you have a fully enclosed space that the Roller will fill without the colour leaking.

Customising Your Palette

You are not restricted to the colours on the palette, you can easily mix more. First select the colour you want to change as the foreground colour and then select the Edit Colour option from the Option menu. But double clicking the mouse over the colour in the palette is far quicker.

The Edit Colours dialogue box is very similar to the Red/Green/Blue colour selection boxes in the Colour settings on the Control Panel. You can select the colours by dragging the slider button and not just by increasing or decreasing the numbers. If you have forgotten how to mix colours on the screen, go back to the section on Colours in the chapter on the Control Panel.

If you are editing shades of grey from the black and white palette all three Red, Blue and Green sliders are fixed together. When you move one, they all move in unison. As there are already

129

Chapter 8 Paintbrush

twenty six shades of grey, it can be difficult to tell whether the shades you add are different from those that are already there.

Once you have created some colours you can save all the colours in the palette in a file that will have a .PAL extension. You save them with the Save Colours option from the Options menu, after giving the file an appropriate filename. You can load the colour file back into your working palette with the Get Colours option.

The Paintbrush File Menu

The New Option

You use the New option to start a new picture, using the current settings of Image Attributes. If you start a picture without saving the previous one, a File Has Changed dialogue box opens with YES, NO and CANCEL buttons.

If you press the CANCEL button, you continue with the existing picture. Pressing YES opens the same dialogue box as you see when you select the Save or Save As options. Pressing NO just begins the new picture, you'll lose any changes you've made since you last saved the one you're working with.

The Open Option

Selecting the Open option opens a File Selection dialogue box. Inside there is a group of boxes labelled Open From. You can selct from: BMP, MSP and PCX file formats.

- BMP

Bitmap format. Used by Windows for wallpaper and the standard file type for Paintbrush.

- MSP

Microsoft Paint format. Paint is an obsolete MS-DOS painting program. Paintbrush cannot save its files in MSP format, so you only need to worry about this format if you have pictures drawn with Paint.

- PCX

This format is widely supported by other drawing programs. However there are several variants of this format so don't be too surprised if Paintbrush can't open a PCX file created by another program.

Selecting one of these boxes is the same as putting the extension into the Filename box. Paintbrush displays just files with a matching extension. Regardless of the extension, Paintbrush will work out the type of file from its contents. So, providing it is in one of these formats, you'll still be able to use it.

The INFO button is only available when there's a valid file in the Filename box; it opens a dialogue box with information about the picture stored in the file:

- The width of the picture (in pixels)

- The height of the picture (in pixels)

- The number of colours. This is the number of colours in the palette used to draw the picture not a count of the colours used in the image.

- The number of planes. You can ignore this setting.

Pressing the OK button returns to the File Open dialogue box.

The Save Option

If you've previously saved your picture to a file, the Save option overwrites the file with the latest version. Unlike Write, Paintbrush does not have the facility of automatically creating back-up files. Once you Save a file, you can't retrieve the previous version.

The Save As Option

Selecting this option opens a dialogue box that contains the standard boxes for Filenames and Directories. Pressing the OK button saves the file.

The INFO button normally shows the same information that Paintbrush displays when you open a file. It seems to use the information in the named file, not the current picture, and so it may not display the correct settings if you are overwriting an existing file. If you've not chosen the file name, it doesn't display anything!

The OPTIONS button expands the size of the dialogue box to show the choice of file types that Paintbrush can store pictures:

Chapter 8 Paintbrush

- PCX

You may have difficulty using a PCX file created by Paintbrush in another program.

- Monochrome Bitmap

Monochrome bitmaps have just two colours - black and white. If you are preparing a colour picture for a black-and-white display or printer, you can save the picture using this option to see what the image will look like.

- 16 Colour Bitmap

This setting is appropriate if your computer has an EGA or a standard VGA viewing screen.

- 256 Colour Bitmap

Some extended VGA (and better) display adaptors can display 256 colours simultaneously. If your computer has one of these, you'll be able to create and display pictures with this many colours.

- 24 Bit Bitmap

Some specialised display adaptors can display over sixteen million colours simultaneously. This requires that each pixel has eight "bits" for the Red, Green and Blue primary colours. Three times eight is twenty-four, so each pixel occupies 24 Bits in memory.

Choosing The Right Colour Option

You should normally save the picture in the format that matches your display. The size of files that Paintbrush creates depends on the number of colours.

You can reduce the size of the file by storing the picture in a format with fewer colours. Since you can't create any more colours than your display can handle there's no point in saving a file with more colours - you'll just waste disk space.

Paintbrush can display pictures created with a higher specification colour display than the one on your computer. It looks at each pixel and 'maps' it to the closest colour that your computer can display. This nearly always results in an acceptable picture. Cleverer techniques than those used

Chapter 8 Paintbrush

by Paintbrush can produce a closer match and are available if you buy specialised 'image processing programs.

The Page Setup Option

If you select this, a dialogue box opens that has the same boxes as those in Notepad, Calendar and Cardfile. You can set up margins and a header and a footer that will be printed on each page of the printed picture. You can use codes in the header and footer to print the date, file name and page number. We cover these codes in the Tip in the Page Setup section of the chapter on Notepad.

When you print a picture, you may imagine that Paintbrush uses only the top and left margin to determine the position of the picture. That's so until the picture is too large to fit on a single sheet of paper. Then, the first page will contain the top-left hand corner of the picture and subsequent pages will contain other parts of the picture, going along and then down the picture until Paintbrush completes it. When that happens, the right and bottom margins determine where Paintbrush splits the picture between pages. Paintbrush does that as most printers cannot print right to the edge of the page. It's up to you to assemble the pieces together, using just the image area on each sheet, to get the completed printout.

The Print Option

When you select the Print option, a dialogue box opens. This includes a group of boxes labelled Quality. If you're using a printer that has draft and proof quality boxes in its Setup screen, then selecting one of these boxes causes the picture to be printed with the printer in the mode you select.

The Window group of boxes has two options: Whole and Partial. These control whether Paintbrush prints the whole picture or just part of it. If you select Partial and then press the OK button to begin the printout, Paintbrush redraws its window just as if you had selected Zoom Out. It then waits for you to select a rectangle by selecting a corner and dragging the mouse to the opposite corner. There is no indication that it expects you to do this. You can recognise that you're in this 'mode' as all the menu items (apart from Help) are greyed out. You have only one chance to select the rectangle so, if you make a mistake, you have to CANCEL the printout and start again from scratch.

The Number of Copies box is initially set to one. If you wish to produce more than one copy, you can insert the number you want in the box. The size of the print file, if you're using the Print Manager, may grow very large as each copy is stored in the file.

Chapter 8 Paintbrush

You can Scale the picture. When you're using Printer Resolution, you should normally leave this at 100% or an exact multiple. That way, you'll ensure that Paintbrush doesn't have to 'interpolate'. That will destroy the advantages that selecting printer resolution brings.

If you select Use Printer Resolution, Paintbrush uses whatever your printer's graphic resolution is set to in its Setup screen. This means that one pixel on the screen matches one pixel on your printer, unless you choose to Scale the picture. This has the advantage of allowing you to control very precisely what the picture looks like but the size of picture will depend on your printer and what resolution it's set to print at.

Otherwise, Paintbrush matches the size of the picture (in Inches or Centimetres) to that you selected in the Image Attributes dialogue box.

Tip: Size Of Printed Images

Oh dear, we need some mathematics! Let's look at an example:

You select an picture size of 5" by 6" in Paintbrush's Image Attributes dialogue box. You select Scale as 100% and leave the UPR (Use Printer Resolution) box unselected. The printed picture will be 5" by 6" and will fit on an A4 sheet of paper.

If you Scale that picture by 200%, the printed picture will be 10" by 12" and will print over four sheets of A4. You'll need to be ready with the sticky tape...

If you select the UPR box, then the size of picture Paintbrush produces depends on your printer's graphics resolution. Let's take the example of an HP Laserjet set to 300 Dots per Inch (dpi). The picture size of 5" by 6" is 480 by 576 pixels as Paintbrush assumes that there are 96 pixels per Inch. But, at 300 dpi, this gives a size of the printed picture of only 1.6" (that is, 480/300) by 1.92" (576/300) - suitable for postage stamp designs although a bit too small for most other uses.

You can Scale the picture by 300%, repeating each pixel three times, giving an picture of 4.8" by 5.76" - that's nearly the original size.

To summarise:

> If you select the UPR box and a high printer resolution in the Printer Setup dialogue box, the picture will be smaller.

Chapter 8 Paintbrush

Use Scale to decide how large the printed picture is. This works even if you select the UPR box.

Tip: Cures For Nibbled Paintbrush Printouts

You've spent ages honing the ultimate Paintbrush picture. You're sure it's a masterpiece and you're all ready to submit it to the Louvre for showing next to the Mona Lisa...

There's just one thing to do; print it. You don't select Use Printer Resolution box and you watch, in horror, as your printer produces a very untidy printout - the font-eating mice are obviously at work again.

To overcome that, you must select the User Printer Resolution box so that Paintbrush and your printer can live in harmony. If that results in a tiny printout, you can use the Scale box - but remember to use only exact multiples of 100%.

When you press the OK button to start printing, Paintbrush opens a dialogue box that shows you the number of sheets that the printout needs. As Paintbrush prints your picture, the dialogue box displays a page counter and a percentage complete. It has a CANCEL button that stops the printout.

The Printer Setup Option

Selecting this option from Paintbrush's File menu opens a dialogue box that allows you to select one of your active printers. Pressing the OK button closes the dialogue box and tells Paintbrush that you wish to use the selected printer.

Pressing the Setup button opens the Control Panel Setup screen for the selected printer. You can alter the graphics resolution, change the paper size and orientation and possibly select Draft or Proof quality. If you press the CANCEL button, Paintbrush continues to use the printer selected before you opened the dialogue box. It doesn't undo any changes you made to the Setups of any printers.

The Exit Option

This option leaves Paintbrush. If you have changed the picture since you last saved it, Paintbrush

Chapter 8 Paintbrush

displays a dialogue box with YES, NO and CANCEL buttons to allow you to save your latest work. Pressing YES saves the picture or opens the Save As dialogue box if you hadn't saved the picture yet. Pressing NO just leaves Paintbrush, you lose your latest work. Press CANCEL to remain in Paintbrush with the latest picture intact.

Chapter 9 - Write

We reckon it must be time for you to get down to some serious writing. You must have got lots of notes to go towards your Journal, not to mention letters you ought to send home. But don't worry, writing won't be so arduous here as it was when you had to do it all long hand.

Write is the writing tool in your kit. It enables you to type text like you would on a typewriter but you can throw the Tippex away! Write is a Word Processor which means that you can delete or change what you have written and only print it out when you are happy with it.

General Features Of A Word Processor

Word Processors allow you to manipulate text. At their lowest level they are purely text editors. You can add bits in, take bits out, even move whole sections around, without having to retype anything. The biggest bonus of all is that you can do all this on the screen before you print the 'hard copy' on paper. Your reader will have no idea of the torturous lengths you have had to go to.

No more paper aeroplanes!

Apart from normal text editing most Word Processors have a 'find and replace' facility. These allow you to ask the computer to look for a specific sequence of characters. A 'look for'

137

sequence can often include special characters for: spaces, end of paragraph markers, page break characters and punctuation as well as ordinary letters and numbers. There is normally a Replace option too, that allows you to type in another sequence of characters which the Word Processor is able to put in place of what you have asked it to find.

Word Processors also give you the means to determine what your printed page is going to look like. You can set margins for all sides of the paper. You can say whether you want all or part of the text to be centred or aligned with the margins on either side. Or the text can be spread evenly across the page by adding extra spaces (that is, justified). You normally also get a few options for how the text will be printed. Bold, underlined, letter or draft quality print, and perhaps subscript and superscript characters for good measure.

If you want more options, you normally have to buy a Desktop Publishing program. DTP packages give you much greater control of the letter shapes and sizes as well as the spacing between them. You can then do the same layouts as a professional Typesetter in a printing firm.

How Is Write Different?

Write has most the facilities of a normal WP plus a few more. Some of these extra benefits give it a fairly big push towards being a DTP program. But by far the biggest benefits come from its ties with Windows.

Windows gives you the option of using the mouse as well as the keyboard. Here, where the keyboard has a major role to play, the mouse is not in competition with it. Both work together for the common good.

The mouse is particularly useful because it helps you move around your file much more easily than you can with the keyboard. It does this by acting as your insertion point's helper. With a click of the mouse button you can move the insertion point to where the I Bar (your mouse's tip inside text windows) is situated. It also helps you select text. You can select anything from single spaces to whole passages. Once selected, you can cut or copy text to the Clipboard, replace it or delete it.

Another advantage of being a Windows program is that you have also got the other Windows Programs like Clipboard and Print Manager to further your work.

The other major facility that makes Write different is Windows' ability to work with different Fonts. Windows has got seven screen fonts. But Write may have more because it will have added the fonts that your printer can print to the list in its Fonts dialogue box.

Necessary Extra Kit

Other than your basic equipment you will also need a printer to get the full benefit from Write. There is nothing to stop you using Write without a printer, you can save all your files to disk. A printer, however, is the only way to get your writing out of Windows world and into your own.

Write Files

Write Files are the same as any other files within Windows. You can open them, save them and print them.

Opening Files

You can select the file you want to Open in the normal way. You can Open a file to read it or edit it as often as you like. Write has the ability to convert files that are either in simple Text Only format (see the Notepad chapter for more details of what Text Only format is) or Microsoft Word format. Microsoft's Word for Windows files cannot be converted directly into Write format, but you can convert them into Word. Write will be able to convert it from Word format.

File Formats

The application that creates a file determines what format the files are going to be in. The format sets the codes for things like end of line, end of paragraph and underlined or bold text. There is, however, no one standard for these codes. This means that every Word Processor can use whatever codes takes its author's fancy. So, for example, one WP could use a code for left margin that another uses for the end of line.

None of this matters if you are only going to use your files with your computer, running your WP software. But if you ever want to give your files to someone else with a different computer, or you want to use them with another Word Processor, things start getting tricky.

The authors of Write have included two different conversions with Write itself. So if you try to open a non-Write file, Write will automatically offer you the chance to convert it into Write format. This appears to be clever because it doesn't even ask you what format you want to convert the file from. But, it is not as clever as all that, even if the file is not in a format that Write can convert, it will still try to convert it if you ask it to. You may be lucky, the file may have been in a format similar to Write or it may be a Text Only file. In either case, you may just

Chapter 9 Write

get the odd funny character in otherwise readable text. On the other hand, you may end up with totally unreadable 'gobbledygook'.

If you ask for conversion the Title Bar will display 'Converting and Loading'. Once the conversion is complete, a text file will look the same whether it has been converted or not. You can treat it as a Write file, use all the Write options and save it as a Write file. If, however, you Save it as a Text Only file any Write codes will be thrown away, never to be seen again. We have only been able to try this out with Text Only files because we don't have Microsoft Word.

Saving Write Files

Saving Write files is the same as saving any other file but with several more options.

Saving Files In Different Formats

It is simple to convert your Write file into either Text Only or Microsoft Word format. All you have to do is select the appropriate box from within the Save dialogue box. If you don't select either the Text Only or Microsoft Word box your file will be saved in Write format.

Tip: Converting Files To A WP Not Compatible With Write

Converting files to other formats can be easy. You need to find a 'go-between' format, and the software to run it, so that you can cross the chasm between them.

To convert your file to another WP format other than Word or Text Only files, you will need:

- a   a copy of Word or another program that can convert Word files.

- b   a go-between format that both your destination software and Word can convert to. Wordstar is normally a good bet but it only supports some of the formatting options that Write uses.

To convert your Write files to XYZ file format:

1. Save your Write file in Word format.

2. Run Word (or whatever program that can convert Word files into Wordstar format) and load the file.

3   Save it in Wordstar format.

4   Run XYZ and load the file into it in Wordstar format.

5   Convert file from Wordstar to XYZ. You may need to restore some of the formatting that was lost in the conversion process.

Make Backups

We have been talking (not to mention shouting and even screaming at times!) about the importance of creating back-up copies of everything you would be loath to lose if the Gremlins attack. If your eyes lit up when you saw that Write had a Backup option and you thought your troubles were over, think again! The Write back-up facility is only a very meagre first line of defence. Unless you have got reinforcements and cavalry behind the lines you could still be a very unhappy warrior. Even if you use Write's Backup option you must still make your own back-up copies on floppy disk, to be safe.

If you select the Backup option, the second time you save your file Write will convert the previously saved copy into a back-up. The latest copy will then be the working copy. So, in effect, you have two copies of the file instead of one.

Write creates two copies of the file by changing the extension of the old version from .WRI to .BKP and giving the working copy the .WRI extension. Write will do this every time you save your file so the .BKP file will always be the previous version to the one you have just saved. If the Write file that you are working on gets corrupted you will be able to fall back on the .BKP file. But, if something goes amiss with your hard disk, you will have lost two files instead of one.

The back-up copy of a file you have converted from Word or Text Only format will be further away from the working copy. The previous saved copy of the file won't have been converted so it will be in a different format. If you have to use that copy, you will have to convert it again.

When Is A .BKP A .BAK Extension

If you are not using the .WRI extension for your Write files your back-up copies will be given the .BAK extension not .BKP. Since .BAK is the normal extension for the back-up copies of

Chapter 9 Write

Word files (which will still be in Word format) this could be confusing. Unless you do something clever with the filenames you will not be able to tell the difference between back-ups of Word files and Write files.

Extensions For Back-Up Copies In Different Formats

Before saving a file in a different format, that you want a back-up copy of, you must knock the extension off the filename. Otherwise, you will create a file with a .WRI extension which is not in Write format.

After saving a Write file without an extension in Word format, the version in Word format will be given a .DOC extension while its back-up (still in Write format) will retain its .WRI extension.

If you don't remove the extension, the Write back-up copy will be given a .BKP extension.

If you are converting in the other direction the same rules apply. Converting a Word file to Write format will give the new Write file a .WRI extension and its back-up copy will retain .DOC on the end of its filename.

If you save a Write file and then save it again as a Text Only file the text file will still be given a .WRI extension with the Write file relegated to a .BKP file. If you want to know which files are in text format and which are in Write format you will have to change the extensions yourself.

Print

The Print option is your file's gateway to the real world. If you select it, you will be given a dialogue box with options of how many copies you want printed and whether you want just a portion printed of a large file.

You can only select a chunk of whole pages to print. There is no way of selecting text that you want printed other than entering the page numbers here.

The Draft Quality box is supposed to allow you to print your file quickly without worrying about the fonts and any other options you may have used from the character menu. After trying all the combinations we could think of and the file looking the same, we came to the conclusion that this option doesn't work. We even came across one printer driver that wouldn't print anything at all if this option was selected. We then installed another printer and found that it did work, but only if the Printer Setup dialogue box lets you select draft or proof (or letter) quality. Even then, it just selects this mode in the printer, all the fonts are still printed. The difference in print quality is entirely dependent on what the printer does.

Printer Setup

You have a direct link to the Printer settings in the Control Panel from the Printer Setup option on the File menu. This means that if you have access to more than one active printer you can select which one you want your Write file printed by. You can also alter settings for the printer to tailor that printer for the file you want to print.

Page Size

Write has no concept of page size, so the Paper Size option in Printer Setup is the only means that you have to set the page size. If you alter the Paper Size and Orientation you should be able to achieve the effect you want.

Repaginate

Repaginate will break your file into pages and number them accordingly. Write can either repaginate automatically or you can check each page break and either confirm or move them.

One of the disadvantages of being able to choose different font sizes is that they alter the number of lines of text you can get on a page. When you select Repaginate it will be sorted out for you. But page breaks (and Page numbers) are only accurate immediately after you have selected Repaginate. Probably the best time to select Repaginate is when you have finished editing the file.

Printing automatically Repaginates the file.

Page Break Markers

Write gives you two different symbols for a page break. There is one marker for a page break that has been put in automatically and one for a manual break that you have positioned yourself. You will need to use a manual break when you want a new page to start regardless of whether the previous page is full or not.

Automatic Page Break

If you don't select the Confirm Page Break box inside the Repaginate dialogue box, Repaginate will go through your file putting in page breaks wherever it feels you need one. These automatic markers look like a small outlined arrow that appears alongside the top line of a new page, in the left hand margin. They are outside the text area so you can't edit them. If you want to alter any you will need to select the Confirm Page Break box in Repaginate and go through each page break in turn until you find the one you want to change. You can then move it with the UP button (or the DOWN button if you take it up too far) in the Confirm dialogue box.

An automatic repagination will put a page break marker at the top of the file. We were a bit worried when we first saw this in case Write had put in an extra page at the beginning. It doesn't do that, but appears to need a starting point.

Page Breaks You Put In Yourself

Once you have moved a page break it becomes a manual one. As well as the arrow in the margin you will also see a dotted line across the file which marks the break.

Tip: Putting In Manual Page Breaks Without Repaginate

While you are typing or editing text, there is a much simpler way of putting a page break into your file. Ctrl+Enter will insert the dotted line to mark where you want the page to be split. When you are ready to sort out the page numbers you can select Repaginate. The dotted lines will be treated as manual page breaks. If you select the Confirm Page Break box you will be given the chance to move these as well as all the others.

If you ask Write to Repaginate your pages automatically, the page breaks you have put in will be left where you have put them. An arrow will be put in the margin to show that they are now page breaks that Write is using.

If you use lots of manual page breaks in a file, Repaginate more often, otherwise Write seems to get itself into a bit of a mess.

One Of The Things We Love To Hate

Repaginate is one of the blackspots of Write as far as we are concerned. Here are some of the reasons:

1   Write doesn't automatically keep track of where you are and increment the pages while you are typing. You have to tell Write to sort out the page numbers with Repaginate whenever you want to know which page you are on.

2   Once you change the file, the page numbers may not be correct (even if you selected Repaginate five minutes ago), until you select it again.

3   You cannot search for an automatic page break and move it. With Repaginate there are no half measures - you either have to do the whole file or nothing at all. You can, however, search for page breaks that you have put in yourself.

4   The page number is not always accurate as a guide to the number of the page that you are looking at. The number of the page will not change until the page break marker reaches the top of the screen. So, you can be looking at text below the page break but the page numbers will still say that you are on the previous page.

5   Write doesn't show you how much room you have got on a page. So, if you are writing a letter that you don't want to be longer than two pages, you will not be given any indication of whether you have reached your limit or not. Selecting Repaginate will only tell you when you have gone over the limit to Page Three. The only way to cope with this is to select Repaginate often so that you know immediately you have gone onto the third page. You can then edit the letter so that it will fit on the number of pages you want.

Editing Text

Editing requires that you are able to move around your file and insert or delete text. The two keys to successful editing are to be able to quickly and easily:

1. Move around the file

2   Select the text you want to work with

If you are using a mouse, you have the scroll bars to move around the file and you can select text with the I Bar. If you need a refresher course on either of these, you will find detailed descriptions in Chapter Three.

If you are using the scroll bars, don't forget that the insertion point doesn't automatically follow.

Chapter 9 Write

This can be an asset if you want to check something further back in the file. You can move there with the scroll bars, check your facts and then carry on typing. Write will return you to where you were instantly. But if you are moving to another part of the file to do some work there it can be a little annoying to find yourself back where you started!

If you are using the keyboard, both the official guide and Write's Help menu have lots of information on keyboard commands. Even if you are using a mouse you could do worse than look at the keyboard commands because things like moving to the top or bottom of your file don't have mouse equivalents that are as easy or quick as pressing two or three keys.

Tip: Selecting Blocks Of Text With The Mouse

In Notepad and Write, if you move the I Bar into the left hand margin it turns back into an arrow. Not the white left pointing arrow that is normally at the end of your mouse, but a white right pointing arrow. If your window background is white it will just look like an outline. While the mouse's tip is a right pointing arrow, the mouse controls do different things:

    A click will select the whole line that the arrow is pointing to.

    A single click followed by a drag will select all the lines that the arrow passes.

    A double click will select the whole paragraph.

    A double click followed by a drag will select all the paragraphs that the mouse passes.

    A Shift + click after you have selected a line somewhere else will select all lines between the two points.

    A Ctrl + click will select the whole file.

No Change Case Command

One thing missing from Write's editing tools is a command that will change the case of a character or block of characters. If you have left the Caps Lock key down by mistake and everything you have typed is in capitals, most WP packages give you the ability to select it and change it to lower case. With Write, however, you have to select it and then type the text all over again in the correct case.

The Undo Option

Here is some really powerful magic. Not only will the Undo option reverse your last action, it will also change its name to mimic what your last option was. It can change between Undo Typing. Undo Editing, Undo Formatting and Undo. The demarcation lines between these four are a little hazy, so we will explore them in a little more depth.

Undo Typing

Undo Typing will undo all the typing you have done since you did anything else. If you type some text and then immediately delete some of it with the Backspace key, Write treats that all as typing. It won't put what you have deleted back but will delete the rest of what you have just typed as well. Deleted text will only be put back if Undo Editing appears on the Edit menu.

Inserting text is treated as typing. If you have been typing continuously and then insert text in the middle of what you have just typed, Undo typing will only delete the inserted text.

Undo Editing

Undo Editing will undo all the options from the Edit and Search menus, plus a few more.

If you have selected a few words and then deleted them by pressing the Backspace or Delete key, you can get them back again be selecting Undo Editing. Also, if you have Cut or Pasted a chunk of your file to or from the Clipboard, Undo Editing will reverse it.

You can also use Undo Editing with the Find and Change options. You can return to the previous Find or reverse the last Change you made. If you have selected Change but have moved some way through the file not changing anything, Undo Editing will return the cursor to where it was before you started that operation.

Undo Editing will reverse any font changes you have just made to a selected block of text through the Fonts dialogue box. You can also change back any indents that you have just changed through the Indents dialogue box.

Undo Formatting

Undo Formatting will undo any option (apart from the Fonts and Indents dialogue boxes) that you have just selected from the Character or Paragraph menus. It will also reverse anything you have done with the Ruler, but only immediately after you have done it. So if you have just

Chapter 9 Write

changed both the indents and the left margin with the Ruler and then select Undo formatting, they will both be reversed to what they were before you changed them. But if you changed the indents, then did some editing and then changed the left margin, Undo Formatting would only reverse the change to the left margin.

Apart from the changes you have made with the Ruler, you do not appear to be able to undo any of the options in the Document menu. You can't even turn the Ruler off with Undo if you have just turned it on.

Undoing What You Have Undone

If you undo something by mistake you can reverse it by selecting Undo again. When you select it a second time it will just be a plain Undo option on the menu.

Cut, Copy And Paste

Cut deletes the selected text from your file and puts it onto the Clipboard. Copy just copies the selected text to the Clipboard, leaving it in your file as well. Once on the Clipboard the text can be pasted back into that file in another place (by moving the insertion point to the position you want the text to go). All the settings of options from the Character and Paragraph menus are carried with the text to its new location. You can just as easily Paste the text into another file altogether. See the Clipboard chapter for more details.

Inserting Paintbrush Files Into Write Files

You can insert graphics that you have created in Paintbrush into your Write file. You just Cut or Copy them to the Clipboard from Paintbrush after selecting the part of the picture you want to use. Smaller pictures are easier to work with but you can work with bigger files too.

Graphics take up more memory than text and by cutting a picture from Paintbrush to the Clipboard and then putting it into Write you will have triplicated the picture so it will take up three times as much memory. If you have other windows open too, and even if you don't, you could be given the 'Insufficient Memory' message. If you get this message and then close all the other windows, you may be able to carry on, if you are lucky!

Colours?

You can only add black and white pictures into Write files. Any colour you use will be translated into black.

Positioning Pasted Pictures

Pictures will be inserted into your file at the left hand margin wherever the insertion point is situated. Smaller pictures will all appear in the window, larger pictures make the file move up so you will only see the bottom portion of the picture.

The entire picture will be regarded by Write as one block (almost like a character except that if you move up or down the file the picture will not move out of view all at one go) by Write. You cannot edit the picture from here, nor can you insert text inside the picture, or anywhere alongside it. Once a picture has been Pasted into Write it creates a sort of cocoon round itself. That whole part of the file, between the left and right margins, becomes a 'picture slot'. This is a 'No Go' area for text. You cannot even put the insertion point into these areas.

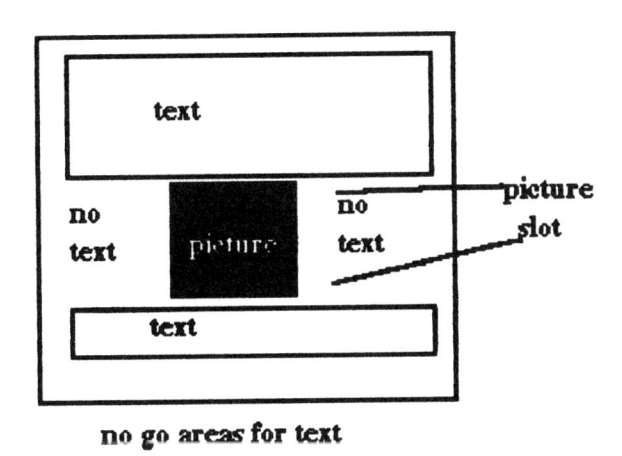

no go areas for text

Pictures in Write files can make the scroll bars inaccurate. If you put a bigger picture at the top of a file, Write will show you the bottom part of the picture on the screen as normal but the scroll button will be right at the top of the track. For a long time we thought there was a problem pasting large files into Write. Then we discovered that you can move higher up and see the whole picture with the Up Arrow key even though you can't get there with the mouse.

Selecting Pictures

Selecting a picture is easy. Just click the mouse, with the I Bar within the picture. Or, if you

Chapter 9 Write

move the insertion point into it (while your picture is still on the left hand margin) with the Arrow keys the picture will be selected automatically. You can also use the right pointing arrow to select pictures but you have to double click the mouse.

Once you have moved your picture away from the left margin there appears to be no way that you can select it with the Arrow keys. So, if you don't have a mouse don't move your picture until you are absolutely sure that you are not going to do anything else with it.

To deselect a picture either move the insertion point off it with the Arrow keys or click the mouse once in the left margin alongside the picture. Clicking the mouse with the I Bar inside a selected picture will have no effect.

Moving Pictures

Animation has not reached Windows yet, so we aren't talking about cartoons. Although we reckon moving Icons would be rather trendy!

You can move your Pasted picture around its slot (after you have selected it of course) in three ways. You can use the Alignment options on the Paragraph menu or the Aligning icons above the Ruler, or you can use the Move Picture option on the Edit Menu.

The Aligning options and icons will only move the picture to the centre of the page or level with the right hand margin. With the Move Picture option you have more freedom of movement although you can still only move it horizontally along the picture slot.

When you select the Move Picture option the mouse's tip will turn into a small bold square (you can control the square with the Left/Right Arrows if you are using the keyboard). A faint outline will also appear around the picture. If you move the small square to where you want the picture to move to, the outline will follow. Clicking the mouse or pressing Enter will tell Windows to move your picture there.

Altering Your Picture's Size

The Size Picture option again uses the bold square in the centre of the picture and the faint outline around it. This time the bold square doesn't do anything until it crosses one of the outline lines and then it picks it up and takes it with it. You can move the small square around either with the mouse or the Arrow keys. We find that using the Arrows Keys is more controllable than the mouse and they also avoid the strong temptation to click the mouse button before you are ready to fix the size!

You cannot move the top line, but you can extend the picture downwards and outwards. If you pick the outline up in one of the bottom corners you can alter the size in both directions at once like you can do with a window. Once you have got the outline to the size you want the picture, either click the mouse or press Enter.

Looking For Something?

The Search menu gives you a way to look for a sequence of characters from amongst the thousands in your file. It also gives you a quick way of moving around your file, if you know where you want to go!

Find

Find allows you to tell Write what you are looking for by typing a 'clue' into the Find What box in the Find dialogue box. You then select the FIND NEXT button with the mouse or press Enter. Find will go away and start looking from your present position. When Write finds the clue, it will put that section of the file on the screen. The word, or sequence of characters that match what you are looking for, will be highlighted. Write will search to the end of the file and will then go back to the beginning and work through until it can't find any more matches for your clue.

You can move back into the Write window with the mouse, or by pressing [Alt+F6]. You can carry on editing, leaving the Find dialogue box on the screen. When you have finished there and want to find the next occurrence of the clue, press [Alt+F6] again. You will then be back in the Find dialogue box ready to start searching either for the same thing or for a new clue.

If you don't need to use Find any more, you can cancel the dialogue box by pressing Esc or you can close it using the Dialogue Box Control button.

What Can You Look For?

You can look for almost anything that might occur in a Write file apart from pictures. You can look for words, spaces, punctuation marks, and even things like paragraph markers that are invisible.

General Guidelines

To find a word, or group of words, type them accurately. If you spell or type your clue

Chapter 9 Write

incorrectly Write will not find it. Write doesn't understand English. So it won't know that if you type 'gix', you really mean fix.

You will need to strike a balance between giving the exact sentence that you are looking for and keeping the search clue as brief as possible. Typing the whole sentence would be time consuming but it would ensure that Write would take you straight there. Typing in a two letter clue, on the other hand, would take a lot less time but you would probably have to stop at every other word and you'd take ages to get to what you were looking for.

You can be fairly brief, however. If you were looking for Windows to check what you had already said you could type just [WIN] and it would find Windows. Mind you, Write would also find 'wind', 'twin' and 'winder' as well. It might be a good idea to think about what other words you have used and adjust the clue accordingly. Otherwise you could be sending Find off on a search where it will find more than you bargained for!

If you are looking for more than one word you may need to put the [^w] code for a space between the words, not an actual space. Although, if you want to look for just spaces, you need to press the Spacebar once for every space you are looking for. We often use this with the Change option while we are writing, to seek and destroy extra spaces that seem to get everywhere.

The Invisibles

As well as the code for a space, there are three others:

[^t] is the code for a Tab character. Suppose you were looking for a word, or sequence of words, that you knew you had tabulated. You could put [^t] in front of your search clue and Write should find it straightaway.

[^p] will find the invisible markers used at the end of paragraphs and on blank lines. This is useful if you think you might have a few stray ones. Likewise, [^d] will find any page breaks that you have put in yourself. The page breaks that Write puts in automatically when you do a Repaginate have a more powerful magic to cloak them. You cannot find them with simple codes.....

Wildcards Again!

Yes, we have got wildcards again. This time there is only one, so that makes it a bit easier.....

Chapter 9 Write

You can use ? instead of any other character in your search clue. So, you can still search for words even if you are not sure how you have spelt them. If you have a habit of misspelling a word, sometimes writing 'devide' when you mean 'divide', you could put [d?vide] into the Find What box. Find will then find it regardless of what the second letter is.

It is probably unwise to use more than one or two ?'s in a clue. You will be increasing the number of matches Write is going to find, by using a ? To widen the search any further is likely to be more of a nuisance than anything else. It is unlikely that you are going to want to find every word beginning with B. Unless you are an Indexer or Lexicographer!

Whole Word Box

If you select the Whole Word box, you will cut down the number of matches that Write will find from your search clue. It tells Write to only show something that matches your clue if it has a space or punctuation mark on either side.

Match Upper/Lower Case Box

Selecting the Match Upper/Lower Case Box will again cut down the number of matches that Write will find from your clue. If your clue contains a capital letter, Write will only find you a match that has a capital letter in exactly the same place. So if you want to find Windows, it won't show you instances where you are talking about the glass filled variety.

We have noticed that Find can sometimes be a bit temperamental. It appears to have its off moments, only finding what you are searching for if it feels like it. This only happens occasionally, and some of those are probably down to us, but there have been times when we knew what we were looking for was there. But Write still came back with the 'Search Text not found' dialogue box.

We can see no apparent reason for these as they appear to be totally random. If this happens to you, double check your clue for spelling and typing. Try to narrow down the search by selecting the Whole word or Match Case boxes. Then try again. If that still doesn't work, try a different clue! But, providing you have got the clue right and you haven't spelt the word that you are looking for differently in the file, Find will come up with it eventually.

Repeat Last Find

This allows you to carry on the search even if you have closed the Find dialogue box. We don't think this is a terribly useful option since you can leave the inactive Find dialogue box on the screen anyway, ready to work whenever you need it. But if you need to see the whole screen, this option will be useful.

Change

This allows you to look for something and replace it with something else. Everything we have said about Find is equally relevant here. But here you can do something with what you have found.

A rather nice feature of these Search options is that they are linked together. If you were searching for something with Find before you selected Change (as long as you have closed the Find box first), your clue will already be in the Find What box when you open Change. You can then just type what you want it replaced with.

What you want your clue changed to can be anything you like. If you are putting in more than one word the space should be a press of the Spacebar, not the code for a space this time. You can even leave the Change To box empty, which will delete whatever you have asked it to find.

In the Change dialogue box are the three extra buttons along the bottom. You could use the Change dialogue box instead of Find because you can just press the FIND NEXT button to go through the file finding things, not changing anything.

The names on the extra buttons are fairly self-explanatory. The only one that has hidden talents is the CHANGE ALL button. That will go through the file, changing every occurrence of your Find clue. If, however, you have a block of text highlighted when you enter the Change dialogue box, the CHANGE ALL button metamorphoses into the CHANGE SELECTION button. Now it will change every clue automatically, but only in the selected area of text.

Go To Page

This is a quick way of moving around your file, if you know where you want to be. You must have already used Repaginate to break your file into pages.

Conjuring Up Odd Characters

One of the things that may brighten up the account of your journey, in more ways than one, is the descriptions of the odd looking characters that you are likely to meet along the way. To help

Chapter 9 Write

your travelogue stand out from the crowd, you have several tricks up you sleeve. These will hopefully make your writing look more interesting. You can choose and change the style of lettering. You can choose to accentuate different characters or whole sections of characters by changing the style, making them bigger or smaller than the rest. Or you can give them attributes.

In Write you have a number of fonts to choose from. As well as the ones that Windows has, you also have any that are available on your printer.

The Fonts that you'll be working with in your viewing screen are rarely portrayed accurately but they will be better on the printout. If, for example, you are working with a large font, the characters on the screen will not reach the right margin. They will look as though they only go halfway across the line. We thought that we had our margins set wrongly but we realised afterwards that it was due to Windows not having WYSIWYG. See Chapter 3 for more details.

You will be given three fonts to choose from in the Fonts section of the character menu (which starts halfway down the menu). You can also choose from any of the others that are available in the Fonts option at the bottom.

How To Change Fonts

You can choose a font at any time, not just when you start writing. When you select a new font anything you type after that will be in the new one. If you want to change the font of text that you have already typed, select the text and then select the font and size that you want to change it to.

If you are using Write for the first time, the best way to make an educated choice from the fonts you have available is to print them all. Although the Windows fonts are displayed in the Font Settings in the Control Panel you won't see the Printer ones there. Printing them will also give you the benefit of being able to see them all side by side.

Tip: To Print All The Available Fonts

Type one line of text into a new Write file.

Copy it to the Clipboard and then Paste it back into the file as many times as there are fonts in the Fonts dialogue box.

Select each line in turn and select a different font for it. Don't worry about Fonts on the list with

Chapter 9 Write

the same name. They are different sizes of the same font.

Save the file and print it.

You can then use this sheet for reference whenever you need it.

The Fonts Dialogue Box

Starting at the bottom of the Character menu, the Fonts dialogue box allows you to select a font and its size.

The Fonts Section

The first font you select will be put into the number one slot in the font section of the Character menu. The second one at number two and the third at number three. After that Windows will show how clever it can be by changing these automatically so that they correspond with the fonts you are using the most. So, if you have been using Helv more often than not, that will be put in slot number one.

The Sizing Section

Between the fonts section and the Fonts option there is the sizing section. These two Options allow you to change the size of the font you are using, or one that you have just selected, without entering the Fonts dialogue box. They are quicker than using the Font dialogue box, but you can only select the next size up or down each time you select either of these options. So they are useful if you only want to make small changes to the font size.

There may be a problem with bitmap fonts, however, because sometimes the sizes that these options think are available are different to the sizes that the Fonts dialogue box actually has available. The sizing options use the sizes that Windows has defined for that font, while the Fonts dialogue box is more interested in the sizes that the printer has defined. So you may be selecting sizes with the sizing options that your printer cannot print. You can check this by:

1. Selecting Reduce Font

2. Entering the Fonts dialogue box

3. Checking the number in the Point Size box in the bottom right hand corner against the

numbers in the Sizes box

Go through the above procedure three or four times. If the numbers in the two boxes always match everything is 'hunky dorey'. If the numbers in the Point Size box diverge from those in the Sizes box your Printer may not be able to print that size. In which case you should avoid using the Sizing option and always alter the size of your fonts through the Fonts dialogue box.

If, however, you are using an outline font, there won't be a problem. See the section on Fonts in Chapter 3 if you can't remember which fonts are which.

Attributes Section

The top section of the Character menu is taken up with Character Attributes. You can turn these on or off by selecting them. They affect the characters regardless of the font and size. You can make characters bold, underlined, italic, subscript or superscript. You can use more than one attribute for any one group of characters. So you could have underlined bold characters or even underlined italic subscript characters if you wanted.

Italic characters are difficult to work with. They lean across the insertion point and make it unclear exactly which character the insertion point is next to.

The Normal option cancels any Attributes you have selected. It will have no effect on the font or font size you have selected.

Using Different Fonts/Attributes In The Same File

If you change the font, font size or attributes, without selecting any text, whatever you type after that will probably be in the new characteristics. Whenever you insert text into your file it will take on the same characteristics as preceding characters. But predicting what characteristics a character will take on when you insert it can be a bit tricky!

The first thing to remember is that spaces and spare lines also take on the characteristics that you are using for the text.

If you have accentuated a few words in the middle of a file in bold, and then you insert a few words immediately in front of it, the insert will not be in bold. If you inserted text immediately after a bold passage the insert will be in bold. But if you leave a space between the bold text and the text you've inserted, the inserted text will take on the characteristics of the space, which will probably not be bold.

Chapter 9 Write

Another example would be if you are inserting a paragraph of smaller text between two paragraphs of text with a larger point size, the last line of the paragraph you are inserting has a habit of reverting to the larger font size. Write doesn't actually make the characters bigger, it just leaves a larger space than it has left between the previous lines. If you select the line and select the Fonts dialogue box, there will not be a number in the Point Size box. Write has lost track of what the size should be. To cure this, put in the point size you are using again, after selecting one or two spare lines below.

Laying Out Your Text

The options in the Paragraph and Document menus are all about how you want your text to appear on the page. They include margins, line spacing, tab stops and text alignment.

The Ruler

Most of the options on these two menus can also be selected from the Ruler's display. The Ruler option on the Document menu will either turn the Ruler on or off. The Ruler has a graphic display for everything apart from the Headers and Footers and the options available from Page Layout. The settings from the dialogue boxes will be shown on the Ruler and any options you change with the Ruler will also be put into the appropriate box. We reckon the Ruler is far easier to work with, but we will go through each option on the menu in turn and describe both ways of selecting and changing them.

The options in the Paragraph menu will affect the paragraph that the insertion point is in. It is only if you want to alter the options for more than one paragraph that you need to select any paragraphs.

Options on the Document menu will effect the whole file. They all have to stay the same throughout the file.

We recommend that you experiment with these options and see what happens when you print your file out. When you are setting-up things like margins or headers and footers which do not actually appear on your screen, this is most essential.

Aligning Text

The aligning options occupy the top of the paragraph menu. They can also be selected from the four icons in the top right hand corner of the Ruler. The Ruler icons give you an idea of what they will do to the text.

The Left Option

Text is normally Left aligned. All lines start at the left margin. They do not normally extend to the right margin because lines are wrapped on the last word that will fit on the line. Text will have an uneven finish down the right hand side. The longer the word that has been pushed down to the next line, the more irregular the right side is going to be. You could alter this by using 'optional hyphens' at appropriate points in longer words.

Tip: Optional Hyphens In Write

You can use optional hyphens to break up longer words that might not fit on the end of a line. This may not just happen to words that get put on the end of a line when you type the text. When you edit, there is no telling where any of the words are going to be positioned on the line.

If you want Write to be able to break up a word, move the insertion point to a convenient break point in the word and press [Shift + Ctrl + -].

Write will only show the hyphen and split the word if it is on the end of a line. Otherwise the hyphen will be invisible.

The Right Option

The Right aligning option will move the text over so that all lines finish at the right hand margin. The left side will then be the uneven one. This is quite strange to work with. The insertion point stays still on the right hand margin and the text moves, which is back to front! We prefer to use Left while we are typing and only Right align it at the end.

The Centred Option

Centred text will be arranged around the central point between the two margins. The extra space that normally appears at the end of a line, if the text is Right or Left aligned, will be split and half added to either end. This is ideal for titles and headings.

The Justified Option

Justified text is spread evenly between the two margins. The extra space that is normally on the end of a line is divided up between all the spaces on the line. Each space is made bigger accordingly. If you ask for justified text on a paragraph that you are just typing, Write will wait until you have typed a whole line and sort out the spacing afterwards. The spacing will not be changed for lines that are not full.

The Line Spacing Options

The line spacing options are the same as the mechanical settings on typewriters. They allow you a limited range of choices for how much space you want between lines of text.

The amount of space allocated for the gap between lines will change depending what font size you are using. Bigger fonts will have bigger spaces between them, even if you have got single line spacing selected.

Tip: Paragraphs That Should Follow One Another...

Paragraphs should follow the aligning and spacing of the previous paragraph. But any spare lines between paragraphs will be treated as paragraphs and are aligned too. As you cannot see them, you might get unexpected results.

For example, you have typed two Left aligned paragraphs and are ready to start the third. You then centre the second paragraph. When you carry on typing the third paragraph, you would expect it to be centred too, as it follows the second one. But it will be Left aligned! It is actually following the alignment of the spare line that you put in to separate the second and third paragraphs, before you centred the second one.

Indents

Indents allow you to start or finish lines somewhere other than the left or right margins. It is useful to indent lists or numbered points so that they are separate from the main body of the text and makes them much easier to read. You can also have a hanging indent, where the top line of each paragraph sticks out to the left. The rest of the paragraph is lined-up against a second indent slightly to the right.

You can have a different indent setting for every paragraph. There are no limits to how many different ones you can have in a file.

To set an indent using the menu option, just type in how far you want the lines to be indented into the Left Indent box (which is inside the Indents Dialogue Box). If you want a hanging indent, type a smaller number into the First Line box. You can also set a Right Indent here. You can use this with the Right Aligning option.

To set indents with the Ruler, drag the small dot inside the right pointing arrow on the Ruler to where you want the first line of the paragraph to start. Then drag the right pointing arrow itself to where you want the other lines to start. For a normal indent you put the arrow level with the dot and for a hanging one you put it further to the right. You can set a right indent with the left pointing arrow. You may have to use the Left/Right scroll bar to find this as it's frequently off the right hand edge of the window.

Headers And Footers

Headers and Footers can contain things like titles, section headings and page numbers. They do not appear in the text area of the page but are stored separately and put into the top or bottom margins. The Header and Footer menu options are in the Document menu.

You can specify where you want them to go by altering the Distance From... box in the Header or Footer dialogue box. If you put in more than a line, or you use a bigger size font than the space allows for, you may need to make the margin bigger in Page layout.

When you select one of these options you are given a clear page as well as the dialogue box. You type what you want to appear in the header or footer onto the empty page, not the dialogue box itself. You can say where you want them to appear with the aligning, spacing, indent and tab options.

If you want your file to have a cover page, don't select the Print On First Page box. Headers or Footers will then be put on all pages from Page 2 onwards.

If you press the PAGE NUMBER # button, your printed pages will be automatically numbered. The page number will appear at the position in the Header or Footer that you were at when you pressed the button. For example, you could have "Page Number" in the footer and then press the PAGE NUMBER # button. Write will then add "(Page)" to the footer. When you print the file, each page will have "Page Number xxx" as its footer.

The CLEAR button removes all the text from a header or footer, allowing you to start afresh. To

Chapter 9 Write

leave the Header or Footer pages, you can either select the RETURN TO DOCUMENT button or close the dialogue box.

Tabs

Tabs work just as they do on a typewriter. They allow you to move the insertion point quickly to predetermined points along the line. The only difference from a typewriter is that when you press the Tab key Write will put in a tab character that you can't see, but you can search for with Find.

When you start work on a file there are tabs already set at half inch intervals for you. They do not appear in the Tab dialogue box or on the Ruler. Any of these that are in front of tabs that you have set yourself will disappear.

These preset Tabs may vary depending what printer you have selected. On one printer we tried, we were only allowed seven preset tabs. When we reached the seventh, the Tab key was stopped from moving the insertion point any further to the right. So, if you are working on a file that you may want to print on two different printers, it might be useful to use your own Tabs rather than relying on the preset ones. Otherwise you may end up with two different layouts for the same file.

You can have two different sorts of tabs. Normal tabs will left align the text in each column. Decimal tabs are useful for columns of figures because the columns will be aligned on their decimal points. There are two ways of selecting a Decimal tab. You can either select the Decimal box underneath a Position box in the Tab dialogue box. Or you can select the tab icon with a decimal point after it from the Ruler display.

Setting Tabs

You can set tabs by typing a measurement into the Tabs dialogue box. They are set from the left margin, so the left hand edge of your window is always 0.

To set up tabs with the Ruler, simply position the mouse's arrow over the point on the ruler where you want that tab to go and click the mouse button. To move a tab on the Ruler drag it to where you want it to go. To remove a tab from the Ruler, drag it straight off. If you want a Decimal tab, you must select the icon first.

Working With Tabs

Once you have put in the tabs you want, they apply for the whole file. If you change a tab it will disorganise any columns that are already there.

It is probably easier to use tabs while you are typing your text rather than during the editing process.

Tip: Don't Tabulate Text Or Figures Already In Paragraphs

It is not a good idea to try to tabulate text that is in the middle of a paragraph. Write may get itself into a mess, particularly if you try to tabulate text that was at the beginning of a line. It will treat the tab character as it would any other character and move it up onto the previous line. It will do this for any word in an effort to get as much as possible onto every line. If you do try to use the Tab key while you are editing, the word that you want tabulated will eventually be moved but only after you have repeatedly pressed the Tab key.

To move the insertion point to a tab position to the right press the Tab key once (as long as you are not in the middle of a paragraph). The insertion point should jump to the next available Tab position.

If the insertion point is actually on a tab position and you press the Left Arrow key the insertion point will leap-frog over the gap and land to the right of any text in the previous tab position. If you press Backspace while the insertion point is on a tab position, it will delete the tab character and move the insertion point with any text that the tab was holding, back to the previous tab position.

The Page Layout Option

The Page Layout option allow you to set and change margins and set the page numbering to start somewhere other than '1'. This allows you to join several files together while printing. You can also change between English and Metric units of measurement.

Chapter 10 The Clipboard

Chapter 10 - The Clipboard

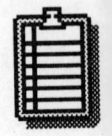

To move information between applications in Windows world, you cut or copy the data into your Clipboard GTi, drive over to the other application and paste it there. You can also use the Clipboard to move information within an application window. The Clipboard window needn't be open - you can Cut, Copy and Paste anyway.

Copying, Cutting And Pasting

You may like to double click the Clipboard icon in the Program Manager and then move the Clipboard window to a corner of your viewing screen. You'll then be able to watch its contents change as you use Windows.

You store whatever you Cut or Copy from an application on the clipboard. You'll see the information immediately appear in the Clipboard window. You retrieve whatever you Paste into an application from the clipboard.

You can't copy more than one thing into the clipboard at a time; it only retains the last item. These high-performance cars always have small boots, don't they? Most of the time, it's easy to pick up one thing at a time, transfer it and then return for more. Paintbrush has Cut To and Paste

From options in its Edit menu that save the cutout straight to a file which by-pass the clipboard.

A Tour Of Clipboard's Menus

The File And Edit Menus

The Clipboard has just three options in its File menu; Open, Save As and Exit.

The contents of the clipboard, in whatever format the application is using, can be saved as a Clipboard file. You normally use a .CLP extension. Saving your clipboard can be useful to store information that you have cut out of a file, so you can reuse it later. Clipboard files can only be opened in Clipboard. If you want to use data you've stored from the clipboard, you must reload the file into Clipboard before you paste it.

The Open option opens a dialogue box from which you can select a file that you previously saved in Clipboard. Clipboard asks you if you want to overwrite the current contents of the clipboard, if there were any. Pressing the OK button copies the contents of the saved file to the clipboard, replacing the clipboard's current contents. If you press the CANCEL button, the clipboard's contents are not disturbed.

Save As saves the clipboard's contents. If you're only saving the clipboard to a file temporarily, you don't have to type a filename, Windows puts DEFAULT.CLP in the File box. If you type a name that already exists, Clipboard asks whether it should be overwritten. If you select CANCEL, you must reselect Save As and then type a different name.

The Exit option just closes the Clipboard window. It doesn't alter the contents of the clipboard.

The Edit menu has only one option: Delete. This opens a dialogue box asking you to confirm that you want to clear the clipboard before doing so. If you press the OK button, you lose the contents of the clipboard for ever. If you Cut data from an application and then clear the clipboard, you'll have to reload a back-up copy of the original file to recover the data you Cut out.

The Official User Guide mentions that you may be able to free memory for other uses by clearing the clipboard. That's true but, unless the clipboard is holding a large Paintbrush picture the memory you'll free will be small. It's probably better to close application windows than to worry about the amount of memory the clipboard is using.

The Display Menu

The Display menu will contain different options depending which application put the data in the clipboard. It will always contain one option, Auto, that will display the contents in a format that you can understand. If there's an Owner Display option, Auto will use this to display the clipboard.

If you've copied data from Write to the clipboard, the Display menu will have three options apart from Auto; Owner Display, Text and OEM Text. The Owner Display option asks the owner, Write in this case, to display the text. If you select this, Write and Clipboard get together and sort out amongst themselves what format in which they will display the text; normally they agree to display it in the correct size and font. Selecting Text just displays the text in the standard font and forgets any formatting like end of lines.

OEM Text is an enigma; OEM stands for Original Equipment Manufacturer although what that has to do with Write is a mystery. It seems to use a fixed width font rather than the standard system font. If you include some pictures, you won't see them when you select Text or OEM Text.

For Paintbrush data, the Display menu has three options; Auto, Bitmap and Palette. Selecting Auto or Bitmap shows the data in the clipboard as a picture. Selecting the Palette option displays the colour palette used for the picture that the cutout came from.

Cutting or Copying data from the other applications with Edit menus - Terminal, Notepad, Cardfile, Calendar and Calculator - all cause the Display menu to have Auto, Text and OEM Text options.

Additional Windows applications that you buy may cause the Clipboard Display menu to have other options. We have found that some of these may not work - this applies particularly with the Owner Display option. It's probably best to leave Auto selected unless you especially need to look at clipboard data from another viewpoint.

Transferring Data Between Applications

Let's look at transferring data between the different Windows applications. The Tool Box chapter shows how to transfer data across The Great Divide between non-Windows and

Chapter 10 The Clipboard

Windows applications.

You can always transfer text data between applications that can use text.

Cutouts created by Paintbrush can be pasted into Write documents, and into card files after you select Picture mode in Cardfile. You can copy a picture back from a Write document to Paintbrush if you are careful to select just the picture.

If you paste Write data that includes a picture into an application that can only handle text, you'll just paste the text.

Numbers from other applications can be transferred to the Calculator as text. Answers from the Calculator's display are copied to the clipboard as text and so can be pasted into most applications. The format of the number is the same as the answer appears in the calculator's display. So, if you select the Scientific view in the Calculator, you can paste numbers in Scientific notation; that is, 100 as 1.e+002.

For additional Windows applications that you buy, the rule is "If it seems sensible, try it"! We've been surprised how well applications from different suppliers work together using the clipboard.

The Print Screen Key

Perhaps you've hit the Print Screen key (on some keyboards, it's a shifted key or labelled PrtSc) by accident when running MS-DOS and found that your printer produces a copy of whatever is on your viewing screen. This is one of the little gems hidden in your computer that you probably never knew about.

Try that in Windows. No printout and a frustrated user, perhaps...

Now, open your window onto the clipboard by double clicking on the Clipboard icon. You'll see a picture of your screen appearing in the Clipboard window. You'll only see part of it but using the Clipboard's scroll bars will allow you to reveal all your screen.

Hit PrtSc again and find the part of the picture which shows the Clipboard window - it will show the contents of the clipboard before you hit the PrtSc key. You'll probably wonder what happens if you press PrtSc when you've a picture of the Clipboard on screen that includes the Clipboard window that includes the.... You get the idea - what does a picture of a picture of a picture look like?

Chapter 10 The Clipboard

Try it! You'll see that nothing untoward happens. Each time you press the PrtSc key, Windows just copies an exact copy of the screen to the clipboard. You may get confused, trying to click on menus that aren't there, but Windows won't.

If you now open the Clipboard's Display menu, you'll see two choices: Auto and Bitmap. This reveals that Windows has merely copied your screen as a Bitmap, nothing more and nothing less. Paintbrush uses Bitmap files so if you copy the clipboard into Paintbrush, it will show a copy of your screen when you pressed PrtSc.

That's just what happens. Once you've got the picture of the screen into Paintbrush it's just like any other image. You can add things to it, like instructions for other people. Or you can mask out things, hiding details that are not needed. Then, you can print it or even transfer it to the clipboard into a Write document.

If you press [Alt + PrtSc], you copy just the active window to the clipboard.

Chapter 11 Notepad

There's an electronic Notepad in the equipment you were issued with at the start of your journey. It's quick and simple to use - just what you need for jotting down brief notes of things that you find out as you explore the world of Windows.

Notepad is a text editor, which is the most basic form of word processor ever invented. You can use Notepad if you don't need pretty looking documents. However, its main role is to provide a simple tool to allow you to create and change Text Only files.

Some Windows users use Notepad to edit the Big Four files that control how Windows is configured.

Notepad - The Basics

Notepad displays the contents of the file in the System font. This is a throwback to the bad old days before Windows 3.0, when nearly all computer generated text looked this bad. Some looked even worse, but that's another story.

There's nothing to stop you from having lots of Notepads open at once, each with a different file open. Make sure you choose suitable filenames so you don't forget what's in each one - it could be embarrassing to find notes on your gambling debts in the middle of your business expenses.

Files You Can Change With Notepad

A Text Only file consists solely of characters that you can see; the letters, numbers and the punctuation marks together with spaces and carriage returns that you can't see. Although you can't see them, they are stored as actual characters in the file. You need the space and carriage return characters to make text easier to read. Few people would use a ring-bound pad that forced them to write like this: "alljoinedupanddifficulttoread".

Notepad And Write

Write can Open and Save files in Text Only format. When you open a Text Only file in Write, you will see a dialogue box asking whether you want to convert the file. If you convert the file into Write format, it will only have one font (10 point Tms Rmn) but you can add others and edit

Chapter 11 Notepad

it just as you would any other Write file. If you don't convert it, by pressing the NO button, you leave the file as Text Only. When you Save a Text Only file in Write, only the text is saved; fonts, margins, tabs and other layout information isn't saved.

Notepad Files

Windows associates all files with a .TXT extension with Notepad. You can give notepads a different extension if you want. If you alter the Filename box in the Open dialogue box from *.TXT to *.* you can look at all the files on your disk. Notepad will not Open a file unless it's a Text Only file.

A Tour Of Notepad

There are only four menus in Notepad.

You can select New, Open, Save, Save As and Print from the File menu. To leave Notepad, select Exit. Printer Setup and Page Setup allow you to select a printer (and set it up) and then alter the page layout. From there, you can describe what header or footer to print on each page as well as set the margins. We'll look at page layout in detail later in this chapter.

Notepad's Edit menu includes the usual Cut, Copy and Paste options. You can also Delete a highlighted block. This is the same as Cut, it just doesn't copy the block to the clipboard. When you select Time/Date, it is supposed to "timestamp" wherever your insertion point is within a file, with the current date and time. We say "supposed" as it just inserts the date.

Select Word Wrap if you're using Notepad as a word processor - it automatically goes down to the next line if the last word is too long to fit on the line. Notepad uses the page size as selected in Printer Setup and the margins from Page Setup, so don't be surprised if it splits lines at strange places - it will look correct when you print the file.

The Search menu includes just two options - Find and FindNext. The Find dialogue box has a box for a clue to be searched for. You can select either to search forwards or backwards. If you select the Match Upper/Lowercase box, Notepad regards upper case (capital) letters as the same as lower case ones during its search. For example, "Windows" would be treated as the same as "windows". Find Next looks for the next match. If you select this before you select Find, it opens the Find dialogue box.

A Do-it-Yourself Change Option

Notepad lacks a Change option. If you have several similar changes to make, you can perform them using the steps below:

1. Select Find and type the clue that you want to replace. Press the OK button to find the first match.

2. Notepad automatically highlights the first match. Type what you want in its place, highlight it (by dragging the mouse over it) and then Copy this to the clipboard.

3. You now have the clue to be found in the Find dialogue box and what you want it replaced with in the Clipboard.

4. To replace each match, select Find Next, delete the original text by pressing the Del key (or selecting the Clear option from the Edit menu) and then paste what you have in the Clipboard.

If you need to do this frequently, you could get Recky the recorder to help you. It will reduce the number of keystrokes to one or two.

Page Setup

Notepad always prints in one font but you can alter the margins and add headers and footers to each page. You can't choose a font, your printer determines it, not Windows. Windows just sends characters and leaves it to the printer to decide which font to use.

Tip: Selecting Fonts In Notepad, Calendar And Cardfile

If your printer allows you to select fonts manually, you may be able to choose a font but you should always pick a fixed width 10 point font. If you don't, Notepad and your printer will fight one another! If you choose a large font, the printout won't fit on the paper. If you choose a small font, your printout will be compressed into the top-left corner of the page.

Tip: Page Setup Codes In Notepad, Calendar And Cardfile

You can insert codes in the header and footer text that tell Windows to include page number,

Chapter 11 Notepad

date and filename. These codes are:

    &d   Today's date

    &t   The current time

    &p   The page number

    &f   The filename of the file

    &l   The header or footer text (following the code) will be justified at the left margin

    &r   Header or footer text (following the code) will be justified at the right margin

    &c   Header or footer text (following the code) will be centred between the margins

You can combine codes in a header or footer. For example, you could have a header with the date and filename, and the page number at the bottom of each page, by typing:

Header: &l&d&r&f
Footer: &cPage &p

We've asked for the date to be left-justified and the filename to be right-justified in the header. For the footer, the page number will be centred.

Tip: Creating A Log

There's another way to Datestamp files other that the Time/Date option in the Edit menu. This one is useful if you want each entry in a file to be automatically stamped with today's date. As before, it should also insert the time but it doesn't.

You simply put .LOG at the start of the file. Each time you Open this file in Notepad, it will automatically add the current date to the end of the file. For this to work, .LOG must be right at the front of the file and it must be in upper case.

Remember that Notepad only datestamps the file when you Open it, not each time you add a line. You have to Save the file and Open it again each time you want to datestamp an entry. If you leave the file open on your desktop all day, adding entries as you go, then only the first entry of the day will be datestamped. Perhaps this is tidier, the choice is yours.

No Large Files Here

There is a limit to the size of files that Notepad can handle. This is approximately fifty thousand characters or about twenty five pages.

Notepad will not let you Open a large file. If you create one in Notepad, say by copying a large block of text from the Clipboard, it will not allow you to save it. You can find out how big a file is by selecting the About Notepad option from the Help menu. When this value exceeds 45,000 you should consider saving the file.

If you wish to edit files that are too big for Notepad, you should use Write. Remember to select the Text Only box when you Save the file in Write.

The Big Four Files

Unless you are very curious about Windows, or need to alter the ways in which Windows works, you'll probably never need to look at the Big Four files.

But if you are, the four files that control Windows' operation are:

- AUTOEXEC.BAT   Your computer executes the commands in this file whenever you turn it on (or reboot). This file is in the root directory of the drive from which your computer boots.

- CONFIG.SYS   This file configures MS-DOS by adding special device drivers and memory management tools. Again, it's in your boot drive's root directory.

- WIN.INI   This file contains settings that control most aspects of Windows operation. It includes lists of programs run or loaded whenever Windows starts, lists of what type of files associate to which applications and details of parameters used by your printers. This file is in the directory that contains Windows.

Chapter 11 Notepad

- SYSTEM.INI   The settings in this file relate to how Windows interfaces with your computer's hardware. It includes details of how Windows drives your display, mouse and keyboard and how Windows should drive your computer's ports. It's stored in the Windows directory.

Quite often, you'll need all the Big Four on screen at once. You can have four Notepad windows open but it's easier to use Syd.

Syd - The System Configuration Editor

To use Syd, you can use the File Run option in Program Manager. If you want him to be instantly available, drag him from the File Manager to a Program Manager group. Syd lives in SYSEDIT.EXE in the SYSTEM sub-directory of your Windows directory. You'll find that he comes with a rather fetching icon.

When you open Syd's window, he displays the four files cascaded in inner windows. After bringing one to the front of the pile, you can print it, edit it and save it.

Syd's editing capabilities are similar to Notepad's but you'll find that Syd has organised his menus and dialogue boxes differently. You can transfer information to and from the Clipboard, find clues and continue a search that you've started, either forward or backward through the file.

Syd lets you organise the inner windows either as tiles or as a cascade and he lets you select one from his Window menu. If you have minimised some of the inner windows, you can organise their icons.

You're probably wondering why we've called the System Configuration Editor 'Syd'. When you save a file, Syd creates a back-up copy of the original file with a .SYD extension. Simple, isn't it!

Chapter 12 - Cardfile

While you're travelling round Windows World, you will find many kinds of weird individuals; Buttons, Menus and even Dialogue Boxes. There are so many of them that it's difficult to remember them all, let alone what they do for you.

You may want a way of organising all this information so that it's all immediately accessible. Cardfile is just the tool you need for this - organising raw data into information.

Understanding Cardfile

You can view Cardfile as a straightforward replacement for a box full of index cards. Or, if you prefer, it's a simple database.

If you want to follow the first approach, fine. Just dive straight in and skip the rest of this section. If you're going to store thousands of cards and you want to be able to get the most out of Cardfile then please read on...

What Is A Database?

Databases store information in Records. One record has all the information about one thing, be it an animal, flower or an antique chest of drawers. You access individual records by using an Index. This is more like a book's table of contents than an index as it just lists the title of each record.

Cardfile uses the term Index Line for the title of each card and the Information Area to describe the rest of the card. Cardfile automates the ordering of the cards - it always maintains the cards in ascending alphabetical order sorted on the contents of the Index Line. You can put anything on the Index Line, not just names; you could even choose to index things such as dates.

Unlike a real card file, where the Index Line is the only quick way to retrieve information, Cardfile lets you search for data anywhere in the Information Area.

Chapter 12 Cardfile

What To Store On Cards

You can store any text on cards. The Index Line must be shorter than forty characters (including spaces, punctuation marks and other special symbols) and the Information Area can hold up to eleven lines of forty characters. As you'll see, you can also store some graphic images as well, although only in black and white (or whatever colours you are using as window text and window background if you have changed them).

You should be aware that Cardfile does not understand the information it stores. For example, "Betty owes me - £1,000,000" has the same significance for Cardfile as "I owe Betty - £1,000,000" although, no doubt, Betty would appreciate the difference!

Organising Your Database

A small database doesn't need much organisation since you can read each card to find the information you're looking for - larger databases (and Cardfiles) require more organisation. You will need to use Keywords and Fields to help you.

Keywords

Keywords help you use the same word to mean the same thing throughout your database. They save typing by replacing longer phrases by shorter ones. They help you retrieve information, which is related, by ensuring that you always use the same names.

For example, if you wish to record all the animals you see on your journey, your database may use "BD" to mean Bird, "MA" to mean Mammal and "RE" for Reptile.

Fields

Fields help you to organise the information inside a record. They allow you to split your records up into different parts and keep the same order for each one. You could, if you were building a database of animals you'd seen, decide that you want to store the name of the animal first, followed by its location and then what you thought of it.

Planning Your Database

Using keywords and fields effectively requires some planning. You must choose your keywords and set aside places in the Information Area for your fields.

For example, you may want to build up information about your fellow travellers. The index line of each card would have each person's name and then fields in the information area could be set aside for:

- Telephone Number

- Address

- How you rated them as companions - using a keyword: 'Good', 'Bad' or 'DTWAB' (that is, Don't Touch with a Barge-pole!)

Looking At Your Database

Perhaps you've seen a gadget that allows you to thumb through index cards while maintaining them in order.

Cardfile attempts to provide something like this but we find it confusing. Shuffling a card to the front leaves all the cards behind it in order and then places all the cards that were in front of that card behind the rest. We said it was confusing, didn't we!

We find it useful to insert a card that has a line of '-' 's as the Index Line to act as a marker. The marker card will be at the front of the deck when Cardfile first loads the card file, so you can use it as a title card. In the database we built on Cardfile, we pasted the Cardfile icon from the Program Manager onto this card.

Starting Cardfile

If you start Cardfile from the Program Manager, it shows you just one blank card. You can then open an existing card file or begin a new one.

If you've turned a card file into a Program Manager icon, or if you double click on a card file in the File Manager, then Cardfile will be run for you. The card file will look just as if it is spread out (cascading, but in the other direction to the way windows cascade) on your desktop, with each index line visible.

Viewing Cards

You can only edit the card at the front of the file. To bring a card to the front, just click anywhere on the card you want. You can also move to the next and the previous cards by using the arrow buttons just below the title bar.

If you want to scroll through all the cards, select the List option from the View menu. This just shows the index line of each card and has a vertical scroll bar that allows you to move rapidly through the cards - the scroll bar moves you instantly through the file, instead of waiting until you let go of the mouse button. If you select a card in the List view by clicking on it, Cardfile will bring it to the front when you change to the Card view.

Searching Through Cards

You can search for cards using the contents of either the index line or the information area but not both together.

You can use the Search facility even if you only know part of the index line or have a vague idea of what is in the information area of the card you want. A card that matches will be brought to the front of the card file.

The Cardfile Search option doesn't look for complete words and ignores case; that is, whether text is in upper or lower case. If you search for "Wall" Cardfile will find cards with "wall", 'Wallflower' or 'swallow'. As we've said, Cardfile doesn't understand what the information means - that's up to you.

If you've started a search that has found a card, but not the one you wanted, you can tell Cardfile to continue searching from that card. Unfortunately, this only works when searching the information area - you must retype the clue if you're searching for matches in the index line.

Changing Index Lines And The Information Area

Once you've got the card you want at the front of the file, you can change the contents of the information area by just positioning the mouse where you wish to type, clicking the left button and typing. If you make some changes to a card, and then want to undo them all, you can use the

Restore option in the Edit menu. This is similar to the Undo in Write and Paintbrush except that it remembers all the changes you make, not just the last one. You must select Restore before you look at another card or save the card file.

To change the index line, you either use the Index option in the Edit menu (press [F6] on the keyboard) or you can double click over the index line.

If you paste a block of text from the Clipboard, and it's bigger than can be stored in a card, Cardfile ignores the entire block.

Adding Pictures To Cards

It is remarkably easy to add pictures to cards. Although our first attempt ended with a blank card and no picture! We didn't realise that the cards are small, less than the size of real index cards, and that the picture you want to paste must be small enough to fit into the Information Area. There's no facility to enlarge or reduce pictures. Each card can have only one picture, adding another merely replaces the first.

You must load the picture into the Clipboard as a bitmap file in either PCX or BMP format. To copy it to a card, you first put Cardfile in Picture mode, by selecting Picture in the Edit menu. You then select Paste from the Edit menu and the picture will be displayed. The Official User Guide says that, once pasted, the picture cannot be moved. We've found that, provided you select Picture mode before moving the picture, you can move the image by dragging it along with the mouse after you've initially positioned it.

You can combine pictures and text, each seems to exist independently of the other. You should position the picture and then type round it because the text goes behind the picture if they clash. Text has to start at the left hand margin, you can only insert spaces and blank lines using the Spacebar and Enter keys. The Arrow keys and mouse can only go where the other two have gone before!

It's probably easier to position the picture at the bottom-right corner of the card, unless you particularly want the picture elsewhere. You can then type a reasonable amount of text without fear that the text will be hidden by the picture.

Printing Cards

You can print either individual cards or a complete card file. To print an individual card, bring it to the front of the deck and then select Print. To print a complete file, select Print All - all the records will be printed. How many cards are printed on a page depends on the settings in the Page Setup.

Page Setup

Before printing, you can set the margins and add headers and footers to each page. We've covered all this in two Tips in the chapter on Notepad.

Merging Card Files

The Merge option in the Edit menu allows you to merge two card files. Open a Card file, then select Merge. You then enter the name of the file you want to merge with into the dialogue box. The cards from that file will each be added to the current file in the correct places. Cardfile doesn't mind if more than one card has the same Index Line so every card will always appear in the merged file.

Autodialling

Cardfile can automatically dial a number on a card. The number to be dialled must be in the Information Area but need not be the first field - Cardfile searches through the card looking for something that looks like a telephone number. You can have your telephone numbers in whatever format you like. For example, 0712221234 and (071)222-1234 both work. There must not be any spaces between the digits.

Preparing To Use Autodial

Your modem must be Hayes compatible. The first time you Autodial, you must set up some options to ensure that Cardfile can communicate with your modem. Press the SETUP button. The Autodial dialogue box doubles in size to reveal boxes that describe which port and the communication parameters Cardfile is to use. You may need to look at the modem's manual to find the correct settings to use but we suggest that, as a first try, you just select the port and leave the others.

Cardfile can also put a prefix before each number it autodials. This can be useful if your modem is on a line that goes out to the outside world through a PABX. You could, for example, enter '9,' as the prefix. That tells Cardfile to dial a nine while the comma is an instruction to wait for two seconds before dialling the number. If you use a prefix, you must remember to select the Use Prefix box the first time you autodial. The number of digits in the Prefix is limited, you can't store such things as Mercury access codes there.

Autodialling A Number

You should leave your telephone on-hook when you select Autodial. You start autodialling by pressing the OK button. Cardfile sends commands to your modem that dial the prefix (if you selected Use Prefix) and then the number. It displays a dialogue box with 'Pick up the phone'. You should then pick up the phone and press the OK button to ask the modem to release the line, allowing you to talk.

Autodialling may seem complicated but it's one of those things that are a lot easier to do than to write about. Try it a couple of times and then decide - it can be a real time-saver and reduces the chances of misreading or misdialling a number.

Chapter 13 - The Clock And The Calendar

There's no link between the clock and calendar other than the obvious one - both work with times and dates. We've combined these two applications as there's only a little to say about the clock and we dislike having nothing to say about anything!

The Clock

Clock displays either a digital or an analogue clock. You can decide whether you want a 12 hour or a 24 hour clock from the International Time Format dialogue box in the Control Panel. The digital clock will reflect your choice but will not display either the am/pm flag or the time zone.

If you minimise the clock, it continues to run. It's surprising how long it takes most users to find this out. We're all so used to just glancing at icons that we tend not to notice that it's ticking along happily, keeping time. You can only change the display from analogue to digital when the window isn't minimised.

A Minimised Clock All The Time?

You may decide that you want the clock to appear automatically as a minimised icon each time you start Windows. We find it so useful that we are going to give you step-by-step instructions. If you follow them carefully, you should have the clock running in no time...

You must alter one of the Big Four files, WIN.INI, in your Windows directory. Before you attempt this, it's important that you back-up this file. Then, even if you make a mistake, you can reload the original file and continue using Windows as if nothing had happened.

Carefully follow the steps below:

    1. Start Notepad and select File Open, then select the Windows directory and type WIN.INI into the Filename box. Press the OK button.

    2. Look for a line near the beginning of this file that begins with:

load=

3. Add 'clock.exe' onto the end of this line. If there were already filenames listed after the equals sign, you must separate them from the entry you've just added by a comma.

4. Save the file.

When you leave Windows and restart it, the Clock will be running at the bottom left-hand corner of your computer's screen. If not, check the line you added to WIN.INI by opening the file again in Notepad. Also, make sure that no icons or windows are obscuring the clock's face.

The Calendar

Every traveller keeps a diary so that they can recall the happy times, big disasters and the little incidents on their journey. It can provide the basic material for that best-selling book and those film rights that every author (yes, even us!) craves for.

Although not a complete substitute for your Filofax, or an el-cheapo eastern substitute, Windows Calendar has some useful features that can help organise your life.

Amongst Calendar's features are:

- You can look at your appointments each day or get an overview of a month at a time

- You can set alarms that can remind you of appointments

- You can print appointment schedules

Calendar - The Basics

When you start Calendar, you see your appointments for today, if you've set the correct time and date. You'll notice that Calendar expects all your appointments to fall neatly into one hour slots. You can change the duration of these slots and when you start your working day but Calendar always divides every day into the same uniform slots.

These slots may be fine for doctors and others who work to fixed appointments. If your life is

Chapter 13 The Clock And The Calendar

less organised, you may have difficulty living within the restrictions imposed by the Calendar. You could divide the day into one hour slots and just note which appointments you have within that hour or you could use fifteen minute slots and leave lots of spares - the choice is yours.

That's not quite the end of the story - you can insert what Calendar quaintly calls 'Special Times' into any day. They appear alongside the fixed time slots.

Besides the time slots, you can add a message for the day. You can only write three lines on each day, so you can't record your life history here. It's easy to copy the message from one day onto the next using the Clipboard. For example, you could copy things that you haven't had time to do on your To Do list.

You can display either a day's appointments or a complete month's schedule. There's little automatic association between the two views of your diary. You can have appointments all day (in the Day view) and not see a thing when you try to see what's happening over the next month using the Month view. The only link is the message of the day and that only appears when you move over a day with a message.

There's limited space for each day in the Month view. You can't type anything against each day. Instead, you can Mark each day with up to five marks. It's up to you to remember what each one means. You cannot change the marks and you cannot see Mark 5 if the day is already marked with Mark 1 as they overlap one another. If you decide to both use time slots to record your individual appointments and to mark days as busy, there's no need to switch Views - you can Mark a day from the day view.

You can ask for an alarm to be set on any appointment. You can do this with another 'doctor-friendly' feature the alarm which can sound from one to ten minutes before every appointment. We suspect that your colleagues might get a little tired of continual BEEPs if you set too many alarms, but you can turn off the sound.

You will only be reminded of appointments by alarms if Calendar is running. If you're going to set lots of alarms, you should consider loading Calendar when you begin running Windows at the beginning of the day. You can do this automatically by adding the Calendar program to the 'load=' line in your WIN.INI file. Have a look at the procedure in the 'A Minimised Clock all the Time?' section earlier in this chapter. This time, the program name is 'calendar.exe'.

When Calendar is minimised, an alarm makes the icon blink. If Calendar is in a window other than the active one, the alarm makes the border flash. When you make Calendar the active window, a dialogue box appears with a polite reminder of what the alarm was for - this is one of the only times that Windows says 'please'!

Chapter 13 The Clock And The Calendar

A Tour Round The Menus

The File menu has the usual New, Open, Save, Save As and Exit options. When you save a calendar file, Calendar saves any alarms with it. Any alarms stored in a file will only go off if the file is in a Calendar window.

You can run as many copies of Calendar as you want, and Open a different file in each. You could, for example, have a business diary and a social diary. If you set alarms in more than one Calendar, they will all go off at the times you set. It doesn't matter whether the window is minimised or not as long as they are open.

When you print your appointments, you can set the margins and add optional headers and footers. We've already covered all this in the Notepad chapter.

You'll see that the Edit menu has Cut, Copy, Paste and Remove options. Remove tidies up your calendar by removing all appointments between two specified dates. Using this avoids your calendar files growing and growing as will happen if you keep adding appointments and don't remove the ones that have already past.

There are just two options in the View menu: Day and Month. Remember that the only links between the views are the message of the day and marks you have set.

You use the options in the Show menu to move round your calendar. Today always returns to today's date, if the clock in your computer is correct. Previous is either Yesterday or Last Month, depending on the view you've selected. Similarly, Next is Tomorrow or Next Month. Selecting Date opens a dialogue box into which you can enter a date that you want to move to in your Calendar.

To set alarms, you use the Set option from the Alarm menu. The alarm is set on the selected appointment and a little bell symbol appears to remind you that you've set an alarm. You can't select this option when you're looking at the Month view.

The Controls option in the Alarm menu opens a dialogue box. You can select the warning that you want to get before an appointment, and decide whether your computer should BEEP loudly or merely politely remind you. Remember that the control settings you select affect all alarms. This includes any alarms set when different settings were in operation.

The final menu is Options. From here, you can choose which mark to put on a day in the Month view and alter the time slots that make up days. You have only a limited choice of marks. You'll

Chapter 13 The Clock And The Calendar

find that the Mark dialogue box shows the marks differently than they appear in the Month view so you'll have to experiment to see what each one looks like.

The Special Time option introduces 'special times' into the current day. You can use these to record appointments that don't fall onto a fixed time slot. Once you add a special time, it is treated just like any other time slot - you can set an Alarm on a special time just as easily as on any fixed time slot.

Selecting Day Settings opens a dialogue box. You can set the time that appears at the start of each day when you first select it and the slots into which you divide the day. If you have made some appointments at quarter or half hour slots and then alter the slot time to one hour, Calendar stills displays the appointments at the correct time. In effect, Calendar automatically creates some special times for you. Which we reckon is rather clever.

Travelling In Time

There are several options for time travellers. You can use the options in the Show menu to move a short distance by using Next and Previous. Or you can use the little buttons, next to the date on either the Day or Month view, to move forwards or backwards. [Ctrl + PageUp] and [Ctrl + PageDown] work in the same way. In the Month view, you can press the Left and Right cursor keys to move one day at a time. The Up and Down keys move forward and backward a week.

For the more adventurous, the Date option in the Show menu allows you to be magically whisked to any date from 1st January 1980 until 31st December 2099.

Chapter 14 - The Calculator

The Windows Calculator is more sophisticated than your average pocket calculator - this chapter will help you to get the best out of it as you travel round the Windows world.

As you'll see, the ability to copy answers to and from the Calculator is handy for doing quick sums while you're using other applications.

What You'll Learn

We'll introduce the Calculator in four stages:

• The Standard Calculator

This is like a pocket calculator with one memory and percentage / reciprocal / square root keys.

• The Scientific Calculator

This combines the common scientific functions (such as SINE, COSINE and LOG) with the functions of a "programmer's calculator" that can calculate in different bases and perform logical operations on numbers.

• The "Statistics Box"

Use this if you want to generate statistics (such as mean and standard deviation) from a list of numbers.

• The Calculator and the Clipboard

Transferring answers between the Calculator and other applications is easy and fun using the Clipboard.

If there's some mathematical terminology you don't understand in the descriptions above, don't worry. We're going to explain most of the available functions in stages. Each stage will build on earlier ones - you'll probably need to read the complete chapter if you want to fully exploit the statistical functions.

Chapter 14 The Calculator

Calculator Basics

When you double click the Calculator icon, it opens with the same View of the Calculator (Scientific or Standard) as it had when you last used it. To switch from Standard to Scientific, or vice versa, just pull down the View menu and click the View you want. The Calculator retains the contents of both the display and the memory when you change View.

When you open the Window Control menu, you'll see that you can't alter the size of the Calculator window. Would you, honestly, be able to press the tiny keys if it was any smaller?

To enter numbers and functions, you can either click the 'buttons' on the Calculator with the mouse or use the keyboard. The more common operations, such as entering numbers, clearing the display or addition and subtraction, use the obvious keys - others may not be so transparent; for example, why use @ for square root?

The help file supplied for the Calculator is easy to follow and lists all the functions and the keyboard equivalents so we'd recommend that you don't bother remembering these - help is but a couple of mouse clicks away!

Using The C, CE And Back Buttons

At the start of a calculation, the C and CE buttons both perform the same function of clearing the Calculator to be ready to start afresh. If you've already entered the first number, the operator (+,-,*, /) and the second number, then CE just clears the last number entered without altering the first number or the operator. The C button clears the entire calculation so that you must enter the first number and the operator as well as the second number.

The Back button acts like the Backspace, clearing the last digit or operator entered so that you can enter another one. You don't need to worry about using the wrong operator, however, because Calculator always works with the last one it sees. If, for example, you pressed 123/*-12 the answer would be 111 (or 123-12) as the / and * operators would be ignored.

None of these buttons affects the contents of the Calculator's memory.

The Memory

The Calculator's single memory can be; cleared (by MC), recalled (by MR), have a number stored in it (by MS) or the number in the display can be added to the memory (by M+). Just

Chapter 14 The Calculator

below the display is the Memory box, which is initially blank. When you store a number in the memory, this box shows an M to remind you that there's something there. If you clear the memory, or you happen to store a zero in memory, or if the memory become zero as a result of using the M+ button, the M disappears.

Using The Standard Calculator

If you've recently used a cheap pocket calculator, you already know how to use the Standard Calculator.

To add, subtract, multiply and divide, you simply Clear the display and then enter the first number, followed by the operator, followed by the second number and then press the = button.

To change the sign of a number you press the +/- button. This changes a negative number on the display into a positive one and vice versa. The Sqrt button takes the square root of the number, so that 49 sqrt gives 7 as 7*7 is 49. Remember that all the operators work on the number in the display. You must select +/- or Sqrt after you've put the number in the display.

The % key not only allows percentages to be worked out but also can calculate discounts, mark-ups and VAT inclusive prices. If you press 234.56 + 17.5 % = the answer will be 284.32; that is, 234.56 marked-up by 17.5%. Similarly, pressing 300.00 - 40 % = will calculate the cost of something with a price of 300.00 after a 40% discount - the display will show 180.00.

The key labelled 1/x takes the number in the display and replaces it with its reciprocal (that is, one divided by the number). For example, 5 1/x gives 0.20.

Using The Scientific Calculator

The basic arithmetic operators are the same as in the Standard view. Two of the operators supported by the Standard view (% and Sqrt) are missing. Sqrt is equivalent to Inv x^y . You can also switch to the Standard view, do that part of the calculation and switch back. You should note that the Scientific view, unlike the Standard view, has 'operator precedence' that alters the more normal 'execute each instruction immediately' style of working.

What's Operator Precedence?

No, operator precedence is nothing to do with telephone operators! It's the technospeak way of

189

Chapter 14 The Calculator

saying that the Calculator has a predetermined order in which it carries out calculations. This order is:

• Operators that work directly on the number in the display, first

• Multiplications and divisions next

• Additions and subtractions last

For example: if you enter 2 + 3 * 4 =, the answer is 14; 3*4 plus 2. The Standard view calculates the answer as 20 as it just carries out each calculation in whatever order you enter it.

Loads Of Brackets

The Scientific view supports brackets. These force the Calculator to do your calculations in the order that you want and not in the order defined by the precedence of the operators. Within a bracket, you can execute not only simple arithmetic but also functions. There's a simple rule for constructing calculations that include brackets: a bracketed section of a calculation behaves just like a number and must be separated from other parts by operators. For example, (2+3)*4 would give 20.

The right-hand box just below the display shows the current level of "nesting" of brackets and is initially blank - showing that no brackets are open.

When you start a bracketed section of a calculation, by pressing the (button, the display shows the number of brackets that are open. When you close a bracket, the Calculator carries out that part of the calculation and the bracket counter decreases by one. If that is the last open bracket, the bracket counter disappears. You never see more than one answer at a time so, for complicated calculations, it's probably a good idea to write out the full expression on paper or in the Notepad before you start. You'd think that you could use the Clipboard to copy a calculation straight from Notepad to the Calculator but you can't.

Tip: Limitations Of Using The Calculator With The Clipboard

The official User Guide tells you that certain Calculator functions can be carried out by inserting codes in the data you transfer via the Clipboard. We've found that, while it's true that some functions are available, it seems a bit hit and miss whether the command that you need is there.

Chapter 14 The Calculator

One surprising omission are the basic arithmetic operators (+,-,*, /). If you try to paste an expression containing these, the effects are completely random but always are incorrect.

Because of these problems, we recommend that you just paste numbers into the Calculator, one at a time, and use our good friend Recky the robot if you have a complex calculation to perform on several numbers.

The Scientific Functions

Pressing PI causes the value of pi (3.14159...) to be displayed. Inv PI displays 2 pi.

X^2 and X^3, square and cube whatever is on the display while X^y expects you to enter another number. Inv X^2 gives the square root while INV X^3 gives the cube root. The Calculator then calculates the original number raised to the second number so, for example, 2X ^ Y4 gives 16, the same as 2*2*2*2.

All the common mathematical functions are available: Sin, Cos, and Tan. Selecting the Inv or Hyp boxes causes the Inverse and Hyperbolic versions of the functions to be evaluated. If you don't understand these, don't worry, neither do we!

Select the correct system of measuring angles, from the Deg, Rad and Grad group of boxes, before using the trigonometric functions. Remember that a right angle is 90 degrees, PI/2 (1.5707...) radians and 100 gradient. You can convert from one type of measurement to another by a slightly devious method; you press Sin, select the new type and then press Inv Sin.

The Ln function calculates the natural logarithm while Inv Ln calculates e (2.718...) raised to the specified power - this is mathematically its inverse function. The Log function calculates the logarithm to base 10 of the displayed number.

N! calculates the factorial of the display so only accepts positive integer numbers - an error message appears if you apply this function to numbers with digits after the decimal point. You use N! to calculate the number of different combinations and permutations of objects. For example, there are 4! (that is, 24) ways of arranging four green bottles, if they are all different.

The Dms button converts the number displayed into degrees-minutes-second format. The answer displayed can be confusing as there are no colons between the degrees, minutes and seconds and no trailing zeros. Let's look at an example: 7.125 will be displayed as 7.073 after pressing the Dms button. If we insert colons and trailing zeros:

Chapter 14 The Calculator

7:07:30.0

Then we can see the answer in a more conventional format. The Dms function can also convert from the degree-minute-second format to a decimal number if you select the Inv box. Again, trailing zeros can be omitted and you can't enter colons.

The F-E button changes the display between scientific and decimal notation; that is, the display of one hundred is either 100 or 1.e+002. You use the Exp button to enter exponents - but remember to follow it with the +/- button if you want to enter a negative one. Very large numbers will be displayed in scientific notation anyway. For example, 1,000,000 F-E will convert one million to scientific notation and the display will show 1.e+006.

Two functions, although in the programmer's section, have other uses. These are Mod and Int. Mod does the other bit of a division - that is, it returns the remainder whereas / returns the quotient, if you ignore the digits after decimal point. Int does just that, it lops off any digits after the decimal point while Inv Int returns just the value after the decimal point. For example, (11 / 4) Int gives 2 - that's the quotient. Notice how we had to use brackets to avoid applying Int to just the 4. (11 / 4) Inv Int will display 0.25; that's just the fractional part of the division. 11 Mod 4 gives 3, the remainder after dividing 11 by 4.

The 'Programmer's' Functions

Some time ago, there was a craze amongst the Boffins for Calculators that calculated things only of interest to themselves. They insisted that they include weird operators with names like Xor and Lsh. Perhaps the writers of the Windows Calculator are in a time warp but, whatever the reason, the Scientific view provides someone (we just aren't sure who) with great fun.

If you're going to venture into these quiet backwaters, you'll have to understand different number "bases" and talk knowledgeably about 'binary', 'octal' and 'hexadecimal' numbers as well as remembering that everyday numbers are 'decimal' numbers.

Here goes! A whole number (programmers are never too worried about the odd digits at the end) can be represented as a sum of the products of numbers (all less than the base) multiplied by powers of a particular base. Wow! For example 1234 in base 10 (decimal) is:

$$1*10^3 + 2*10^2 + 3*10^1 + 4*10^0$$

Programmers like to work in a notation that is closer to that employed by computers that only

Chapter 14 The Calculator

understand 'On' and 'Off' signals. There are three such bases:

• Binary

This is so close to the computer that you can hear it breathing. You write everything out using base 2, which only has the two digits 0 and 1. Each digit in a binary number is a 'bit'. The trouble is that large numbers tend to be a bit (pun intended) unwieldy.

• Octal

This was the first attempt to make binary numbers easier to write. Someone realised that if you combined each group of three bits together, you could write everything more compactly whilst remaining close to the computer. It's called octal since three bits have a maximum value of seven, so the base of this system is eight.

• Hexadecimal

When microcomputers first appeared, they operated on eight bits at a time. Using octal notation wasn't very tidy, because eight isn't a multiple of three. Grouping four bits together was the solution.

Four bits can take values between zero and fifteen and so this base needs sixteen digits. Employing 0 to 9 is obvious but what about the other six? Someone, somewhere decided that the best solution was to use the first six letters of the alphabet. So, hexadecimal digits are:

0,1,2,3,4,5,6,7,8,9,A,B,C,D,E and F

There are buttons labelled A to F and boxes for Hex, Dec, Oct and Bin. These select the number base that the Calculator is to work in. They also act as conversion functions since a number displayed in one base can be re-displayed in another simply by pressing one of these boxes. For example, if your computer told you that a particular program occupied memory locations A123 to B897 (hexadecimal) you could find out how large it was by selecting Hex, entering B897 - A123, giving 1774 in hexadecimal. To convert that to decimal, simply press Dec, giving 6004 bytes as the size of the program.

When you've selected a base other than decimal, you'll notice that the Deg, Rad and Grad boxes change to Dword, Word and Byte. Pressing one of these will not alter the answers to calculations but just alters the number of digits displayed:

Chapter 14 The Calculator

Setting	Binary	Octal	Hexadecimal
Byte	8	3	2
Word	16	6	4
Dword	32	11	8

What about the Or, And, Xor, Lsh and Not buttons? These all perform so-called logical functions. They all treat the numbers displayed as binary numbers and apply logical operations on each bit independently.

- And

This operator combines two numbers in such as way that only if a particular bit is on in both will it set the bit in the answer. For example, 110 And 011 gives 010.

- Or

The answer produced by this operator is a number where the bit is on if either number has a particular bit turned on. For example, 110 Or 100 gives 110.

- Xor

Xor stands for 'Exclusive OR' and the answer is a number where each bit is on if only one number has the bit on. For example, 110 Xor 101 gives 011.

- Lsh

Lsh stands for 'Left Shift'. You should enter another number after pressing this button. The answer is a number with each bit shifted towards the left (more significant) end by the amount specified by the second number. This operator has the effect of multiplying the original number by two to the power of the second number. For example, 101 Lsh 10 gives 10100, which is 4 (that is, 2 to the second power) times the original number.

If you press Inv Lsh, you 'Right Shift' the original number. The answer is the number shifted right (towards the least significant end) and is equivalent to dividing the number by the power of two specified. For example, 101001 Inv Lsh 11 gives 101.

Notice that Lsh requires you to enter the value for the shift in the selected number base and how Inv Lsh loses digits from the right.

- Not

When you press Not, each bit in the displayed number will be inverted - that is, 1 becomes 0 and 0 becomes 1. For example, 101 Not gives 1.....11010.

The Statistics Box

To start with, we had difficulty understanding the Statistics Box. We were confused by the strange labels in the dialogue box - RET, LOAD, CD and CAD. We wondered what assembler instructions, Compact Disks and Computer Aided Design had to do with statistics!

What Is The Statistics Box?

Let's begin at the beginning... Whoever wrote the Calculator decided that they wanted you to be able to calculate common statistics easily and without having the write down intermediate answers. Their solution was simple and rather clever - they've provided a sort of electronic notepad on which you can write numbers.

To calculate the statistics, they added some buttons to the main Calculator. These take the numbers in the notepad, apply the standard statistical formulae and place the answer in the Calculator display. To make the whole thing easy to use, they realised that you would need to transfer numbers to and from the Calculator as painlessly as possible.

Opening The Statistics Box

Like Pandora's box, you must open the Statistics Box to reveal the delights inside. You do this by pressing the Sta button that appears on the left of the Scientific view of the Calculator. In response, a small dialogue box opens. This is the Statistics Box which will remain open until you explicitly close it or close the Calculator window. To reselect the Statistics Box, after using the Calculator, you can either press the Sta button or merely click somewhere within it.

You can't alter the size of the Statistics Box. If the single sheet of notepad becomes full then scroll bars appear that allow you to access any of your data. If you minimise the Calculator, the Statistics Box goes with it but it retains all the values written on it.

Controlling The Statistics Box

Along the bottom of the Statistics Box are four buttons:

Chapter 14 The Calculator

• RET

This stands for 'Return' and makes the Calculator the active window but leaves the Statistics Box open. You will only use this button if you are using the keyboard as clicking anywhere in the Calculator window has the same effect.

• LOAD

This copies a number that you have selected from the Statistics Box back to the Calculator display. To select a number, merely click over it; it will be highlighted. If you're using a keyboard, select the number using the Arrow keys and then select the LOAD button with the Tab key.

• CD

Stands for 'Clear Data' and deletes any number that you have selected from the Statistics Box. Once deleted, you can't get it back. Different from the other CD's, isn't it - you can't get rid of them at all...

• CAD

Press this button only if you are sure that you want to wipe the entire Statistics Box clean. It stands for 'Clear All Data'. The Calculator doesn't ask you to confirm this drastic action - it just goes right ahead and deletes all your data. You have been warned!

Just below the buttons is a counter of the number of entries in the Statistics Box. We aren't sure of the maximum number you can load, we got bored trying to fill it up after about two-and-a-half thousand.

Copying Numbers To The Statistics Box

The only way to load numbers into the Statistics Box is via the Calculator display. You can either press the DAT button or hit the [Insert] key on your keyboard.

You can either type each number in, transfer it and then type the next one or, you can store the answers from calculations - it's up to you. If you're into doing your statistics with binary, octal or hexadecimal numbers, you'll be pleased to hear that you can do these...

Right, Now For Some Lies...

If our memory is correct, it was Disraeli who said 'There are lies, damned lies and Statistics!' Having loaded the Statistics Box, the Calculator is ready to tell some lies.

Although there are only three buttons (Ave, Sum and S) you can calculate all the common statistical functions:

Button	Function
Ave	Average
Inv Ave	Mean of Squares
S	Standard Deviation, population parameter (n-1)
Inv S	Standard Deviation, population parameter (n)
Sum	Sum
Inv Sum	Sum of Squares

The most useful functions are Average and the Standard Deviation with population parameter (n-1), which indicates the amount of variation between the individual numbers in the Statistics Box. A higher Standard Deviation indicates more variation.

Putting It Together...

Let's suppose that you want to find your average daily mileage for a five day journey. You know the mileage each day:

Thursday	2.3
Friday 20	9
Saturday	5.8
Sunday	2.3 - you had a day off
Monday	19.7

Follow these steps:

1. Open the Statistics box by pressing the Sta button.

Chapter 14 The Calculator

2. Load the mileages by entering each number onto the Calculator display and then pressing the Dat button.

3. After you've entered all five numbers, you should see them in the Statistics box and the counter should show '5'.

4. Press the Ave button on the Calculator. The average, 14.2 miles, will appear in the Calculator's display.

Other Uses For The Statistics Box

If, like us, you've got a devious mind, you can think of more uses for the Statistics Box than just calculating statistics.

Because it's so easy to transfer answers between the Calculator and the Statistics Box, you can use it to provide additional memories for the Calculator.

A word of caution is necessary before you imagine that you have an almost unlimited memory bank: you can't label numbers in the Statistics Box, so you can only tell entries apart by looking at them!

It's probably best to restrict its use to storing readily identifiable constant values that are going to be used frequently in a particular calculation. That way, you won't find yourself dividing by the distance to the Sun when you meant to divide by the distance from London to Aylesbury...

The Clipboard And The Calculator

You can copy and paste between the Calculator's display and the Clipboard and from there, to and from most of the other Windows applications.

Let's give a step-by-step guide to getting a number from an application (we'll use Write in this example), dividing it by 3 and then pasting it back to replace the original number:

1. Clear the Calculator's display

2. Select the number from the Write document and Copy it to the Clipboard

3. Use the Edit menu's Paste option to load it into the Calculator's display

4. Divide the number by 3, leaving the answer in the display

5. Using the Edit menu in the Calculator, copy the answer back to the Clipboard

6. Reselect the original number in the Write document and Paste the new answer over it.

That's all there is to it...

Chapter 15 - The Terminal

You can use Terminal to explore the delightful world of computer communication and to share your experiences with other travellers as you explore Windows.

No Computer Should Be An Island

Terminal allows your computer to communicate with others; either across the room or across the world. It's a lot easier sending data over potentially dangerous and difficult terrain than it is making the journey yourself.

Most people find that communicating with other computers is one of their most fascinating applications. Once you get 'on-line' and begin sending and receiving data to and from other people, you'll understand us saying: no computer should be an island. Indeed, you may well wonder why it took you so long to discover these delights and how you managed to survive in such an isolated place, cut off from the bright lights of the rest of the world.

Who's Out There?

When you look into the different types of services available, you'll be amazed at their variety as well as the ease with which you can access them.

To list just a few:

> You can share data with colleagues and friends.
>
> You can send and receive electronic mail (the buzzword is E-mail).
>
> You can chat to other computer users via Bulletin boards.
>
> You can use many information services including share prices and company results, timetables for trains and airlines as well as more specialised ones such as chemical hazard databases.

The Downside

Like all promised Utopias, this one has some problems that, unless you prepare for them, may cause you unnecessary frustration and expense.

One is 'complexity' and the other is 'money'! Traditionally, computer-to-computer communication has required a high level of expertise and considerable expenditure.

Luckily, the developments of the last few years, not least the introduction of user-friendly programs like Terminal, have largely eliminated the need for technical expertise. Even if you've never connected anything to your computer, you should be able to talk to most of the available services after reading the 'Getting On-line' section later in this chapter.

Whilst the cost of equipment required to get on-line has fallen significantly over the last few years, the same cannot be said of the costs of using services. It's worthwhile planning your use of time you spend on-line to ensure that you use it as effectively as possible. Again, this chapter contains some useful guidelines.

Transferring Files

Terminal has other roles than turning your computer into a Terminal. By far the most important of these is to allow you to receive (the jargon word is 'download') and send ('upload') files between your computer and another.

Let's explore this in a little more detail...

Chapter 15 Terminal

The simplest approach is just for one computer to send the data as if it was listing it on paper and for the other computer to 'capture' all that data and store it in a file. Sometimes, the computer you connect to lacks special facilities and so you must employ this very basic approach - Terminal includes several features that can be useful to help ensure it works as well as possible.

If you're luckier, the other computer understands a 'File Transfer Protocols' to ensure that complete files can be transferred quickly and easily. These make sure that:

- Each side agrees on when to start and when the transfer is complete.

- The receiver is able to ask the sender to pause while it writes some of the data to disk.

- The receiver knows when to interpret characters in the file and when not to. A file may include invisible characters (as a program file or a formatted Write file will almost certainly have).

- The receiver knows how to detect and correct errors that may occur during the transfer.

Before You Start...

To talk to computers across the room or within your office, all you need is a cable. Usually, if you're going to be communicating between two computers, rather than logging in to a mainframe, you'll need a so-called 'Null Modem' cable. Oh, an obvious thing, you must make sure that the other computer can run Terminal or a compatible communication program such as Datastorm Technologies' Procomm.

If you're being more adventurous and want to use the telephone system to communicate with another computer, you'll need a Modem. If you're buying one for the first time, make your life easier by ensuring that it's 'Hayes' compatible. If you've already got a modem, and it's not Hayes compatible, then you'd better find its manual - you're going to need it!

It would be nice if you could just connect your cable or modem, start up Terminal and get on with what you want to do. Nice it maybe, real-life it ain't!

The reason - every computer designer seems to have forgotten that his masterpiece would have to communicate with others. Talk about the Tower of Babel - it's more like an entire city full of Towers.

Luckily, there are bodies called CCITT and EIA that try to bring order to this chaos. Although

Chapter 15 Terminal

they haven't totally succeeded, they have at least restricted the number of choices down to a more reasonable level.

They have succeeded, for example, in insisting that everyone agrees on a standard for the electrical characteristics of the signals employed. The RS-232 standard ensures that you can connect two computers together without either of them damaging the other - a good first step, we'll sure you agree! But this is real-life, and for some specialised applications, there are other standards (such as RS-422 and IBM's Coax and Twinax) but you can forget these - Terminal only understands how to use RS-232.

They also succeeded, for a time, in ensuring that everyone used the same plugs and sockets. These are twenty-five pin 25 way 'D' connectors - the shape of the outer shell gave them their name. IBM has however, confused everyone by, firstly, using D connectors for both RS-232 ports and parallel (printer) ports and, secondly, by changing the RS232 port to nine pin connectors on the IBM PC/AT and PS/2 computers. You can tell which is the RS-232 and which is the printer port by looking at the 'sex' of the socket on your computer - the RS-232 will have pins (male, geddit?) and the printer port will have sockets (female). Convertors are readily available between the non standard 9-pin RS-232 ports and the standard 25-pin connectors if you need to extend a cable or use an existing modem cable.

Unfortunately, there are still many choices available for how to transfer data and what data means what. So, before you can communicate with a particular computer, you must ensure that the two computers understand each other. You use the Settings menu to do this.

Settings

Most people's reaction on looking at the Settings menu in Terminal is to panic... But, honestly, it really isn't as complicated as it seems. Each option opens a dialogue box. Let's look at each of these in turn:

Phone Number

You can ask Terminal to pause between dialling parts of the telephone number by inserting a comma. This is useful if your computer connects to the telephone network through a PABX or if you use the Mercury network. For example, '9,0712221234' requests an outside line, pauses and then dials the number.

If you are using a Hayes compatible modem, you can also switch between tone and pulse dialling in the middle of the telephone number by using 'T' and 'P'. For full details, consult

203

your modem's manual.

Terminal Emulation

The simplest advice we can give is to check what terminal the other computer is expecting to communicate with. If you can't find out, leave the initial setting unless strange characters appear on your screen.

Terminal Preferences

Leave the initial values unchanged unless Terminal truncates lines, you only see the received data or you encounter a 'staircase' effect where the beginning of each line appears further and further to the right.

You'll need to alter the 'Buffer Lines' setting only if you can't use a file transfer protocol (see below) or if you are short of memory.

Function Keys

The Function Keys are particularly useful if you are logging on to a mainframe or information service. These services frequently need you to type commands and user identifiers that are the same each time you log on. You should never store your password in a Function Key as anyone could press it and then use your account.

For each function key, F1 to F8 (along the top or the left of your keyboard) you can type a Key Name and a Command that will be sent from your computer whenever you press the key. If you select the Keys Visible box, the Key Names will be displayed as buttons on the bottom of the Terminal window so that you can press them by clicking the mouse.

If you need more than eight function keys, you are able to define up to four groups of eight, called 'levels'. You can switch between groups of function keys by including ^SL1 to ^SL4 in the Command box. You then need to select the corresponding Key Level button to define the new function key group. If you do this, we suggest that you display the function keys so that you can keep track of what the function keys will do on each level.

Text Transfers

If the computer you are communicating with doesn't support any of the file transfer protocols, you will need to use this option to set up parameters to allow transfers to be done. Unfortunately, which settings are appropriate depends entirely on the other computer so the best advice we can give is to use 'trial and error' to find the correct settings.

Binary Transfers

Terminal supports two of the most common transfer protocols: XMODEM/CRC and KERMIT. You have a hidden choice as well; XMODEM/CRC can automatically handle the XMODEM/Checksum protocol.

Our advice is to use XMODEM/CRC but to be aware that mainframes and UNIX computers are more likely to support the older KERMIT protocol.

Communications

These settings describe the interface between the computers at the basic hardware level. They include such things as which port to use, the speed, the precise format of data and how to control the flow of data.

You should check these settings on the other computer and choose a matching set on yours. If you have a choice of Baud Rate, go for the highest which works reliably as data will then be transferred quicker.

If you can't find out the settings for the other computer, a reasonable guess is to try 1200 or 2400 Baud, 8 Data bits, 1 Stop bit, No parity and Xon/Xoff flow control. If these settings don't work, see the Oh, It's Not Working section for help.

In theory, you can use COM3 and COM4 for communication. But, since the original IBM PC only had COM1 and COM2, you may run into problems as some clones set-up the additional ports differently.

Modem Commands

You'll only need to alter these if your modem isn't Hayes compatible or isn't one of those listed. We could say that 'all you need to do is to find the appropriate commands in the modem's manual' but experience suggests that this exercise is likely to need a large amount of effort and a fair measure of luck. We did tell you to buy a Hayes modem, after all...

Saving The Settings

Having carefully crafted the settings you need, you don't want to have to go through the same laborious process each time you need to access the same service. You don't have to, Terminal can save all the settings into a file.

If you regularly communicate with several different computers, it's worth saving the different settings that each needs as separate files. To keep your files organised, it's a good idea to save these files using filenames that reflect which computer they refer to.

Getting On-Line

You're ready to go on-line and send data whizzing half-way round the world... Typically:

1. You must make sure that you plug all the cables into the correct connectors (COM1 or COM2 RS-232 ports, depending on which you've selected in Terminal). Also, turn on your modem.

2. If possible, you should check that the other computer is ready.

3. Now start Terminal, loading the appropriate file of settings.

4. If you're logging on to a host computer (that is, a computer providing a service for you) you must dial its number, wait for it to answer and then follow the log on instructions. These may require that you:

   Get the attention of the computer by typing Return.

   Type your User Identifier.

   Type your Password.

   Type the name of the service you wish to use.

5. If you're answering a call from another computer, you must have sent the modem the appropriate command to put it in 'auto-answer' mode. Terminal doesn't have a menu option to do this, you must define a function key with the command that your modem needs. For Hayes modems, this is '+++ATA'.

6. You should check communication with the other computer by typing a short message. If there is a human at the other end of the link, they can reply to your message with a suitable acknowledgement like 'Hi, not you again!'

Welcome To The Wonderful World Of Talking Computers

Right, you're on-line and raring to get out there and talk to all these wonderful services. This section explains what you need to do to maximise the benefit and minimise the cost. Don't forget that you have to pay for using these services when your telephone bill arrives! Turning on the Timer, by selecting the Timer Mode option in the Settings menu, can help by reminding you how long you've been on-line.

Using On-line Services

When accessing a bulletin board for the first time, you may need to 'register'. Usually, this is just so that the operator of the bulletin board system (the jargon term is 'sysop') knows who is using his system. Once registered, you may find that more facilities are available to you. If you eventually download lots of files, you may find that the Sysop asks you whether you've got any interesting files to upload. It is illegal to upload files on which you do not own the copyright - you have been warned...

Registering for an on-line information service may be more complicated - there will almost certainly be a subscription fee. Normally, a usage fee will be charged as well as the cost of the telephone call. There may be other fees if you store data on the system or use 'gateways' into more specialised services.

Many on-line services are as far away as the USA - but most of the larger services provide local telephone numbers that then link to the national and international data networks.

Sometimes, you may have to communicate with a computer at the telephone exchange before you enter this network. If the service you use is one of these, you'll receive instructions when you subscribe and most services run help desks (operated by humans) if you need assistance.

Most on-line services have two access methods:

- A menu 'tree' that begins with a start-up menu, then has subsidiary menus that access groups of services and then finally give you access to the individual services.

- A whole raft of strange sounding names for each individual service.

It's tempting to explore, using the menus, but BEWARE - you're paying for every second! If you know which service you need, try to get its name from the guide provided when you subscribed or use the menus just for the first access and then use the service's name.

Transferring Files

When the computer you are communicating with can use a protocol supported by Terminal, you should use the options to send and receive 'Binary' files even if you are transferring a file containing text.

If you can't, then you must talk to the operator of the other computer and discuss the procedure you will both follow to ensure that when one computer sends the file, the other is ready to receive and store it. You should also agree a method of deciding when the transfer is complete.

Using a built-in file transfer mechanism avoids most of these problems. Both computers will wait for each other, so you can start either one first. They also agree between themselves when the transfer is complete.

Compressing Files

You may wonder whether you can reduce the time it takes to send files by squashing them before transmission and un-squashing them at the other end. The answer is 'Yes'. Two methods can be used:

1. You can use a file compression programs to compress the file before you send it, then the operator of the other computer can use another program to decompress it. The best program is LHARC that is available from most 'shareware' suppliers who advertise in the computer press. LHARC combines compression and decompression into one program. ARC, an earlier program, is still in use by many bulletin boards. You might need copies of both programs.

2. You can use a data compression modem. Look for modems with MNP 5 or V42 bis.

You are probably thinking that you can compress a file with LHARC and then further compress it with V42bis but compression doesn't work like that! Don't compress anything that is already compressed, it will only get bigger...

Chapter 15 Terminal

Whether you use a program or a modem with data compression depends on your budget. It will also depend on the other computer. You will need a compatible program or modem.

Sending Just Part Of A File

The View Text File option in the Transfer menu allows you to see a Text Only file in the Terminal window. You can then select a block of text, just as you can within the other Windows applications. Terminal's Edit menu has an additional option, Send. Send copies the selected text, not to the Clipboard, but to the modem.

There are a couple of problems with Send. Firstly, you send the data 'as is', not using a file transfer protocol. Secondly, the Terminal buffer can only store a maximum of 400 lines or about seven pages. Initially, Terminal only stores 100 lines but you can increase this in the Terminal Preferences dialogue box in the Settings menu.

Oh, It's Not Working

This is where we tell the truth - you are most unlikely to get your computer talking to another on the first attempt. There are simply too many variables, all of which must be correct.

Don't get downhearted - about two million people have been through the same experience, and nearly all have come out of it smiling. What's more, most of them didn't have this section to help them!

To ensure success, you must put on your detective's hat. Remember, all good detectives must be thorough and persistent.

Recognising that failure comes in degrees, we've divided our guide to communication detective work into two parts:

- Nothing works at all

- It nearly works

If you've established a link, you're already half-way home. If not, read the next section first. Then, if you aren't happy with the link you've made, read the section after that as well.

209

Nothing Works At All

Don't panic! The first thing to check is that you have connected everything, turned everything on and that the other computer is ready to talk to you.

You may have a simple wiring problem or have a problem with the computers themselves. The testing strategy below will give you the ability to establish the cause.

Remember, though, you only need to read what follows if you have a problem. If, as we hope, your link works (or at least, nearly works) then you can skip this entire section.

How To Test The Communication Link

There are several ways of testing a communication link. Many people get by using a `poke and see' philosophy but we don't recommend that way. There are just so many configurations that you have to be either very lucky or very dedicated to solve wiring problems trusting in the laws of probability.

There are three ideas that you need to understand before we start:

1. Terminal sends and receives data serially, that is, one bit at a time. This explains why there are so few wires in the cables that connect computers.

2. Flow control methods (which we met in Settings) act like traffic lights controlling the flow of data. Each computer needs enough time to receive and display data sent by the other. There are two types of flow control: Xon/Xoff and Hardware. Xon/Xoff operates by sending special characters; Xoff means stop and Xon means restart. Hardware flow control uses extra wires in the cable to get the same effect. It may take several wires to allow each computer to tell the other what it's doing.

3. Within the world of data communication, computers and all other devices are either 'Computers' (sometimes, 'Hosts') or 'Terminals'. Cables wired in a straightforward way; that is, pin 1 to pin 1, pin 2 to pin 2, and so on, can connect computers to terminals. If you are connecting computers to computers (or terminals to terminals) you need to change around some of the wires. We've already mentioned that if you are connecting two computers directly together, you use something called a Null Modem cable - which does just that.

We are going to suggest that you enlist the help of a 'BOB'. BOBs and their equivalents are

Chapter 15 Terminal

readily available and are ideal for giving you that professional image that really will impress your friends! They let you look at what is happening inside your link and provide the means to correct anything that is wrong, without you having to fork out for an electronic engineer's toolbox.

What Is A BOB?

A BOB is a Break Out Box, which is a box with a 25 way RS-232 serial plug and socket at either end. On top, it will have a row of switches down the middle with one or two lines of holes on either side of them with a row of LEDs (Light Emitting Diodes or little bulbs) that correspond to some or all the holes. There will be some patch wires and you may also get an RS-232 extension cable with two more 25 way serial plugs/sockets on either end.

Alternatives To BOBs

A fully fledged BOB is expensive, £90 to £120 or more, but if you combine two units to give you the same facilities as a BOB you can cut the price to somewhere between £30 and £50. If you can afford a fully fledged BOB, fine, if not look in the mail order catalogues for a Mini Tester (RS-232) and something called a Wiring Box.

The Mini Tester will have the lights, whilst the Wiring Box will enable you to swap wires over without using a soldering iron. These, or a BOB, will enable you to test your link and get the wiring right. You can also use your link with the BOB in the middle until you can get a proper wire made up.

All you need is to plug the Mini Tester into the Wiring Box. You can then plug your computer in one end and whatever you want to communicate with in the other. You do exactly the same if you are using a BOB. Plug your computer into one side, with the computer or modem you want to send data to in the other.

If you are connecting to a modem, you may find that the modem itself has a set of LEDs that perform part of the function of the Mini-Tester. We say 'part' as they will monitor what the modem sees, which is not necessarily what your computer is seeing.

What Does A BOB Do?

A BOB will allow you to see the data going across the link and all the flow control lines. When the BOB detects a signal on any wire it will either turn the relevant LED on or change their colour, depending on whether you have got one or two coloured LEDs. If data is not getting

Chapter 15 Terminal

through the BOB, it will allow you to change the connections between your computer and the other device, e.g., you can change pin 2 to pin 3 by putting a temporary wire to join them together. These temporary wires are Patches or Jumpers.

Your Testing Strategy

We've assumed that you can change the set-up of, and see what is happening to, both ends of the link. When you're setting up a link with another computer, that's probably true. If you can't easily access the other end of the link, or if you're using a modem, you may have to skip some tests that need you to alter the set-up of the other device.

Step 1 - Checking that your computer is working

1 A

> Start Terminal, deselect Xon/Xoff flow control from the Communications dialogue box in the Settings menu. Then plug your BOB or equivalent between your computer and the other device. Make sure that all the little switches are ON so that it connects both sides of the BOB together and check that the LED lights monitor the signals.
>
> No lights? - go to Step 1B
>
> Flickering lights? - go to Step 1C
> Some lights on? - go to Step 2
>
> No lights at all? - check that your computer is on, that you've plugged all connectors into the correct ports and that you have Terminal in a window.
>
> If you still have no lights on, go to Step 1D

1 B

> Switch all the switches off on the BOB and plug in the patch wires so that the `pairs' of wires swap with each other. That is, Pin 2 goes to pin 3, 4 goes to 5 and 6 goes to 20 on the same sides. This configuration is called 'loop-back' and allows you to test just your computer without worrying about the other end of the link.
>
> Whatever you type on your computer's keyboard will be sent back to your screen if your computer is working correctly. If the Local Echo button in the Terminal Preferences

dialogue box is on, you should be 'seeing double'.

Each time you press a key, you may see the LED connected to pin 2/3 flicker - you are seeing the data. If you feel like seeing this in slow motion, try reducing the Baud rate to 110 in the Communications dialogue box. Don't forget to reset it to the correct value afterwards.

If nothing gets through, go to step 1D

1 C

If some lights are on but they flicker on and off when you move the connecting cable, especially if you started with an intermittent problem, you have probably got a faulty connection in either the cable or the connector.

1 D

Re-check everything. If you don't find an obvious problem then your computer probably has a fault and so should be repaired.

2 - Testing Compatibility

2A

If three or four of the lights come on, your computer is probably working. Before unplugging the BOB, draw a quick diagram so that you can remember which lights came on. Note the colour of the lights because that may be useful later.

2 B

Repeat the same thing on the other device by plugging the opposite side of the BOB into that and again note down which lights are on.

If no lights are on, check that you have:

   Turned the other device on and that it is ready to communicate with your computer.

   Run the correct software, if relevant, and have checked that it is properly set-up.

Chapter 15 Terminal

If the other device has more than one serial port, check that you have plugged the BOB or equivalent into the port that the software is working with.

If these all seem right and you still have no lights on:

The other device may not be functioning properly, so get it repaired.

2C

Compare the two diagrams you have drawn of the lights at each end of the link:

If there are no overlaps, i.e., a totally different set of lights come on for each side, move to step 3.

If there is an overlap i.e., one or more of the same lights are lit on both sides, move to step 2D.

2D

If one or more lights are overlapping it is because both pieces of equipment are terminals or computers and you will have to swap some wires round. To do that:

Make a note of which lights are lit on both sides.

Plug the BOB or Mini Tester and Wiring Box into your computer.

If you are using a BOB turn all the switches OFF.

If you have a clash on Pins 2 or 3, use a couple of patch wires to swap these lines. You connect pin 2 on your computer's side to pin 3 on the other and vice versa. To start with, the flow control wires each go back to the other one in the pair on the same side. That is, you wire pins 4 and 5, and 6 and 20 together on both sides. Link pins 1 to pin 1 and pin 7 to pin 7.

Test the link by connecting the other device to the BOB or equivalent, type some characters on your keyboard and see if you can send data both ways across the link.

If you have a clash on Pins 4 or 5, swap over these two links so that Pin 4 goes to 5 and Pin 5 goes to Pin 4.

Chapter 15 Terminal

If you have a clash on Pins 6 or 20, swap over these two links so that Pin 6 goes to 20 and Pin 20 goes to Pin 6.

For safety reasons, it's important to ensure that pin 1 and pin 7 on each end of the link are always connected to their matching pins at the other end, no matter what other inter-linking is done.

Normally, pin 8 is not connected on your computer but if it is needed by the other side it can be linked into pin 6 on the same side.

Try sending characters down the link and, if successful, try transferring a file. If not, move to Step 3.

3 - Setting the Speed and Flow Control Method

If data is still not getting through:

Disconnect the flow control wires (if they aren't already) by pulling out the wires that go to pins 4/5 and 6/20.

Set the flow control to None (in the Communications dialogue box) and set the Baud Rate to the slowest speed that both machines can tolerate. Don't forget to change the flow control method and the Baud rate on the other device too, after you've made a note of the current settings.

Try sending some more characters. They should get through this time. If not, it's worth checking both ends of the links to make quite sure that you haven't made a silly and easily corrected mistake. We are all humans, after all!

If the link now works, you need to find out whether it was a problem with the Baud rate or the flow control setting (or both) that stopped data getting through.

First you need to test the Baud rate setting by increasing the speed on both sides in steps. Go up one level at a time until you get to a rate where nothing gets transferred. You now know the fastest speed that the link between these two particular pieces of equipment will work at and you can set it back to that.

Now you need to look at the flow control setting. It depends what methods the other device can use. If it can use Hardware, you'll have to plug a patch wire into the relevant holes on the BOB or Wiring Box (pin 4 on your computer across to either pin 4 or 5

215

Chapter 15 Terminal

depending on whether the other device is configured as a computer or a terminal).

You can then try the link again but you will not know whether your choice of flow control works until you get the other device to say it doesn't want any more data. You can get it to do that by sending enough data to fill up the buffer (which might take a long time!) or, if it is a computer you could use the PAUSE command that some communication programs have, In Terminal, there's a Pause option on the Transfer menu.

If your computer stops sending more characters (possibly, after a short delay) you know that you've chosen the correct flow control method. If it carries on sending data, you know that it doesn't work.

If it doesn't work, try both flow control methods (Xon/Xoff and Hardware) before settling for None. You'll find that, while None works most of the time, it can be unreliable.

After these tests you will know both what speed and what flow control method this link likes to use. Don't forget to note down what links you made in the cable and the settings you used on the other device. Save the current Terminal settings, so that you'll know what to do if you need to communicate with this device again.

It Nearly Works

How often have we heard this, closely followed by 'I give up!' when all attempts fail...

In this section, we explain how you can get a link to another device working reliably and with the minimum of effort. Overleaf there's a table that lists the symptoms, their probable causes and then what you should do to get the link working.

Chapter 15 Terminal

Symptom	Cause	Solution
Data goes across the link, but all characters are incorrect	The Baud rate is wrong	Check the Baud rate on the other device, then alter your settings
Approximately every other character is incorrect	The Parity setting is wrong	Check the parity (odd, even, none, mark or space) used by the other device. If this isn't possible, set your parity setting to None and deselect the Check Parity button in the Communications dialogue box
Each character you type appears twice, like this: 'sseeiinngg ddoouubbllee'	Both you and the other device are 'echoing" - your computer is echoing your keystrokes and the other device is echoing back the characters it is receiving	Either you or the other device must turn off echoing. You can deselect the Local Echo button in the Terminal Preferences dialogue box
You receive characters but can't see what you are typing	Neither you or the other device are 'echoing"	Either you or the other device must turn on echoing. You can select the Local Echo button in the Terminal Preferences dialogue box
Data you type or receive is double line spaced	Your computer is incorrectly interpreting a 'new line" character. So it's going down a line after the other device has already issued that instruction	Deselect both CR -> CR/LF buttons in the Terminal Preferences dialogue box
Data you type or receive looks like a 'staircase' going down the screen from left to right	Your computer isn't interpreting the 'new line' character. So it's not going down a line and moving to the beginning of the next one	Select both CR -> CR/LF buttons in the Terminal Preferences dialogue box
Some characters, such as '£' and '#', are not displayed correctly	The computer you're communicating with is using a different language to that used by your computer	You can use the Translation box in the Terminal Preferences dialogue box to match the language to that used by the other device. You can, for example, select 'Spain' even if your computer uses 'United Kingdom'
Normal characters look correct but some special control characters do not	Terminal can 'emulate' (jargon for behave like) several different terminals. It's set up for the wrong type	Find out whether the emulate a VT-100 or VT-52 and then select the corresponding button in the Terminal Emulation dialogue box. If not, then push the TTY button and ask the user of the other computer to set it to the simplest type of terminal that his program can emulate
Not all characters on long lines are visible even if you use the horizontal scroll bar.	The other computer is sending 132 character lines but Terminal is only storing the first 80.	Select the 132 Columns buttons in the Terminal Preferences dialogue box.

217

Chapter 16 - The Recorder

When we introduced Recky (your friendly robot) we mentioned that he (are robots hes, shes or its?) was a willing slave and would make your life easier and more fun. This chapter shows you how this versatile little fellow can help you use your kit in Windows without leaving your armchair.

What Does Recky Do?

After you've spent some time using Windows, you'll find that there are some jobs that you do everyday. If they always involve the same steps, it's time to ask for Recky's help as he'll perform them over and over, just like a computerised pianola.

Unlike a pianola, you can teach Recky to perform almost any job. To do that, you must be a good teacher and show him what you want him to do. Unlike most students, Recky has an infallible memory, so he will never forget - unless you tell him to.

Some Jobs Recky Could Do...

Lots of Windows users just use Recky to organise their desktops when they start Windows each day. Another common job is to ask Recky to do all the steps needed to select a particular printer. As you'll see later in this chapter, you can even add Recky files as icons (in the Program Manager) that you can just double click to get Recky started on a job. So, you could have icons labelled Laser Printer and Dot Matrix.

Getting The Most Out Of Recky

Recky doesn't know what he's doing - he just does it parrot fashion - so it's up to you to make sure that he does what you want. This places a heavy burden on you - you must know (in detail) what steps to perform in what order, so that you can teach Recky. It means that you must know how to use the application that you want Recky to use. There's no escape from exploring the terrain for yourself before you send Recky off on a job.

Recky is an obedient student, perhaps almost too obedient. To avoid mistakes, it's worth rehearsing what you want to teach Recky so that he can recall it later without embarrassing slip-ups. For any teacher, there's nothing worse than a student repeating his teacher's mistakes in front of others!

What Is Recky Recording?

If you think about it, everything you do in Windows can be reduced to combinations of pressing keys, moving the mouse and pressing the mouse buttons. (Wow, put like that, why have you just read over two hundred pages?)

The designers of Recky recognised (try saying that quickly!) that you might want him to replay your actions either at the speed you performed them; say, to demonstrate a procedure; or as fast as possible - to get the job done. You tell him which when you teach him the job or, if you change your mind, you can alter the setting later.

Recky records mouse movements by recording the mouse tip's position on the screen or within a window. He is completely blind to what is on the screen. This has some important implications that we will explain in the The Problem Page section at the end of this chapter.

Recky is only happy in Windows world. If you run a non-Windows program while recording, Recky disregards everything you do until you return to the safety of the Windows world.

Chapter 16 The Recorder

What's A 'Macro' Doing On A Micro?

When you start using Recky, you'll meet Macro in the menu and everywhere else after that. No doubt you, like us, wondered what a Macro was. Those with a scientific background will recognise 'macro' as the opposite of 'micro', that may seem even more confusing, so read on...

We found out that Macro is shorthand for 'Macro Instruction', which explains it totally, doesn't it?

OK, we told you a little white lie! One of us knew all the time what a Macro was and is old enough to remember when men were men and computers were programmed in assembly language. Yes, there really are some of us still alive! In those dim and distant days, programmers got a bit tired of typing the same sequences of instructions again and again. Also, their programs were decks of cards that weighed a ton and fell to bits at the merest provocation - you Windows users don't know how good you have it!

Eventually, somebody had the idea of replacing the more common sequences of instructions with single 'macro instructions' that told the computer: 'look, replace this single card with the sequence of instructions that (say) adds two numbers'. Later, somebody else realised that you could define your own sequences once and then use them often, even in different programs. The result was shorter programs, happier programmers and the word 'macro' entering the language.

Chapter 16 The Recorder

That's just what Recky's doing - allowing you to replace a long sequence of instructions with a shorter one. The long sequence is the job you want carried out and the shorter sequence is the one that you use to tell Recky to perform it for you.

Macros Within Files

Recky allows one file to contain many different Macros. It is similar to a Cardfile containing more than one card or a Write file having many pages. You need this:

1. To allow you access to many Macros without having to load each one from a separate file.

2. To allow Macros to be 'nested' inside one another - see the next section.

Within a file, each Macro has a name and a shortcut key, either can be changed later. It's a good idea to use both. The name is useful to identify the job that the Macro performs. The shortcut key means that each Macro in the file can be accessed with just one keystroke.

You can assign nearly any key as a shortcut key. You enter the key you want to use in the Shortcut Key box in the Record dialogue box. It has a hidden list of options that includes all the special keys like PageUp, PageDown and the function keys along the top of the keyboard. Most of the time, you'll need to select one of the Ctrl, Shift and Alt boxes as most keys (such as letters, numbers and punctuation marks) are already used when running other software. You need to choose a combination of keys different to that you're using with any other program. Don't use just Alt and another key as Windows already uses most combinations.

Each shortcut key must be unique. Recky complains if you try to define a Macro with the same key as one that already exists. You can only have one copy of Recky open.

It's a good idea to call your Macros by meaningful names, and assign them mnemonic shortcut keys, so that you can instantly access them without having to open the Recorder window. For example, a Macro to remove old appointments in the Calendar could be called 'Tidy Calendar' and use [Ctrl + T] as its shortcut key.

What's Nesting?

Most explanations of 'nesting' use the Russian Doll analogy - those toys that are a doll with a smaller doll inside it, and then a smaller doll inside that and so on...

It's a good description of what's happening - one Macro contains another. If a part of the job that

Chapter 16 The Recorder

one Macro performs needs to follow the same steps as one you've already created, you can simply use it's shortcut key to perform those steps. You might imagine that each Macro nested inside another must be 'smaller' (that is, simpler and with less steps) than the one outside. You may also imagine that one Macro can only contain one Macro - just like the original dolls.

Not so! It's possible to have a Macro that just records that you've pressed one shortcut key and then another; like two dolls inside one. Each of these can then perform an involved job; like a larger doll inside an outer one.

A word of caution - recording nested Macros can get very confusing as the steps within each nested Macro will be replayed as you record the Macro. Our advice is to plan what each part each Macro is to play in performing the complete job and to rehearse a few times before you record them. The Macro Description box is a good place to note which Macros nest within this one.

You cannot open Recky's window to start another Macro when he's recording. You can only use the shortcut key to begin a Macro that you want nested inside another. You must select the Enable Shortcut Keys box in the Record dialogue box and select it from the Options menu, before you record a Macro that will contain others.

Merging Files Of Macros

Recky includes a facility to let you merge files. Merge will add the Macros from another file into the list of Macros displayed in Recky's window. For example, if the Macro list already contains Macro A and B and the file you want to Merge contains Macros C, D and E, the list will then show all five Macros: A to E.

You need to use Merge if you want to nest a Macro from one file inside a Macro stored in another file. You (to say nothing of poor Recky) would get hopelessly confused if you could change files when he was recording.

Telling Recky What To Record

Before looking at how to tell Recky what to store when recording a Macro, let's clarify the roles of three similar dialogue boxes: Preferences on the Options menu, Record and Properties (both on the Macro menu).

You'll normally just use the Record dialogue box. If you find that Recky always seems to give you the wrong initial settings then the Preferences dialogue box allows you to change them. The

Properties option can be used to change some of the details you typed in the Record dialogue box after you've recorded a Macro. Luckily, all three dialogue boxes use the same terms to mean the same thing so we'll just look at the Record dialogue box.

The boxes we're interested in are Record Mouse, Relative To and those inside the Playback box.

The first two relate to what mouse actions will be recorded (nothing, just clicks and drags or everything). You can record movements as relative to the window; so that, if the window moves, the Macro will still work. Or, you can also record them as relative to the screen; useful if you want to click the mouse outside a window; as you would do when laying out your screen.

The Playback inner boxes control where you can play the Macro (either to any application or just back to the one that was running when it was recorded), the playback speed and whether you want to enable the shortcut keys. We explain the box labelled Continuous Loop in 'Creating A Rolling Demo', later in this chapter.

Running Macros From The Program Manager

You can run a Macro directly by double clicking on an icon in the Program Manager window. It allows you to select a particular Macro from within a file containing more than one Macro.

Follow the steps below:

1. Record your Macro and save the file.

2. Run the File Manager and copy the file containing the Macro to the group in the Program Manager where you want it to go.

3. If you double click on the icon now, it will start Recky and open the file - not run the individual Macro.

4. Select the icon and pull down the Program Manager's File menu, then open the Properties dialogue box.

5. You will see two boxes, Description and Command Line.

6. Edit the Description to reflect what the Macro does. This will be displayed below this Macro's icon within the Program Manager window.

7. At the beginning of the Command Line box, insert [recorder.exe] followed by [-h] then the code for the shortcut key - see below - and then a final space. After you've finished, the box should look something like:

   recorder.exe -h ^F12 c:\windows\test.rec

8. After you click the OK button, the icon should have the name of the Macro you want to run.

9. It's a good idea to exit Windows now, after selecting the Save Changes box, to save the position of the icon.

Shortcut Key Codes

Shortcut key codes consist of two parts: the first part shows the combination of Shift, Control and Alt used:

   Control is ^

   Shift is +

   Alt is %

The second part is one of the keys on the keyboard. If you are using function keys, make sure that you have called them the same name as in the Record dialogue box hidden list. For example, the shortcut key code '^F12' stands for [Ctrl + F12] and '^%A' stands for [Ctrl + Alt + A].

Creating A Rolling Demo

If you need to show off some Windows programs, Recky can help you avoid the tedium of repeating the steps over and over.

Normally, Recky must be told when to start and, when he's finished, he doesn't know what to do next. To keep Recky repeating a job you need to select the Continuous Loop box in the Record dialogue box. This will turn Recky into a pianola with an endless loop of music - repeating the same thing over and over...

If you want to ensure that nothing can stop Recky, you should deselect Control-Break Checking

Chapter 16 The Recorder

in the Options menu. Now, the only thing that can stop Recky is death - that is, turning the computer off or rebooting! You should only use this feature if your Macro doesn't alter any data while it's running.

The Problem Page

We hope that we've given you a feeling for what Recky is and how he can help you - now it's time for some 'home truths' which show that Recky is not always a sweet, innocent little fellow.

Recky Hates The Mouse

Recky would be much happier if the mouse could not be used when recording a Macro. He shows his displeasure by consuming vast quantities of disk space when you mouse around.

To avoid this, you should use the keyboard alternatives whenever practicable when recording Macros. For example, to select bold text in Write, you should type [Ctrl + B] rather than pulling down the Character menu and then clicking on Bold.

If you do use the mouse, and the window is near the bottom of the screen, the pop-down menus can become pop-up menus! Your carefully crafted Macros tend not to work when what was a downward mouse movement suddenly becomes an upward one.

Recky Doesn't Like Movement

Remember that Recky can't see what's on the screen so any movement (of windows, icons or whatever) can completely alter the outcome of running a Macro...

If a Macro moves something on the screen, running it again may have completely different effects (probably, undesirable) to running it for the first time.

Recky Gets Confused By Overlapping Windows

You can replay a Macro that is set to playback to the Same Application even if that application is not the active one. If you happen to have placed another window over the one that Recky is working with, Recky will stop the Macro and complain.

Part 4

The Back Pack

Chapter 17 - The Windows Tool Box

We'll begin by looking at how you turn an MS-DOS computer into one using Windows, explain how to keep your computer running smoothly and then we'll look at using MS-DOS applications inside Windows.

Installing Windows

Installing Windows on a computer is simple and straightforward. Don't rush into it, set aside enough time and just follow the on-screen instructions. Even on a slow computer, it will only take about twenty minutes.

Do I Need To Install Windows?

If you're lucky, someone has already installed Windows on your hard disk. The simplest way to see whether you need to install it is to try running it! At the MS-DOS command prompt, type:

[win] and then press Enter

If you get a message saying 'Bad command or file name', someone may have installed it without telling MS-DOS where it is. To check this, you should look on your hard disk for a directory called something like \WINDOWS. From the MS-DOS command prompt, type the command that lists the files in your root directory, making sure that you press the correct slash keys. The command is:

[dir \ /w] and then press Enter

You should see a multi-column list of names. If WINDOWS or WIN is amongst them, someone has loaded Windows for you. To test that you can run Windows, you need to change to the directory that contains the Windows files and then start Windows from there. If that directory is WINDOWS, you'll type:

[cd \windows] and then press Enter() [win] and Enter

Chapter 17 The Windows Tool Box

If that doesn't work, but you think that Windows is installed, then you should ask the person who supplied the computer.

Before you start using Windows, please have a look at the 'Running Windows For The First Time' section later in this chapter.

Preparing To Install Windows

You should check:

- That your computer can run Windows

- That you have a full set of Windows disks, the official User Guide and a copy of this book(!)

- That you have backed-up your computer's hard disk

- That the data on your computer's hard disk is clean and tidy

- That you have an MS-DOS 'emergency restart' disk

Let's look at a couple of these in more detail...

Can My Computer Run Windows?

If you're lucky enough to have an 80486 computer with 8Megabytes of extended memory, about 100 Megabytes of free disk space with an XGA (that's better than VGA) screen, Yes! You'll be running Windows as its designers intended and you'll get good performance.

At the other extreme, we've had Windows running on an 8086 machine with 640 Kilobyte of memory, 3 Megabytes of free disk and a CGA screen. It runs quite well but you may wonder what this talk of increased productivity is about while you wait for windows to open and you have to deal with Out of Memory dialogue boxes every few minutes.

We reckon that you need at least an 80386SX computer with 640 Kilobytes of conventional and 2 Megabytes of extended memory, 15 Megabytes of free disk space and a VGA screen.

Even if your computer has a lower specification than that, it's still worth trying to install Windows. If you find it's too slow, you can always delete all the Windows files and continue

Chapter 17 The Windows Tool Box

working with your old applications. Or you could take the opportunity to upgrade your computer!

Backing-Up And Checking Your Hard Disk

Just to be sure that any important data is safe, we recommend that you back-up all the files on your hard disk before you install Windows. There's very little danger, we've installed Windows on half a dozen different machines without losing a single byte. We just like to be cautious when it comes to protecting data. There's a section on back-ups later in this chapter.

You should also check that all the files on your hard disk are valid. Sometimes, particularly after a crash, MS-DOS will not be able to keep your files organised. But, even if this happens several times, MS-DOS can carry on working. You may eventually, however, either run out of disk space or lose a file or two. It's a good idea to tidy up your disk before you install Windows so it can start with a clean slate. Again, there's a section later in this chapter that covers this in more detail.

Creating An Emergency Restart Disk

We've never seen a situation where the computer couldn't be used after attempting to install Windows. But, in line with our policy of suggesting ways in which you can protect your data, we suggest that you create an Emergency Restart Disk. We'll show you how to make one later in the chapter.

Installing Windows

You've established that your computer can run Windows, found the Windows disks, backed-up your hard disk and checked its health. You're ready!

You now have a choice of routes to choose from. You can either:

> Follow the instructions in the Users Guide and feed disks into your computer for about ten minutes.

> OR

> Load all the files on the Windows disks onto your hard disk in one go and then sit back.

Which method you choose is up to you. If you just want to get Windows working NOW and

229

Chapter 17 The Windows Tool Box

you'll be happy with its initial configuration, then follow the first route. If you're going to add new equipment or try different configurations of Windows, then following the second route avoids the need to find the disks again later. There's a price to pay for this - five megabytes of disk space, to be precise. You are, in effect, storing the Windows files twice.

Whichever method you choose, you'll need to know whether the floppy disk you're going to use is a:, b: or whatever. If you have just one floppy, you can safely assume that it's a:. Otherwise, you could probably assume that the drive you usually load software from is the a: drive and the other one is b:. There are exceptions, so when all else fails, you may have to try each drive letter and see whether your computer accesses the correct disk drive.

If you choose the more flexible method, first create a directory on your hard disk called \WINFILES by typing:

[md \winfiles] and then press Enter

Then, copy each of the original Windows disks into this directory by using the MS-DOS Copy command. If you're loading from the a: drive, type:

[copy a:*.* \winfile*.*] and then press Enter

Repeat this for all the disks. You needn't type this command for each disk. Simply press [F3]; MS-DOS will remember the last command and repeat it.

Don't be tempted to try running Windows straightaway. Even if you do, it won't work. The installation program, Setup, does some work on the files before Windows can be run.

Using Setup To Install Windows

If you're using the official installation method, you must insert the first Windows disk into one of your computer's drives, log onto it and then run Setup. If you are using a:, you'll type:

[a:] and then press Enter

[setup] and then press Enter

If you're using the alternate method, you change to the directory that holds the Windows files and then run Setup. You'll type:

[cd \winfiles] and then press Enter

[setup] and then press Enter

When Setup runs, you see a series of text screens and then, halfway through the process, Windows takes over and several windows appear. Setup must use this peculiar hybrid as it must first get some basic Windows software working before switching to the friendlier Windows world from the unfriendly MS-DOS one.

If you take each screen in turn and just follow the instructions, you should find it easy to get Windows running on your computer. Don't skip a screen just because you don't understand it - they are all important.

First Installation Screen

If this is the first time you've seen Windows, we've tried to give you enough information here to allow you to install Windows. However, this is not really sufficient to allow you to get the best out of Windows. For that information, you should read the earlier chapters of this book. If you already know the basics of working with Windows, you'll find that you can skip most of this section. Start reading from the Second Installation Screen section.

This is an introductory screen and explains some keystrokes that you can use from all the other screens:

[Enter] performs an Action

Pressing Enter tells Setup that you are happy with the options that it has displayed. It will remember these settings and move onto the next stage of installing Windows.

For each group of settings, the first time Setup displays them is the only chance you have to change them within Setup. If you accept incorrect settings, you'll probably still be able to run Windows and make any changes from there, but you should be careful not to get trigger happy with the Enter key.

[F1] displays Help

Pressing [F1] only works when Setup is waiting for you, not when it's busy copying files or setting up data on your hard disk. Until Windows takes over, pressing the [F1] key will cause Setup to display a single screen of helpful information. To continue after you've read the help screen, press the Esc key.

[F3] abandons Setup

After displaying a message asking you to confirm that you really want to leave, Setup returns you to MS-DOS. If you do abandon Setup, Windows will be only partially installed and so you should not attempt to run it. Instead, you should delete all files in the directory that you asked Setup to install Windows in, and in its SYSTEM sub-directory. Then re-run Setup. [F3] is always active, even if Setup if busy copying files or setting up information on your hard disk.

Second Installation Screen

After a short pause, the second text screen appears. Near the bottom you will see a highlighted pathname. This is the directory to which Setup will copy all the files and will be where you will start Windows.

Setup gives you an initial directory name - c:\WINDOWS. If you wish to install Windows on a different disk drive or in a different directory, you can change Windows' location by editing the name. When the pathname is correct, press Enter.

The most common reason for choosing a different directory name is that you already have one version of Windows installed and are upgrading to a newer one. If so, you should see the section on Upgrading Windows later in this chapter. Setup searches your hard disk looking for Windows but it may not always find it. You should carefully read the message that appears on this screen to help you decide what to do next.

Third Installation Screen

Between displaying the second and third screen, your computer's monitor may lose synchronisation for a split second. This is perfectly normal and happens when Setup tests what type of monitor your computer has.

The third screen is probably the most frightening of those displayed by Setup as it refers to the basic hardware and software of your computer. Normally, you don't need to involve yourself with these and that's true here. Setup employs some pretty clever techniques that allow it to determine what it needs to know about your computer automatically.

If Setup finds out what it needs, then it will display your computer's configuration. You just press the Enter key and move on. Don't expect it to know that your computer is a XYZ computer with an ABC monitor, Setup just looks at your computer's general configuration and deals with a few specific makes and models that Microsoft knew had quirks.

Sometimes, Setup's tests fail to identify your computer. If so, you may have to tell it yourself.

Chapter 17 The Windows Tool Box

Occasionally, you may receive a separate disk with the information which Setup needs. Now's the time to rummage round the packing case looking for that all-important little disk.

Even if Setup says it can determine your computer's configuration, it's wise to check that the tests have produced the right results.

Setup looks at:

- Your computer. It determines if it is a standard PC-DOS / MS-DOS computer, one of the listed exceptions or whether it needs a disk from its supplier.

- Your display. If your computer can support more than one video mode, Setup selects the one with the highest resolution because that will make Windows look its best. Higher resolutions show more detail so your computer may require some time to open windows. If it has a higher resolution mode than VGA, you may find it best to select a lower resolution mode until you're happy with Windows' performance.

- Your mouse. If your mouse can behave like a Microsoft mouse, we suggest that you use it as one.

- Your keyboard. The choice here is between a PC/XT or PC/AT keyboards, one of the exceptions or to use a special disk from your supplier.

- The keyboard layout. Setup uses the information which MS-DOS maintains about the keyboard. It may show that you have a US keyboard even if you don't. You can change the keyboard layout setting from within Windows.

- The language that your computer is using. Again, Setup may tell you that your computer is using US English even if it isn't. You can easily change this setting from within Windows.

- The network (if any) that your computer is attached to. If Setup fails to find a network when one is attached, you may need to upgrade the network software to a version that is 'Windows aware'.

When Setup first displays the information it's found out about your computer, it highlights the 'Above list matches my computer' message at the bottom of the screen. If you are happy that the list matches your computer, just press the Enter key. If not, the Up Arrow key can be used to move the highlighting to the entry you wish to change. Pressing the Enter key from there will display the list of choices which Setup has available. When you've found the one you want,

Chapter 17 The Windows Tool Box

press the Enter key again. You'll then be able to move the highlighting on to other options by using the Up Arrow and Down Arrow keys. When you've finished, move down to the 'Above list. ..'entry and press the Enter key.

Fourth Installation Screen

This is the last text screen. Once Setup has got a description of your computer, it can then copy just enough Windows software onto your hard disk so that it can use Windows to install the rest of it.

At the bottom of this screen, a status line shows you which file Setup is copying to the Windows directory.

Fifth Installation Screen

Between the fourth and fifth Installation Screen, Windows takes over your computer. It displays a pretty heading along the top of the screen and fills the remainder with a rather natty blue graduated background. It's all reminiscent of those slides with graphs that people spend fortunes creating and then never use.

If this is the first time you've seen Windows, try moving the mouse. The arrow should follow it around. Then, with the arrow pointed over the HELP button, try pressing the left mouse button. You'll notice how the arrow seems to press the on-screen button.

A window will open with Help information. Unless you want to take this opportunity to explore the Help system, just press [Ctrl + F4] to close the Help window.

The window in the middle of this screen has three small buttons:

- SET UP PRINTERS

    Press this button (that is, move the arrow over it and click the left mouse button) if you want to tell Windows about your printers. If you prefer, you can leave this until later.

- SET UP APPLICATIONS

    Press this button if you wish to tell Windows about the applications already on your hard disk. Later in the installation, you can then select some or all of the Windows or non-Windows applications. You may leave this until later.

- READ ON-LINE DOCUMENTS

Press this button if you want to read the latest information on Windows.

Since you'll be in a hurry to get Windows going, you'll probably decide not to do any of these things. That's fine, it's as easy to do them later when Windows is running as it is while you're installing it. The on-line documents contain information that is not available elsewhere. It may be worth controlling your enthusiasm for a further five minutes while you glance through the latest news on your version of Windows.

Sixth Installation Screen

We'll continue to call what Setup displays 'screens' although, since Windows is now in charge, they are just windows displayed on a common background.

If you're following the official installation method, this is where the disco music should start as you'll be shuffling disks for about ten minutes. The rule is simple: Windows asks for a disk, you find it, load it into the same drive you started the installation from and then press the OK button. After two or three disks, you should be doing this automatically. After the five or six disks it takes to complete the process, you may be an experienced disk jockey but you'll certainly be a slightly worried one. You'll be asking: Where are these files going? Will my disk have any space left?

If you've loaded all the files onto your hard disk, go and get a cup of coffee. Your computer will be busy talking to itself for about five minutes. Setup copies the files from the directory you initially loaded them into to the directories that Windows uses when it runs. It decompresses some files as it copies them.

Near the end of all this copying, the message in the dialogue box changes from 'Copying files' to 'Installing fonts'. Setup is loading the fonts that come with the basic package. If you have purchased further ones from other sources, you can add them later from the Control Panel.

The next step is quite dramatic. Setup begins with a blank window and then adds each group and program icon individually to build an initial window for Program Manager. The first time we saw it perform, we wondered whether Windows had taken flight and gone off into its own world, leaving ours for ever.

Chapter 17 The Windows Tool Box

Seventh Installation Screen

At this stage, some basic Windows software is running, the files that Windows needs are on your hard disk and the Program Manager has an initial set of icons.

You may think that that's all there is to do. But, as we said at the beginning of the book, Windows isn't independent - it relies on MS-DOS.

A Diversion Into MS-DOS Land

MS-DOS, despite its age, is quite an advanced operating system that can be 'extended' and 'configured'. In simple language, these terms mean that new parts can be added to it and that some parts can be changed to behave in different ways.

The designers of MS-DOS recognised that you (the user) wouldn't want to configure your computer manually each time you switch it on. They provided two files that automate this: CONFIG.SYS and AUTOEXEC.BAT. MS-DOS looks at both files every time you turn on (or reset) your computer. Those who have read the earlier chapters will remember these as two of the Big Four.

CONFIG.SYS tells MS-DOS about additions to the basic system and sets various internal controls in the system. AUTOEXEC.BAT holds commands which MS-DOS executes automatically just before the command prompt appears. Both files are in the root directory of the hard disk you boot from. They needn't exist at all if your applications don't require any extensions or changes to basic MS-DOS.

To run efficiently, Windows needs to both add parts and set some controls. It therefore wants to modify both your Config and Autoexec files. It could just go right ahead and do that, but Microsoft would be inundated with calls from angry users.

Why is this? The answer, in a word, is 'TSR' programs. No, it's not a reference to a defunct plane of the 1960s, but stands for Terminate and Stay Resident. TSRs cheat MS-DOS into believing that they've stopped running whereas, in fact, they are still there. If this sounds like a Gremlin, you're dead right on two counts: One, it's a tricky trick to play on poor MS-DOS and Two, they can cause the other sort of Gremlin, crashes.

You can only get away with fooling MS-DOS into living with TSRs if you are careful in the order they get loaded and you configure MS-DOS to accept their quirks. How do you do this? You alter the Config and Autoexec files.

Chapter 17 The Windows Tool Box

So, Windows needs to change your Config and Autoexec files and so may any TSRs that you are using. You must resolve any conflicts yourself. Setup gives you the chance of looking at what it wants to do to these all-important files before stamping all over them with seven league boots.

CONFIG.SYS And AUTOEXEC.BAT - Your Options

Setup gives you three choices. You may ask it to:

- Go ahead and make the changes itself

- Let you look at and edit the changes and only then make them

- Not change either file but save suggested changes in files for you to look at later

Leaving Setup In Control Of Autoexec And Config

You can safely let Setup go right ahead and alter both Autoexec and Config files if your system is running straightforward applications and you have no TSRs loaded. You'll know if an application is a TSR if it is available while you are working in other applications whenever you press a special keystroke.

If you let Setup alter the files, it copies the current contents of your Config and Autoexec file to files in your root directory called CONFIG.OLD and AUTOEXEC.OLD. The Help system is not very helpful on this; it mistakenly says that these files have .BAK extensions.

Reviewing Autoexec And Config

If you decide that you'd like to see what Windows is going to do before letting it go ahead, select the second option. This opens a dialogue box with two little boxes with scroll bars and two buttons, labelled CONTINUE and CANCEL. If you press CONTINUE, you're telling Setup that you've finished editing, so don't press that yet. CANCEL will return you to the same dialogue box that you saw when you chose what you wanted to do to your Config and Autoexec files.

The top box displays what Setup proposes to do with your Autoexec file and the bottom one shows what's in there now. Setup links the two boxes; if you move within one box, using the scroll bars or the Arrow keys, the other box shows the same section of the other file. This works both ways round.

Chapter 17 The Windows Tool Box

You'll notice that Setup has put the changes it wants to make in lower case but, apart from that, it's up to you to find the changes it wants to make. You can edit the altered file, or simply look at the changes, by moving the arrow into the upper box. Once there, you have most of the normal Windows editing functions; you can move round using the mouse or Arrow keys, insert and delete text and even delete blocks by highlighting them and then pressing the Del key. When you've finished editing the Autoexec file, press the CONTINUE button.

It's then the turn of the Config file to receive your attention. You'll see that the dialogue box looks identical - it behaves in exactly the same way. The top box has Setup's changes, the lower box has the current file. When you've finished, press CONTINUE.

Setup then alters both files, having first renamed your existing files to .OLD extensions.

Creating Copies Of Autoexec And Config

The third option, where Setup simply creates files that contain the changes without touching your Autoexec and Config files, is useful if you don't want Setup to change them. If your computer is on a network or if you use memory management software like Quarterdeck's QEMM, the files may contain highly specific information. It's unlikely that Setup understands its importance.

Setup opens a dialogue box with boxes for the names of the changed files and three buttons; SAVE, DON'T SAVE and CANCEL. CANCEL returns you to the same dialogue box that appeared when you decided what to do to your Config and Autoexec files.

SAVE saves the changes that Setup would have made to your Autoexec and Config files to the two files named in the boxes. You can change these names by moving the mouse over them, or pressing the Tab key if you're using the keyboard, and then typing the names you want to use. The files will be stored in the Windows directory. These boxes only accept a few characters; you may not be able to store the files in sub-directories of your root directory.

The DON'T SAVE button does just what it says - it doesn't save the changes. Changes will be lost for ever. Unless you've installed Windows already, and are just creating another copy on your hard disk, it's a good idea to at least glance at what Setup would like to do.

Tip: Recovering from Windows Induced Amnesia

If you allow Windows to do its own thing and then you find that your computer doesn't boot, you'll have to use an Emergency Restart disk.

If you're lucky, you'll find that you can access the hard disk. If so, restore the Config and Autoexec files from the .OLD versions and then reset again. If not, you'll have to rebuild your the programs and files you had on your computer from your back-ups.

Eighth Installation Screen

If you selected the Set up Printers option in the Fifth screen, Setup displays a dialogue box to allow you do that. If not, Setup skips this screen.

The dialogue box is the same one you use to set up printers from the Control Panel. You can just glimpse the Control Panel itself in the background. Read the Printers section of the Control Panel chapter for more details.

You must find out, and then give Setup, the following information:

- What printer you have or what printer it can behave like or 'emulate'

- Which port (serial or parallel) it will be connected to

If you only have one printer, that's all you need. If you have more than one, you should decide where you want to connect each printer. If you decide to share ports between printers, you'll have to decide which one to make active and which to leave inactive. You can only print on active printers.

After you've pressed the INSTALL button, you should scroll down the list until you find the printer that matches yours, either because it is the same as yours or because your printer can emulate it. If you followed the official installation procedure (from floppy disks), Setup will ask for the disk that contains the software that Windows needs to drive your printer. After installation, you're given the opportunity to configure the printer. You can tell Windows about any options installed on the printer and what paper size and graphics resolution to use when you print.

When you've finished, press the OK button. If you press the CANCEL button after you've installed a printer, your Windows directory will still contain the files that Windows needs to drive the printer. If you're short of disk space, you should delete these later.

Ninth Installation Screen

If you selected the Set up Applications option in the Fifth screen, Setup displays a dialogue box to allow you do that. If not, Setup skips this screen.

Since you have only just loaded Windows, it's unlikely that there are any Windows applications already on your hard disk. You can also set up non-Windows applications that you want to work with from within Windows.

We'll cover this in detail later, as it's a function of the Windows Setup application.

Tenth Installation Screen

If you selected the Read On line Documents option in the Fifth screen, then Setup opens a window that contains the file with the latest information. You are using Notepad to look at the README.TXT file in the Windows directory.

The first page of the file gives simplified instructions for using Notepad. Then there are sections dealing with running Windows on particular computers and with particular peripherals. The file ends with a list of other on-line documents that you can open from Notepad when Windows is running.

Eleventh Installation Screen

You're nearly there! Just this one and then you can get a well-earned cup of coffee or even something a little stronger.

What you see here depends on whether you allowed Setup to make changes to your Autoexec and Config files. If you did, there are three buttons: REBOOT, RESTART WINDOWS and RETURN TO DOS. If you were mean and didn't allow Setup to alter your files, then you only get two buttons: RESTART WINDOWS and RETURN TO DOS.

If you expect that pressing the REBOOT button will reset your computer, you're wrong... MS-DOS lacks a way (at least, a deliberate way) of resetting your computer. All it can do is to shut everything down, display a rather lame message and then wait for you to do the dirty deed yourself.

Why do you need to reset? Returning to MS-DOS land for a few moments, you'll recall that MS-DOS executes the Autoexec and Config files whenever you reset. Now, that's the only time when MS-DOS looks at the contents of the Config file and the only time when you can safely execute the commands in the Autoexec file. So if you change them, you must reset your computer for any changes in MS-DOS's configuration to be made. That's why Setup asks you to reset after it has changed the files.

Pressing RESTART WINDOWS does just that; it restarts Windows just as if you'd typed [win] followed by pressing Enter at the MS-DOS command prompt.

The RETURN TO DOS button leaves Setup and returns to the MS-DOS command prompt. We suggest that you do this, rather than dive straight back in to Windows, so that you can back-up the Windows files you've just installed onto diskette or tape.

Running Windows For The First Time

You're raring to go... No, we aren't about to tell you that you have to do five other things before you can start Windows for the first time. You can dive straight in!

To start Windows, simply type:

> [win] and then press Enter

Ninety-nine times out of one hundred, this will start Windows. If not, then see the First Aid Kit chapter for a cure.

Windows will display a start-up screen, clear that and then display the Program Manager window in the middle of the screen. If Windows recognises your mouse, you will see an arrow in the middle of the screen. Moving the mouse should cause the arrow to move. Again, see the First Aid Kit chapter if your mouse is ill.

You're in Windows World and it's now up to you to explore as much or as little as you choose. The earlier chapters explain the language of Windows, how to get things to happen and how to use the basic tools of this ever-growing world.

Running Setup Once Windows Is Installed

Setup has FOUR separate functions:

- You run Setup to install Windows - that's the one you've met.

Chapter 17 The Windows Tool Box

- You can use Setup to install a new version of Windows.

- If your computer can't run Windows because you made a mistake when you installed it or subsequently, you may be able to restore it by using Setup to change options such the type of display you are using.

- Setup (called Windows Setup now) can be started from within Windows to add new software or to allow Windows to continue working if you change the configuration of your computer's hardware.

We'll deal with two of these here: for details on using Setup if you can't run Windows, turn to the First Aid Kit chapter.

Installing A New Version Of Windows

When you run Setup, it checks to see whether you have installed Windows on your hard disk already. If you have, it displays the directory where it found the installed Windows files and asks whether you want to overwrite the files.

At this point, you can either allow it to go ahead and overwrite your files or you can change the directory name displayed.

If you don't change the directory name, Setup will upgrade your copy of Windows to the version on the disk or in the Windows files directory. You'll see a special text screen, telling you that it's copying some files, and Setup will then invite you either to reset or return to MS-DOS.

Important: We've only tested an upgrade from version 3.00 to 3.00a of Windows ourselves. You should check with your supplier to find what to do when Microsoft release other versions.

You can also keep the older version on your disk to make sure that all your software runs under the new one. Once you are happy, you can delete the old version to free up disk space.

To keep two versions, you change the directory name. Setup installs the new version from scratch, taking you through all eleven installation screens. You'll then have two versions of Windows on your hard disk.

The version you've just installed will be a 'raw' one. The colour scheme and Program Manager groups will be set up just as they were when you initially installed Windows. If you've made any changes to Program Manager groups, changed colour schemes or if any Windows software has updated WIN.INI then you should copy the WIN.INI file from the old directory to the new one. You should also copy PROGMAN.INI and all files with a .GRP extension. If you've made changes to SYSTEM.INI then you should make those again in the new directory - don't copy this file from the old directory.

Windows Setup Explained

You use the Windows version of Setup:

- If you change any of basic hardware of your system. This includes its display, keyboard, mouse and network.

- To allow Windows to use existing Windows and non-windows applications.

In either situation, you start Windows Setup by double clicking the Windows Setup icon in the Program Manager group called Main.

Changing Basic Hardware

Windows Setup shows you the configuration that Windows is running with. To tell Windows of a change in your computer's hardware, select Change System Settings from the Options menu.

A dialogue box will open with four box:

- Your display. Remember that in its highest resolution mode, your computer may require some time to open windows.

- Your keyboard. The choice here is between a PC/XT or PC/AT keyboards, one of the exceptions or you may use a special disk from your supplier.

- Your mouse. If your mouse can behave like a Microsoft mouse, we suggest that you use it as one.

- The network (if any) to which your computer is attached. If your computer can't communicate with your network, you may need to upgrade the network software to a version that is 'Windows aware'.

To change one of these, select the appropriate box in the Change System Settings dialogue box and open the hidden list. If you're using the keyboard, select the box using the Tab key and display the list by pressing Enter.

Changes are not immediately carried out. After you've made changes, Setup allows you to restart Windows so that these can take effect.

Adding New Applications To Windows' Repertoire

Windows Setup other role is to add new applications to Windows so that they appear as icons within the Program Manager window.

Whilst most Windows applications come with installation programs that automatically add icons to Program Manager groups or create new groups, a few do not. Windows Setup can deal with these. It also knows about many non-Windows applications and can add icons for these.

When you select Set up Applications from the Options menu, a dialogue box opens that has two buttons, OK and CANCEL, and a list box with a hidden list. The list has All Drives, Path Only and the hard disk containing Windows.

Windows Setup is asking where it should search for applications. If you select All Drives, it will search through all directories on all drives. Selecting Path Only will start a search through those directories that appear in the MS-DOS PATH command. Selecting just the one hard disk could be useful if your computer is attached to a network. It restricts the search to files on your own hard disk, not to all those that you have access to over the network.

It may take a few minutes to complete the search. To keep you occupied, Windows Setup displays a little bar chart showing its progress and lets you know each time it finds an application. Eventually, you'll see another dialogue box that has two boxes, separated by three buttons labelled ADD, REMOVE and ADD ALL. This dialogue box also has OK and CANCEL buttons.

Look at the left box. It lists all the applications that Windows Setup found. Your mission, should you choose to accept it, is to decide which applications you wish to set up to be runnable within Windows. You add all those listed in the right hand box when you eventually press the OK button.

You'll find some peculiarities in the list:

- Even if an application is already set-up for Windows, it will still appear in the list.

Chapter 17 The Windows Tool Box

- Windows Setup doesn't recognise all the standard Windows applications.

- Windows Setup only recognises the non-Windows applications that have been pre-programmed into it.

- The list may include programs that are parts of others. For example, a spelling checker may appear separately from the word processor of which it is a part.

You should only add applications if you are sure the one you select is the 'main' component of an application and that you want to run it within Windows. Select applications by clicking the left mouse button while the arrow is over their name. Don't add everything in sight, you'll get a hopelessly cluttered Program Manager window.

You can add more than one application by selecting each one and pressing the ADD button. Alternatively, you can select more than one, by clicking the mouse button over each one, and then press the ADD button. Clicking the mouse button over a selected application deselects it. Although this behaviour is unusual, it's sensible.

If you've added an application to the right-hand list by mistake, selecting it in the right-hand box and pressing the REMOVE button will remove it. The ADD ALL button should be treated with caution. Be prepared to REMOVE a large number of applications if you use ADD ALL.

When you press OK, Windows Setup adds icons to Program Manager groups for the applications you selected. It puts all the icons for Windows applications in a group called Windows Applications. Windows Setup puts non-Windows applications in a group called, logically enough, Non-Windows Applications. If these groups don't exist, Windows Setup creates them before adding icons to them. You'll see Windows Setup minimising Program Manager groups after changing them, so you may need to reopen them later.

Windows Setup treats some non-Windows applications as 'Utilities'. The names of these programs are followed by 'Utility' in the list boxes. When you run a Utility, having added it to the Program Manager, Windows will open a dialogue box for you to enter the command line parameters that most utilities use. It will be just as if you type the program name followed by the parameters from the MS-DOS command prompt.

Housekeeping For Windows

You've installed Windows, possibly added some more applications and now you're free. Free to explore Windows, free to enjoy the extra time that Windows will give you. You are no longer tied to your computer's way of working...

Yes, and No... If you fancy danger and don't mind losing all your work in a millionth of a second, then fine. If not, then there's some housekeeping that ensures that you can carry on enjoying Windows for years to come, secure in the knowledge you've covered yourself from most disasters.

Like the other kind of housekeeping, you'll find it better to do Windows housekeeping regularly. It won't take long and it will develop into second nature.

This section shows you how to carry out three of the most important tasks. You should:

- Back-up your computer's hard disk every week.

- Check the data on your hard disk every week.

- Build an Emergency Restart disk each time your hardware configuration changes.

If you're working to a deadline, or if the data on your disk is particularly important, you need to do your housekeeping more often. That's due to a well-known variant of Murphy's Law: 'Your computer will fail when you need it most!'

Backing-Up Your Hard Disk

Unless you have a more up-market back-up device like a tape-streamer, you must be prepared to act like a disk jockey; feeding disk after disk into your computer. If you are going to use the MS-DOS BACKUP command, all the disks must be formatted. If you're lucky enough to have a program like Central Software's PC-Tools, the disks needn't be pre-formatted, the program can format each one as it uses them. Whichever program you use, you must have sufficient disks available. You can estimate how many disks you're going to need by running CHKDSK and seeing how many bytes your files occupy. Divide that by the size of the disks your computer uses:

Type	Size (in bytes)
5 1/4' low density	360,000
5 1/4' high density	1,200,000
3 1/2' single sided	720,.000
31/2' double sided	1,440,000

The manual for the back-up program you are using will show you the command you must type to start the back-up. If you're using the MS-DOS BACKUP command, it is:

[backup *.* a: /s] and then press Enter

Label the disks and put them safely away. For extra security, you should store your back-up disks away from your computer.

Checking Your Hard Disk

It's very simple to check your hard disk using the MS-DOS CHKDSK command. You just type:

[chkdsk] and then press Enter

After some seconds of furious disk activity, your computer either shows you the amount of free and used disk space or displays some error messages. If everything's fine, then you've nothing further to do.

If there are some problems, it's time to make sure that you backed-up the disk as you're going to ask MS-DOS to fix the problems for you. Even if CHKDSK displayed messages whilst it was running that showed that it was correcting problems, it hasn't yet.

Ninety-nine times out of a hundred, it manages to repair the damage and you can carry on. But, there are ninety-nine other people running CHKDSK when you are, so check your back-ups before moving on!

To ask MS-DOS to repair the damage, type:

[chkdsk /f] and then press Enter

It will make some repairs itself but may ask whether you want to convert lost clusters into files. MS-DOS makes files from fixed sized chunks - these are clusters. Lost clusters are those that MS-DOS believes belong to files, it's just forgotten which one. If you say No, MS-DOS throws the data in these lost clusters away and returns the space that they occupied back to the pool of free space. If you say Yes, MS-DOS finds the lost clusters. In other words, it takes the space and turns it into files with meaningless names like FILE0000.CHK. Unless you suspect that a lost cluster includes critically important data, we suggest that you always type No.

Having repaired the disk, you should rerun CHKDSK just to be sure that your disk is in perfect

Chapter 17 The Windows Tool Box

health.

Important: If, having run CHKDSK a second time, it still reports errors, there's a distinct possibility that your disk is severely damaged. We have known a second try at repairing a disk, by running CHKDSK /F again, to destroy all the files on the hard disk. You should back-up all your files before running CHKDSK /F a second time.

Tip: Running CHKDSK From Within Windows

You can check your hard disk by running the MS-DOS CHKDSK program within Windows, if you are using MS DOS version 3.3 or later. Earlier versions are more unreliable, sometimes reporting errors which aren't there.

You should never ask it to repair a disk by using the /F parameter. Always do that from the DOS prompt.

Creating An Emergency Restart Disk

Before you start using Windows, and every time you upgrade your computer's hardware or the version of MS-DOS you are using, create an Emergency Restart Disk. When you use this disk, it's just like mouth-to-mouth resuscitation for your computer.

You'll be able, almost always, to restart a dead computer provided there's nothing wrong with it's hardware. No matter what state your hard disk gets itself into, you can rebuild your system from your ER... disk and your back-ups. We call this an 'ER...' disk as that's probably what you'll be saying as you realise that you need to use it!

Your ER... disk should have just enough software to allow you to boot from it and to recover your back-ups. You create it on a blank, unformatted disk by using the MS-DOS FORMAT command with an option which means: Copy the system files to this disk. If you are using the a: drive, type:

    [format a: /s] and then press Enter

Don't forget that you should copy the program to your ER...disks that you use to recover your back-ups. If you're using the MS-DOS BACKUP command, you will need a copy of

RESTORE.COM. You'll find this file in your root directory or in the directory that contains the MS-DOS commands. Look in \SYSTEM, \MSDOS or \DOS.

You should also include a copy of the FORMAT program so that you can reformat your hard disk, should that be necessary.

You may find it helpful to include a program that can test your computer but most of these are too large to fit on your ER... disk. One exception is Quarterdeck's Manifest. Although it can't tell you precisely what's wrong with your computer, Manifest lets you check how much memory your computer has and displays various hardware details.

After you've built your ER... disk, test it whilst your computer is still healthy. Reset your computer after putting the ER... disk in drive a:. Your computer may display a message asking you to type the date and time and will then display an 'A>' command prompt. You should not run Windows or any other application at this point - your ER... disk merely allows you to boot your computer before restoring your back-ups.

If you are using an IBM PS/2 computer, you also need to ensure that you keep the Reference Disk for your computer up-to-date.

Preparing For Disasters

Besides the files on your system, you also need to consider how to back-up and restore the partition table on your hard disk and, if you have an IBM PC/AT or compatible, the contents of the CMOS RAM. Although vital, these items cannot be backed-up and restored automatically by MS-DOS programs. You'll either need additional software (such as Quarterdeck's Manifest) or you'll need to do some work to restore them manually.

Your ER... disk should let you restore both the partition table and the contents of CMOS RAM if the gremlins damage them.

What's The Partition Table?

The IBM PC family was designed to allow more than one operating system to share one hard disk. Although this feature is now rarely used, it does provide a means of splitting hard disks into multiple volumes.

If your computer has than one hard disk volume (that is, if you can log onto hard disks with letters other than c:), you should check whether these share the same hard disk. If so, your hard disk has been 'partitioned' and you need to record the settings in the partition table.

Some versions of MS-DOS include the FDISK program that can read the partition table. You can make a note of the settings so that, after you've booted from your ER... disk, you can type the settings in manually. To find these settings, type:

    [fdisk] and then press Enter

The numbers you want to record will be displayed if you select option 4 - Display partition data. If there is only one partition displayed, then you'll know that you can format that hard disk as one MS-DOS volume if a crash makes this necessary. If there's more than one, you'll have to run FDISK to recreate the partitions if you ever need to format your hard disk.

Unless you have a disk repair program, you cannot assume that any data on your hard disk is safe if you have to run FDISK to recover from a crash. You should always restore the contents of that disk from your latest back-up.

What Is CMOS RAM?

IBM PC/AT or compatible computers, and most 386/486 clones, have an area of memory which stores essential data about the hardware configuration of your computer. The battery that supplies the clock/calender powers the CMOS RAM as well, so its contents will be retained even when you turn your computer off.

Occasionally, a crash may damage the data held there. Apart from the minor inconvenience of making you set the date and time, corruption of this memory can stop your computer accessing its hard disk.

To avoid this possibility, you should learn how to read and restore the contents of CMOS RAM. It's easiest to use programs like Central Software's PC-Tools or Norton's Utilities.

Even if you can't purchase additional software, most clone computers include a built-in program called a BIOS as part of their basic software. You should refer to the operating instructions for your computer to find how to use the BIOS to read and set the various CMOS RAM settings. You may find that you need to press a special key when you turn on your computer.

What's In The BIOS?

When you turn your computer on, the first thing it does is to run the BIOS - that's an abbreviation for Basic Input/Output System. This program looks at what equipment your

Chapter 17 The Windows Tool Box

computer has, loads MS-DOS from disk and then hands your computer over to MS-DOS.

MS-DOS and Windows need answers to questions like:

- How many disk drives are there?

- How big are they?

- How much memory does your computer has? Does it all work?

- Where is everything within your computer?

Here is the catch question... If your computer doesn't know where everything is to start with, where is the information stored? It can't be on the disk, because your computer doesn't know how to read that yet. It can't be built-in to the BIOS program because you can have different sorts of disk drive. The answer - this data is stored in CMOS RAM. One important piece of information that is stored there is what disk drives your computer has.

Your computer will have one PRIMARY disk drive (usually drive a:) and some SECONDARY ones (these may be b: and then the hard disks c:, d: and so on).

When you boot, the BIOS will try loading from the PRIMARY disk drive first. Your a: drive will burst into life, only for the BIOS to find that there is no disk. The BIOS then moves on to the SECONDARY drives until it finds your hard disk. It will read the first part of MS-DOS and then that will load the rest. The BIOS program also reads the time and date from your computer's clock and sets up the clock used by MS-DOS.

Most BIOS programs include a facility to allow you to select which drives you want as PRIMARY and SECONDARY. You may have noticed when you start your computer there is a message like `Press ESC to run SETUP'. This SETUP program is a totally different one to Windows Setup. The message that your BIOS displays varies from computer to computer. If you are fortunate enough to have a copy of your computer's hardware manual, you may find additional information there on how to use SETUP to change CMOS RAM settings.

Look at what the settings are and copy down the numbers on a piece of paper. You may find that to look at the settings, you have to say that you want to change them. If so, you may also have to save the unchanged settings. Put your note of the settings in a safe place - preferably where you can find it again!

Some older computers do not have a `SETUP' option in the BIOS program, they need an

Chapter 17 The Windows Tool Box

additional program on disk. This program is normally called `SETUP' (what a surprise!) and you should make sure that you copy this program onto your ER... disk. If this program was just on your hard disk you could find yourself in a `Catch 22' situation. The CMOS RAM settings may not allow the BIOS to look at your hard disk, and you can't change it because you can't run the program from your hard disk. If you find that the PRIMARY disk drive setting is corrupted in the CMOS RAM, you may need to disconnect the battery for a short time. When you boot your computer, the BIOS will then use settings that will at least allow you to read floppy disks.

The CMOS RAM Battery

Occasionally, the battery that supplies power to the CMOS RAM and the clock/calendar goes flat. If that happens, the effect is just as if the data has been damaged - your computer will have forgotten the date and may not be able to boot. Luckily, the clock seems to stop just before the battery goes flat so you'll have some notice.

When this happens, it can be very confusing. Your first reaction is to call in the supplier to repair your computer. If you do, ask them to replace the internal battery with an external battery pack so that you can replace it yourself when it next goes flat.

Running Non-Windows Programs

We've suggested that you don't run MS-DOS programs from within Windows. Nonetheless, there are occasions when you may want to run a program that is not available in a Windows version. It seems a pity to leave Windows, run the program and then restart Windows.

For these occasions, three methods are available. You can run non-Windows programs:

- From the Program Manager's File Run menu option.

    Simply type the full pathname, filename and extension of the application. When your application ends, you return to Windows.

- From the DOS Prompt.

    After you double click on the DOS Prompt icon in the Main Program Manager group, Windows creates a computer within a computer. The screen will clear and you'll see the familiar MS-DOS command prompt. After each program ends, you return to the MS-DOS command prompt. To return to Windows, you type:

Chapter 17 The Windows Tool Box

[exit] and then press Enter.

- By adding them as icons in Program Manager groups.

If you want to run the same program frequently, you can add it as an icon to a Program Manager group. That way, running the program is as easy as double clicking its icon. When the program ends, you return to Windows.

Tip: Before Running Non-Windows Programs

Before running a non-Windows program, particularly one that you haven't tried running under Windows before, we'd suggest that you save any work in open (or minimised) windows.

That way, you'll be able to carry on with your work even if the non-Windows application doesn't agree with Windows.

There are just two more things you need to know:

Windows lets you exercise control over non-Windows programs. Each program can have a Program Information File, or PIF, which stores the settings you've decided on.

AND

If you have a 386 computer, and are running Windows in 386 Enhanced mode, you can run non-Windows programs within windows.

What Are PIF Files?

You may be surprised to find, when you select the Program Manager's File Properties option, that the command line for a non-Windows program isn't always the program name itself.

If Windows Setup added the application or if somebody who knows Windows added it, the command line is likely to be a file with a .PIF extension. These PIF files contain information about the program that Windows uses to ensure that non-Windows programs can live in harmony with Windows programs in Windows World.

You can create your own PIF files for non-Windows programs that you add yourself by using the

PIF Editor. There's a file called _DEFAULT.PIF (yes, the first character really is an underline) that contains the initial settings of all the options.

Basic PIF Editor Options

Depending on whether Windows is running in Real/Standard or 386 Enhanced mode, the PIF Editor displays a different dialogue box. You can create a 386 Enhanced mode PIF file even if you're running in Real or Standard mode, but your non-Windows program may not run until you switch to 386 Enhanced mode.

Some options are common to both modes. The Program Filename is the full pathname, filename and extension of the program to be run. You can decide on a Window Title. In Real/Standard mode, this will just appear under the icon when the program is a minimised icon. In 386 Enhanced mode it will also appear in the title bar when the program is running in a window. If you leave this box blank, Windows uses the program name without the extension.

You can list Optional Parameters that are not optional - whenever you run the program, they get added to the command line. You can decide a Start-up Directory; this creates the illusion for the non-Windows program that it started in that directory. You will normally select that you want to Close the Window on Exit.

PIF Editor In Standard Mode

In standard mode, the PIF Editor allows you to specify:

- Whether the program is text-only and uses only a single display page or requires graphics or multiple display pages.

- The amount of conventional and extended memory your non-Windows program will use.

- Whether the non-Windows program directly modifies the hardware controlling your computer's serial ports and keyboard or whether it uses equivalent MS-DOS functions.

- Whether you intend to use the PrtSc key to transfer snapshots of non-Windows screens to the clipboard. Select No Screen Exchange if you do not want to take snapshots.

- Whether you want to switch back and forward between Windows and the non-Windows application whilst it is running. Select the Prevent Program Switch button if you don't intend to do this.

• Which keys your non-Windows applications needs that Windows normally reserves for its own use. You just list here those keys that would normally be interpreted by Windows when your non-Windows application is running. All other key combinations, such as [Alt + F], go straight to your program.

PIF Editor In 386 Enhanced Mode

Windows provides more control over non-Windows applications when it's in 386 Enhanced mode. There's so many settings that they're divided into two parts, one labelled Advanced. You get to these advanced settings by pressing the ADVANCED button in the dialogue box.

The basic options allow you to decide:

• The amount of conventional memory required by your non-Windows application. If the program operates more efficiently with more memory, you can ask for a larger amount than your programs need to run by typing a number into the Desired box.

• Whether your non-Windows program will initially run full-screen or in a window.

• Whether you want your non-Windows program to be able to run in the Background - that is, to continue running when it's a minimised icon.

• Whether you want your non-Windows application to have Exclusive use of your computer when it's running as the active window. This stops multi-tasking and is useful when the non-Windows application needs constant access to your computer's hardware. If you select this option, background Windows applications will not continue running when your non-Windows program is in the active window.

The advanced options determine:

• The priorities to be assigned to Foreground and Background tasks. A foreground task is that in the active window, background tasks are the rest.

• The amount of expanded and extended memory that your non-Windows program requires and the maximum amounts it can be allowed to occupy.

• Whether the expanded, extended or conventional ('application') memory is Locked into physical memory or whether Windows can treat the memory as able to be paged to and from disk. You should only lock memory for an application that uses interrupts or must respond to external events.

Chapter 17 The Windows Tool Box

• Whether your non-Windows program uses the high memory area; that is, the area between 640 Kilobyte and 1 Megabyte.

• The Display Options options are only applicable to some types of display. You should deselect the Emulate Text Mode box only if the display gets garbled. The Video Memory options determine how much video memory your non-Windows application will need - this depends on what video mode your application operates in. The Monitor Ports options may be used if your application directly accesses the display controller hardware. Windows will look at the controller registers and 'track' changes. If you close the window of a non-Windows application and subsequently reopen it, Windows will then be able to restore the correct settings to the registers before re-displaying the window. If you deselect the Retain Video Memory box, and your non-Windows alters video modes, you will free memory for other tasks. Against this, you may lose the display of your non-Windows application if Windows runs short of memory.

• Whether you want to be able to close (that is, stop) your non-Windows application even if it is active. You should only select the Allow Close When Active box if your non-Windows application never alters any data on your hard disk. If it can store data, then you could cause serious data loss if you stop the application when it is in the middle of a sequence of disk operations.

• Whether your non-Windows application can support the Fast Paste option when Windows pastes data to it from the Clipboard. If in doubt, leave it deselected.

• Which keys your non-Windows applications needs that Windows normally reserves.for its own use list just those keys that would normally be interpreted by Windows when your non-Windows application is active. All the other key combinations, such as [Alt + F], go straight to your program.

• The key you will use to make your non-Windows application active. This key, called the Application Shortcut Key, will be recognised whenever you press it (even if you're running another Windows or non-Windows application) so you should take care to choose a unique combination of keys. You press the actual combination of keys that you want to use; the PIF Editor displays the keystroke as a code using 'Ctrl', 'Alt' and 'Shift'.

Choosing PIF Settings

With so many settings, it's easy to get overwhelmed and end up getting lost in a maze of interrelated options. You should follow the general principle of only altering any settings if it's absolutely necessary.

If you need guidance on a particular setting, the help pages for the PIF Editor are quite enlightening.

The Window Control Menu For A Non-Windows Application

In 386 Enhanced mode, when you run a non-Windows application in a window, the Window Control Menu has two extra options. You'll also find that pressing [Alt + Spacebar] when a non-Windows application is running full-screen converts the program's display to a window before opening the window control menu.

The two extra options are Edit and Settings. You use items in the Edit hidden menu to transfer data between the clipboard and your non-Window application. Settings opens a dialogue box which duplicates some settings you initially set up in the PIF Editor. You can also Terminate your non-Windows application from here, if you selected the Allow Close When Active box in the Advanced PIF options.

Using The Clipboard With Non-Windows Applications

It's amazing, when you think of the different worlds that they inhabit, that you're able to transfer data between Windows and non-Windows applications.

The gateway between the two worlds consists of the Clipboard and the options on the Edit hidden menu.

To copy data from a Windows to a non-Windows Application, use the Edit Cut or Copy options to load the Clipboard with the data. Then, when you select the Paste option from the Edit hidden menu, you transfer the data to your non-Windows application. That's all there is to it!

To copy data the other way, from a non-Windows application to Windows, you must first select Mark from the Edit hidden menu. You then drag out a highlighted area that you want copied. You don't have to use the Edit menu, you can just drag the mouse over the area you want to copy.

Next, select Copy from the Edit hidden menu. That loads the data in the Clipboard, ready to be transported to whichever Windows application needs it. You simply choose Paste from the Edit menu from there and the data is pasted before your eyes.

Chapter 18 - The First Aid Box

On your travels round Windows' world, you may need assistance to deal with little accidents. In the real world, you'd just say 'Ouch!', get out your first aid kit and carry on.

So, here it is; your very own Windows First Aid Kit. We haven't included plasters or aspirins but we hope you find that it soothes cuts and bruises and cures headaches just as effectively.

We won't be giving you all the answers here but we've covered the most common ills. The prescriptions given here will allow you to continue using Windows even after a disaster. Please don't give up on Windows, the gains are greater than the pains!

Running Windows If WIN Doesn't Work

We've said that running Windows is as easy as typing WIN at the MS-DOS command prompt. Normally, Windows displays its start-up screen and then, after a short delay, you see the Program Manager's window. Away you go, either to the far corners of Windows world, or perhaps, just a little way in to write a quick postcard.

Don't panic if Windows doesn't run; there's normally a simple explanation. You should first check:

- That you've installed Windows on your computer.

Look for a directory called \WINDOWS and see if it contains about 85 files. You should find it contains a file called WIN.EXE.

- That MS-DOS knows where Windows is.

To check that the directory containing Windows is on the path, type [path] and then press [Enter]. If so, MS-DOS knows where it is.

- That your computer can run Windows.

You should have a hard disk, at least 640 Kilobytes of memory and a CGA (or better)

Chapter 18 The First Aid Box

display.

• That you're not using TSR programs, like Borland's Sidekick, that you can run from inside other applications.

If you find such programs, edit your Autoexec and Config files so that they don't get run.

If you don't know how to do these checks, see the Learning The Lingo and the Tool Box chapters. If Windows doesn't run, your computer may be one of those on which Windows works, but only if you set its Mode.

Windows Modes

Windows has three modes: Real, Standard and 386 Enhanced.

These are:

Real: This mode ensures maximum compatibility with earlier versions of Windows. It can run on computers with 8088 or 80806 processors.

Standard: This mode requires a 286 processor and at least 1Megabyte of memory.

386 Enhanced: The 'deluxe' mode. This requires a 386 processor and 2 Megabytes of memory.

You set the Mode by adding a parameter onto the WIN command you use to start Windows:

[win /r] - starts Windows in Real mode

[win /s] - starts Windows in Standard mode

[win /3] - starts Windows in 386 Enhanced mode

If your computer can support 386 Enhanced mode, you should use that in preference to Standard mode as Windows then uses Virtual Memory.

Chapter 18 The First Aid Box

Tip: What's Virtual Memory?

When Windows runs in 386 Enhanced mode, it can give you more memory to work with than is available on your computer. Sounds like magic, doesn't it?

Windows does this by setting aside an area on your hard disk and then swapping parts of your data back and forth between memory and disk. To avoid you having to wait while it does this, Windows uses clever techniques that allow it, most of the time, to predict which parts of your data are in use and which parts are not being accessed.

If you want to get the most from Windows when it's swapping, you can help it by setting aside an area of your hard disk for it's exclusive use. The official User Guide shows you how to do this. You start Windows in Real mode and run a program called SWAPFILE.

No Life In Your Mouse

The following may help if your mouse is not its normal perky self. It may also save you some very expensive vet bills!..

- Check that you've connected your mouse

- Some mice can emulate (behave like) other types of mice

Check whether your's is one of these. If so, you need to find out how to make it emulate a Microsoft mouse. Typically, your mouse may need you to hold down one of its buttons while you turn your computer on.

- You may have selected the wrong type of mouse when you installed Windows

Run the Windows Setup application. If you do change the type of the mouse, don't forget that you'll have to restart Windows to see whether the change solves the problem.

No Display?

If you've selected the wrong display, Windows might not give you anything on the screen. Or, you might get a pattern like a television out of tune. You should find out what type of display you have and then run Setup from the MS-DOS command prompt.

Chapter 18 The First Aid Box

Tip: Using Setup from MS-DOS

Windows Setup can run from the MS-DOS command prompt, rather than within Windows itself. You should change your current directory to the one containing Windows, type [setup] and then press Enter.

Running Setup from MS-DOS allows you to correct configuration errors which stop Windows running. You could find it a life-saver. For example, it can be used if you select an incompatible display type and then can't use Windows.

Running Setup in this way only gives you the Hardware Configuration screen. You can change configurations, then reset your computer and try again.

Unrecoverable Application Errors

The most common Gremlin you will experience is the Unrecoverable Application Error or UAE. It strikes when Windows thinks an application running within it is trying to do something either fishy or downright dangerous. Windows is trying to protect itself from an application that has gone wild. That's not to say that badly written applications are to blame for every UAE. Sometimes, Windows and the application simply don't agree. It happens even within Windows' close family!

Whoever is to blame, you're the loser. While protecting itself, Windows doesn't seem to care about what you, the user, might want to do. It just says 'Enough is enough' and stops the application it disagrees with, without so much as a 'by your leave'. To be fair, Windows has other things to think about. In particular, it has its own integrity and those of the other applications to consider.

You'd imagine that was it, you'd lost nothing other than that application. You'd think that you could rerun the application, open the back-up file (that you saved not long ago) and carry on... But the problem goes deeper than that, the application may have told Windows things, like which system resources it needs. It will have intended to tell Windows when it has finished with them. But, the UAE stops it in its tracks. Sure, Windows will try to tidy up but the job seems beyond it in all but the simplest circumstances.

A UAE leaves Windows in an unstable state. You won't know whether Windows is coming or going! It may run perfectly happily. Or, more likely, it has got itself into more of a mess trying to sort out the mess that resulted from terminating the original application. Whatever the outcome, it's definitively best to play safe.

After A UAE...

Following a UAE, you should always:

- Get out of Windows FAST!

The safest way is to select the Exit option from the Program Manager's File menu. If there are any open applications running with files that need saving, this will make them each active to allow you to save any work you've not recently saved. Be careful. If you don't have to save a file, don't!

If you get another UAE whilst exiting, Windows really is in a mess. So, don't save any further files.

- Once you've returned to the MS-DOS command prompt, reset your computer.

We've found that MS-DOS may also be affected by a UAE. While MS-DOS commands may seem to work, there's a good chance of getting another UAE when you restart Windows. Resetting your computer cleans the slate and forces all of MS-DOS to be loaded afresh.

- Check your hard disk when your computer has been reset.

It's important that you detect and repair any problems before you continue. See the Checking Your Hard Disk section in the Tool Box chapter to find out how to use CHKDSK to check your disk.

- Only after running CHKDSK, and correcting any errors that it highlighted, should you run Windows.

- If, when you rerun Windows, you still get UAE's, it may be best to turn off your computer. Leave it for five or ten seconds and then turn it back on.

We've found no hard evidence, but we've found that doing this seems to improve subsequent reliability. It's almost as if, occasionally, Windows gets in such a state that even resetting doesn't erase all of the problem from memory.

Tip: Lots Of Unrecoverable Application Errors

If you experience, on average, more than one UAE a day, it may be because your computer isn't a true clone of the IBM PC family. You may find that your supplier can supply you with a disk containing special drivers for your model of computer. If not, you should try running Windows in another Mode. If your computer has a 386 processor, try starting Windows with [win /s] rather than just [win].

If that doesn't improve reliability, you may have something wrong with your computer. Get it checked.

Crash Recovery

Windows crashes more often than it should...

Don't Panic! Most crashes are quite harmless. You may lose your work since you last saved your current file. But you've recently saved your file, haven't you? If not, you'll soon develop the habit of saving your work every few minutes and then, when the inevitable crash does happen, you'll just restart (following the guidelines given later) and carry on.

Recognising A Crash

Apart from times when Windows refuses to listen to either the mouse or the keyboard, there are other possibilities. Windows may:

- Refuse to respond to the mouse but it happily continues when you press keys

- Unexpectedly exits back to MS-DOS

- Cause your computer to reset

- Starts doing 'strange' things like misinterpreting keystrokes or mouse clicks.

Whatever happens, you'll soon know about it!

Chapter 18 The First Aid Box

After A Crash...

The steps you should follow after a crash are similar to those after a UAE. You should:

- If you're still in control, get out of Windows FAST!

The safest way is to select the Exit option from the Program Manager's File menu. If there are any open applications running with files that need saving, this will make them each active to allow you to save any work you've not recently saved. Be careful. If you don't have to save a file, don't!

If you get a UAE whilst exiting, Windows really is in a mess. So, don't save any further files.

- Once you've returned to the MS-DOS command prompt, reset your computer.

We've found that MS-DOS may also be affected by a crash. While MS-DOS commands may seem to work, there's a good chance of getting a UAE when you restart Windows. Resetting your computer cleans the slate and forces all of MS-DOS to be loaded afresh.

- If you can't talk to Windows, you'll have to reset your computer.

Before you reach for the Big Red Switch (well, on IBM PCs it's red and it's large) or press the [Ctrl + Alt + Del] key combination to reset your computer, check that you can't use the keyboard to exit from Windows. Doing that is much safer.

- Check your hard disk when your computer has been reset.

It's important that you detect and repair any problems before you continue. See the Checking Your Hard Disk section in the Tool Box chapter to find out how to use CHKDSK to check your disk.

- Only after running CHKDSK, and correcting any errors that it highlighted, should you run Windows.

- If, when you rerun Windows, you still get problems, it may be best to turn off your computer. Leave it for five or ten seconds and then turn it back on.

Chapter 18 The First Aid Box

Disaster Recovery

This section explains how to recover from the 'Nightmare Scenario' - where a crash leaves your computer in a state where it can't boot from its hard disk.

The good news is that this rarely happens; all three of us have been using Windows intensively for over eighteen months and we've only ever had this happen once. Even then, it happened when we were trying out some new software so we don't know for sure whether the crash was Windows' fault.

The bad news is that when it does happen, it leaves you feeling numb with shock. We've seen assessments of the stress factors of everyday life; things like divorce, losing your house and so on. We reckon that finding your computer doesn't boot must be up near the top of such a list.

You should ALWAYS check your hard disk's health after a crash by using CHKDSK - see the Tool Box chapter. Never be tempted to hurry on. If you do, your hard disk could suffer a sort of creeping paralysis that is very difficult to detect and even more difficult to cure.

Disaster Recovery - Initial Steps

No matter how bad you feel, always stay calm and try the following:

- Try resetting your computer again...

  You can either try the [Ctrl + Alt + Del] key combination or press the Reset switch, if your computer has one.

  Simple perhaps, but our experience shows that this is a very effective cure. Normally, you'll breathe a sigh of relief and vow to keep your back-ups up-to-date for the rest of your life - or until you next forget to do them!

- Even if that doesn't work, turn your computer off, leave it for five or ten seconds and then turn it on again.

  Again, a simple but usually effective cure. This may work, when resetting fails, because your computer is starting from scratch rather than remembering the tangle it had been in.

Chapter 18 The First Aid Box

Disaster Recovery - Before You Panic

You're probably now getting worried. Your boss may be looking over your shoulder and you're close to panic... Don't panic (yet!) we're still here to help.

This is where your ER... (Emergency Restart) disk comes into its own.

Even if you didn't make one, it may not be the end of the road. You may find somebody with a computer that is compatible with yours and be able to persuade / bribe / cajole them into letting you use their ER... disk or let you build one. See the Tool Box chapter for details on how to do that.

When you use the ER... disk, it's just like Mouth-to-Mouth resuscitation for your computer. Follow the steps below:

- Put the ER... disk in a disk drive, normally a:, and boot your computer by pressing [Ctrl + Alt + Del] together or by pressing your computer's Reset switch.

    Your computer should read the disk and, after a few moments, display a prompt: 'a>'. You may be asked for the date and time.

    You are now, at least, talking to your computer. Do a directory listing of the floppy disk by typing:

    [dir a:] and then press Enter

    If your computer doesn't display a directory listing, and you're sure that you typed the command correctly, then it's likely that your computer is ill. Call in the doctor, sorry, call an engineer!

    If that worked, it's safe to assume that your computer with its monitor and keyboard are working. Your only problem will be what to do about your hard disk.

- You should now ask your computer to try reading its hard disk. Type:

    [dir c:\] and then press Enter

    Your computer should display a list of the directories in the hard disk's root directory. If it does, then you should run CHKDSK to check your hard disk. When that works, you know that all your work is probably safe. The reason your computer didn't boot may be that some of the MS-DOS files have been corrupted.

After logging onto your hard disk, you can try copying the system files from your ER... disk to the hard disk. See the manual for the version of MS-DOS that you are using for details on how to do this. If this is successful, try resetting your computer, check your hard disk and then run Windows.

- Your computer may access the hard disk (look at the little light on the hard disk drive) but then cannot read its directory.

If that happens, it's likely that you have a hardware problem or that your computer has corrupted some of the data on your hard disk. Unless you have a disk repair program, you should find your back-ups and then call in the doctor. After your computer is returned to health, the doctor may prescribe a reformat of your hard disk. If so, you'll have to reload all your data from your back-ups.

- If your computer doesn't read your ER... disk, or if it doesn't access the correct hard disk, then your computer's CMOS RAM may have lost its memory.

If you have a SETUP option in your BIOS or your ER... disk includes a program to set up the CMOS RAM, you should reset your computer and then start the SETUP routine in BIOS by pressing the specified key. Check the settings in the CMOS RAM, change them if necessary and then try resetting your computer. If your computer's BIOS doesn't have a SETUP option and your ER... doesn't include a program to set up the CMOS RAM, try disconnecting the battery that supplies the CMOS RAM. That will force your computer to use the factory settings. If neither of these methods work, you should call in the doctor. As before, the doctor may prescribe the drastic medicine of reformatting your hard disk, so find your back-ups.

Cures For Windows Traveller's Diseases

We're now going to look at three common diseases that Windows travellers can suffer from:

- Out-of-Memory Disease

- Out-of-Disk Space Sickness

Chapter 18 The First Aid Box

- Slowness Syndrome

While none of these complaints are fatal, prevention is definitely better than cure, so this section concentrates on vaccines rather than medicines.

Out-of-Memory Disorder

The obvious cure, buying more memory, is worse than the original disease as it can lead to Memory Addiction that is expensive and difficult to resist. It may cause you to go on raids of other users' computers - just to get another Megabyte. It may even lead to your computer's death from a heart attack (that is, power supply failure) if your computer becomes overloaded with memory.

The proper cure is to avoid running too many programs at once within Windows. That way, your computer can remain lean and fit.

The About item in Program Manager's Help menu opens a dialogue box that shows the amount of memory that Windows has available for your programs and data. If you are using 386 Enhanced mode, don't be surprised if Windows seems to have found more memory than your computer has. The figure shown includes both the real memory in your computer and the virtual memory that Windows creates on your hard disk.

You should avoid wallpaper. We know it's pretty but it's a memory hog. When Windows places a window over your wallpaper, it puts a copy of the wallpaper in memory. To a lesser extent, the same thing happens whenever you overlay one window on top of another, particularly if you're using Paintbrush. The cure is to keep your Windows desktop as tidy as your real desktop!

If you've installed either Smartdrv or RamDrive (see the Slowness Syndrome section later in this chapter) then you've reserved memory for their exclusive use. That's fine, the performance of your computer when running Windows will be significantly enhanced. If you get tight on memory, you can always just reduce the amount of memory they use whilst retaining most of the benefits they bring.

If you're running Windows in 386 Enhanced mode, don't forget that Windows is using a part of your disk to extend the memory you have available. It may be worthwhile using a disk compaction utility so that Windows can use more of your disk as a 'swap' area and hence give you more virtual memory to work with.

Shortness Of System Resources

Sometimes, you'll see an Out of Memory dialogue box when you know that you have plenty of memory available. Windows has several sorts of memory under its control.

Often, the first one to run out is the pool called 'System Resources'. You can see how many System Resources are available by selecting the About option in Program Manager's Help menu. The figure shows what percentage of the total available Windows has free. If this drops below about 15%, you're heading for a problem. Closing windows will release System Resources for other programs.

Out-of-Disk Space Sickness

You'll have to adopt a strategy of deleting files from your hard disk if they aren't in use. The Space Traveller's Guide to overcoming Space Sickness suggests the following cures:

- Delete .TMP files

After a crash, Windows applications may leave temporary files on your hard disk. These are just working files and contain no useful data so you can safely delete them all. Don't delete these files from the File Manager if there are other applications running - you might delete a working file of an application that's actually reading or writing data on your hard disk.

- Consider deleting Write back-up files

If you have allowed Write to create back-up files, that's those with .BKP and .BAK extensions, you may find that your hard disk quickly fills up with old back-up files. We're not suggesting that you need to delete them all, be as selective or as brutal as your lack of disk space requires.

- Consider Archiving or Compressing Paintbrush files

Graphics files (that includes Write documents and Card files with pictures) take a lot of disk space. If you have such files that are no longer in active use, consider archiving them to disk or tape and then deleting them from your hard disk. As an alternative, these files are ideal candidates to be Compressed. Compressed files occupy much less space but are nearly as accessible as the originals. You may need additional software, such as LHARC, but such programs are available as Shareware for very little cost.

Chapter 18 The First Aid Box

- Consider deleting unused MS-DOS applications

Now you're using Windows, you'll be loath to return to your old non-Windows applications. You may be able to back-up these programs and then delete them from your hard disk. Don't forget that most application programs consist of more than just the program file itself. For example, a word processor may have separate files for its spelling checker and printer driver. You should back-up and then delete these files as well.

- Consider deleting some of Windows files

There are many files that Setup loads when you install Windows on your hard disk that you will rarely use. You can reduce the disk space that Windows occupies from 4.9 Megabytes to about 2.2 Megabytes if you drastically prune these files. Generally, don't prune more than you have to. You'll find that the other cures we've suggested are more effective.

If you decide to delete any Windows files, take back-ups before you delete them. If you later decide to reinstate any files, restoring these back-ups is simpler than following the official User Guide instructions on how to expand files from the original Windows disks.

You can delete all the files with .BMP extension if you don't mind living in a Windows World without wallpaper. The Windows games (Solitaire and Reversi) may be amusing but they can go after you've got bored with them. The on-line documents could be deleted after you've printed them, they've the files with .TXT extensions.

You may find that you never use some of the standard applications, like Notepad or Calendar, so they can go. Don't forget that they each have both a .EXE file for the program and a .HLP file for their help information.

If you can live in a fontless world, most of the .FON files in the SYSTEM subdirectory can be deleted. Leave HELVE.FON or you won't be able to read such essentials as dialogue boxes and help screens.

We've included the table overleaf to show which application use which files. Your Windows directory may contain different files, depending on your computer's hardware and the version of Windows that you're using.

Chapter 18 The First Aid Box

Contents of \WINDOWS Directory

SETUP	EXE		CALENDAR	HLP	*Calendar	
SETUP	HLP		CLIPBRD	HLP		
WINHELP	HLP		CONTROL	HLP		
WINHELP	EXE		NOTEPAD	HLP	*Notepad	
WIN	INI		PBRUSH	HLP	*Paintbrush	
SYSTEM	INI		PIFEDIT	HLP		
WIN	COM		PRINTMAN	HLP	*Print Manager	
CONTROL	INI		PROGMAN	HLP		
RAMDRIVE	SYS	*Ramdrive	RECORDER	HLP	*Recorder	
SMARTDRV	SYS	*Smartdrv	REVERSI	HLP	*Reversi game	
EMM386	SYS	*386 Enhanced Mode	SOL	HLP	*Solitaire game	
WINVER	EXE		TERMINAL	HLP	*Terminal	
PROGMAN	EXE		WINFILE	HLP		
WINFILE	EXE		WRITE	HLP	*Write	
CALC	EXE	*Calculator	CARDFILE	HLP	*Cardfile	
CALENDAR	EXE	*Calendar	PYRAMID	BMP	*wallpaper	
CARDFILE	EXE	*Cardfile	CHESS	BMP	*wallpaper	
DIGITAL	FON		WEAVE	BMP	*wallpaper	
CONTROL	EXE		BOXES	BMP	*wallpaper	
NOTEPAD	EXE	*Notepad	PAPER	BMP	*wallpaper	
PBRUSH	EXE	*Paintbrush	README	TXT	*on-line document	
PIFEDIT	EXE		NETWORKS	TXT	*on-line document	
RECORDER	EXE	*Recorder	PRINTERS	TXT	*on-line document	
RECORDER	DLL	*Recorder	WININI	TXT	*on-line document	
REVERSI	EXE	*Reversi game	WININI2	TXT	*on-line document	
PRINTMAN	EXE	*Print Manager	SYSINI	TXT	*on-line document	
SOL	EXE	*Solataire game	SYSINI2	TXT	*on-line document	
WRITE	EXE	*Write	SYSINI3	TXT	*on-line document	
MSDOS	EXE	*MS-DOS Executive	3270	TXT	*on-line document	
TASKMAN	EXE		MOUSE	SYS		
CLIPBRD	EXE		PROGMAN	INI		
CLOCK	EXE	*Clock	MAIN1	GRP		
PBRUSH	DLL	*Paintbrush	ACCESSO0	GRP		
TERMINAL	EXE	*Terminal	GAMES	GRP	*games	
CALC	HLP	*Calculator	_DEFAULT	PIF		

Contents of \WINDOWS\SYSTEM Directory

SETUP	INF		WINOA386	MOD	*386 enhanced mode	
KERNEL	EXE		SWAPFILE	EXE	*Swapfile	
GDI	EXE		WIN386	PS2	*386 enhanced mode	
USER	EXE		WIN386	EXE	*386 enhanced mode	
WIN	CNF		KRNL286	EXE		
SYSTEM	DRV		WINOA286	MOD		
VGA	DRV		DOSX	EXE		
KEYBOARD	DRV		VGACOLOR	GR2		
MOUSE	DRV		VGA	GR3		
VGASYS	FON		CGA40WOA	FON		
VGAOEM	FON		CGA80WOA	FON		
SOUND	DRV		EGA40WOA	FON		
COMM	DRV		EGA80WOA	FON		
VGAFIX	FON		SYMBOLE	FON	*Symbol font	
VGALOGO	RLE		HELVE	FON		
VGALOGO	LGO		COURE	FON	*Courier font	
LZEXPAND	DLL		TMSRE	FON	*Tms Rmn font	
WINOLDAP	MOD		ROMAN	FON	*Roman font	
WIN87EM	DLL		SCRIPT	FON	*Script font	
SYSEDIT	EXE	*System Editor (SYD)	MODERN	FON	*Modern font	
KRNL386	EXE	*386 enhanced mode				

271

Slowness Syndrome

We've called slowness a 'syndrome' rather than a disease as it can have several causes. Whatever the cause, the result is the same: you get frustrated and cease to enjoy life in Windows World.

The Truth About Improving Windows Performance

Let's tell the truth. Even if you follow all our suggestions for speeding up Windows on your computer, you are unlikely to make a substantial improvement to its performance.

Despite the huge leaps in performance over the last ten years, remember that Windows puts any computer through its paces. It pushes your computer to its limits on all fronts: memory, processor speed, disk speed and video speed. Making improvements on one front is unlikely to improve the performance dramatically. You need faster hardware to do that!

Cures for Slowness Syndrome

The official User Guide gives many, detailed, suggestions. We'll just summarise them here:

- Configure all your Memory as Extended

If your computer has additional memory beyond 640 Kilobytes, it will either be configured as Expanded or Extended.

Accessing Expanded memory is slower than accessing Extended memory but some major MS-DOS applications, such as Lotus 1-2-3, only support Expanded memory. If you configure all your memory as Extended, Windows will perform better.

If you can run Windows in 386 Enhanced mode, you can set aside part of your Extended memory to act as Expanded, for those applications that need that. The official User Guide tells you how to install EMM386.SYS in your computer's CONFIG.SYS file.

- Install the Smartdrv Disk Cache Program

You can install SMARTDRV.SYS in your CONFIG.SYS file - the Official User Guide tells you how and suggests settings for the optional parameters.

Smartdrv is a disk cache program that works out what parts of your hard disk you are using most often and holds them in memory. Then, when Windows needs the data, Smartdrv delivers it from memory, so avoiding the delays associated with reading the disk.

It's a clever little beast. It has to work out, merely by watching what Windows does, which parts of the data you've finished with for good and those that are going to be used again in a few moments. It then uses the memory that hold those parts that you've finished with to hold the data it thinks you're going to need.

Smartdrv isn't always right. Sometimes, it may slow your computer down by moving large chunks of data to and from your hard disk that are only going to be used once.

- Install the Ramdrive RAM Disk Program

The Windows package includes another program that uses your computer's RAM for disk storage. You can install RAMDRIVE.SYS by following the instructions in the official User Guide.

Ramdrive simulates a disk drive by setting aside an area of memory. Instead of reading or writing to the disk, it reads and writes this memory area. It's different to Smartdrv because that stores part of your hard disk in memory.

An ideal use for this simulated disk drive is to store the temporary files that Windows creates. To do this, you must include a command in your AUTOEXEC.BAT telling Windows to use this disk. Typically, this command should be:

[set temp=d:\]

The drive letter you use, d: in the above example, may need changing if your computer has more than one hard disk volume. It will be the next letter along from the last hard disk letter.

If your computer has limited memory, it's best to use just Smartdrv. Access to temporary files will be speeded up anyway.

- Compact your Hard Disk

As you use your computer, MS-DOS creates and deletes files. When it creates a file, MS-DOS decides where to put your data. When you delete a file, MS-DOS doesn't move other files to fill the gap, it just leaves holes. If files grow, they may clash with other files. When that happens, MS-DOS just continues the file either at the end of the disk or, more likely,

Chapter 18 The First Aid Box

by re-using the space left behind by a deleted file. Eventually, your hard disk looks like Swiss cheese, with files, holes and more files scattered all over.

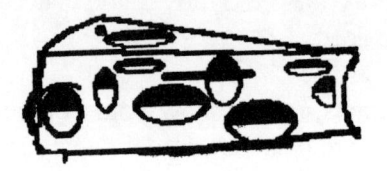

Windows likes files. It likes to create lots of files. Most never see the light of day but are erased almost as soon as they a recreated. MS-DOS tolerates this behaviour with good humour - it just goes on allocating space on the disk as always - splitting files when they clash with others and filling in gaps.

Your computer reads or writes most files from beginning to end. When MS-DOS splits a file into pieces, the disk drive must find the next chunk before it can continue reading or writing the file. For large files, and Windows can create very large files, the time taken in finding each piece can easily double the time it takes to read the file.

The result of this is to slow down your computer.

MS-DOS itself doesn't provide a solution. You need to buy a disk compaction utility, such as Compress, in Central Software's PC-Tools. These utilities take all the files on your hard disk and then shuffles them so that every piece of each file is together. They also move all the files up to the 'beginning' of the disk so that the free space is all at the 'end'.

You can do the same thing by backing-up your hard disk, deleting all the files and then restoring all your data. We wouldn't recommend doing that unless your computer is running very slowly and you can't buy a compaction utility.

- Use a Permanent Swap File

If you're running Windows in 386 Enhanced mode, you should create a Permanent Swap File (PSF). As we've seen, Windows can use disk space as Virtual Memory and so expand the amount of memory your computer can work with.

Chapter 18 The First Aid Box

A Permanent, as opposed to a Temporary, Swap File is an area on your hard disk set aside for Windows' exclusive use. As only Windows has access to this area, it can by-pass MS-DOS and transfer data much faster.

To create a PSF, you must start Windows in Real mode. To do this, type: [win /r] from the MS-DOS prompt.

Then, select the Run option from Program Manager's File menu. Start the SWAPFILE.EXE program. It looks at your hard disk and finds the largest empty hole. As an initial setting, it assumes that you want to use half of this hole for the PSF. You can change this from the dialogue box.

If your hard disk fills up after you've created a PSF, you can change its size by running SWAPFILE again.

- Alter the Order of Directories in your PATH Command

One of the commands that you'll find in the AUTOEXEC.BAT file, executed each time you boot your computer, is PATH. PATH is followed by a list of directories. MS-DOS searches each directory in this list, one after another, whenever it or Windows runs a program.

You should change the PATH command so that the directory containing Windows appears first in the list. That way, MS-DOS can find Windows programs faster as it will look in the Windows directory first.

You can change this from within Windows, using either Notepad or Syd.

Index

Active printer, 102
Active window, 38
Adding a printer, 103-104
Adding applications -Windows setup, 244-245
Adding colours, 111
Adding files to program manager, 59-60
Adding fonts, 105-106
Adding programs to program manager, 56, 59
Airbrush tool, 122
Alarms - calendar, 184-185
Aligning text -write, 158-160
Altering picture size -write, 150-151
Altering the size of a window, 34
Applications - adding, 244-245
Applications - non-Windows, 252-257
Archive attribute, 77
Archiving files, 87, 269
Arrange icon button - task list, 68
Arrange icon option - program manager, 65
Arranging your windows automatically, 39
    manually, 39
Associate option - file manager, 82
Attributes of fonts, 45
Auto arrange option - program manager, 64
Autodialing- cardfile, 180-181
Autoexec.bat, 173,236-238, 241, 273
Automatic page breaks,144

Back-ups, 87
Background - coloured, 117
Background colour, 118
Background colours, 126
Backing up - hard disk, 246-247
Backing up write files, 141-142
.Bak files, 141-142
Basic equipment, 5
Battery - CMOS RAM, 252
Baud rate - terminal communications settings, 205
Before running non-Windows programs - tip, 253
Benefits of Windows, 13-15
Binary file transfer - terminal, 208
Binary transfer - terminal settings, 205
BIOS, 250-251
BIOS setup, 251- 252, 267
Bitmap fonts, 47-48, 156
.Bkp files, 141-142
.Bmp files, 130 BOB, 210-211
Bookmark - help, 52
Border width - desktop, 113

Brackets - calculator, 190
Brush shapes option, 127-128
Brush tool, 127-128
Bulletin boards, 201

Cables null modem, 202
    types of, 210
Calculator, 187-199
    brackets, 190
    clearing, 188
    memory, 188-189
    programming functions, 192-95
    scientific, 189-197
    scientific functions,191-192
    standard, 189
    statistical functions, 197
    statistics box, 195-198
Calculator and clipboard, 167, 198 -199
Calendar, 183-186
    alarms, 184-185
    dayview, 184
    menu options, 185-186
    month view, 184
    moving around, 186
    page setup, 171-172
Cancel button - task list, 68
Cancelling dialogue boxes, 41
Cancelling highlighted text, 32
Cardfile, 175-181
    autodialing, 180-181
    editing, 178-179
    index line, 175-176
    information area, 175
    marker card, 177
    modems. 180
    moving around, 178
    page setup,171-172
    paintbrush cutouts, 167
    pasting pictures, 179
    pasting text, 179
    pictures, 179
    printing, 179-180
    restore, 179
    search,178
    merging, 180
Cascading windows, 39
Case changing - write, 146
Centred text - write, 159
Change all button - write, 154
Change attributes option - file manager, 76
Change in notepad, 171
Change option - write, 154
Change selection button - write, 154

Index

Changing case - write, 146
Changing fonts - write, 155-157
Changing hardware - Windows setup, 243-244
Changing program description, 62
Changing program icons, 62
Changing program manager groups, 63
Character attributes - paintbrush, 124
Character attributes - write, 155, 157
Checking - hard disk, 247
CHKDSK, 247-248,262, 264
Choosing a palette, 117
Choosing file type - paintbrush, 132
Choosing from dialogue boxes, 42-44
Clearing - calculator, 188
Clearing - clipboard, 165
Clicking the mouse, 29-30
Clicking the mouse - arrow, 30
Clicking the mouse - Ibar, 31
Clipboard, 164-168
    clearing, 165 delete, 165
    display formats, 166
    non-Windows applications, 257
Clipboard and calculator, 167, 198-199
Clipboard files - saving, 165
Clock,182-183
    menu options, 182
    minimised, 182-183
Closing a menu, 36
.Clp files, 165
CMOSRAM, 249-250, 267
CMOS RAM - battery, 252
Codes - page setup, 171-172
Colour eraser tool, 126
Colour palette, 109-110
Colour schemes - ready made, 109
Colour selection box, 118
Colour settings - control panel, 109-111
Coloured background, 117
Colours
    adding, 111
    creating, 129
    customised - control panel, 110, 112
dithered,111
    mixing, 110-111
.Com files, 58
Communication link testing, 209-211
Communication parameters, 101
Communication settings - terminal, 205
Compacting your hard disk, 273-274
Config.sys, 173, 236-237, 241, 272
Configuring printers, 102, 105
Confirm on delete - file manager, 74, 86
Confirm on mouse operation - file manager, 86

Confirm on replace - file manager, 86
Confirm on subtree delete - file manager, 86
Confirmation option - file manager, 85
Control panel, 94-113
    colour settings, 109-111
    date time settings, 99
    desktop settings, 112-113
    fonts settings, 105-106
    international settings, 95
    keyboard settings, 99
    mouse settings, 100
    port settings, 101
    printer settings, 102-105
    sound settings, 99
Converting files to a WP not compatible with write - tip, 140-141
Converting from write format, 140
Converting text only files, 169
Converting to write format, 140
Copy disk option - file manager, 87-88
Copy option - file manager, 75
Copying a help topic, 52
Copying cutouts, 121-122
Copying cutouts - tip, 122
Copying the screen, 168
Country - control panel, 95
Courier font, 123
Crashrecovery, 263-264
Crashes, 7, 263
Create directory option - file manager, 73
Creating a log - tip, 172
Creating a RAM disk may rename drives - tip, 24
Creating an archive, 87
Creating backups,5-6
Creating colours, 129
Creating groups in program manager, 63
Cross references - help, 51
Cures for nibbled paintbrush printouts - tip, 135
Cures for terminal ills, 217
Currency format- control panel, 98
Cursor - blink rate, 114
Cursor - definition, 30
Curve tool, 128
Customised colours, 110, 112
Cut and paste - paintbrush, 120
Cut and paste - write, 148
Cutout tools - general, 121
Cutouts - copying, 121, 122
Cutouts - sweeping, 121

Data bits - terminal communication settings, 205
Database, 175-177
    fields, 176-177

ii

Index

keywords, 176
records, 175-177
Date format - control panel, 97
Date time sent - print manager, 93
Date time settings - control panel, 99
Datestamp in notepad, 172
Day view - calendar, 184
Dealing with the unexpected - tip, 80-81
Default printer, 102
Definition - cursor, 30
Definition - menu, 33
Delete - clipboard, 165
Delete - print manager, 91
Delete option - file manager, 75
Deleting a print job, 91
Deleting directories, 74
Deleting groups in program manager, 63
Deleting highlighted text, 31
Deleting programs, 60
Deselect all option - filemanager, 79-80
Desktop - control panel, 112-113
    border width, 113
    icon spacing, 113
    pattern option, 112
    sizing grid, 113
    wallpaper option, 112-113
Desktop publishing, 138
Device contention options, 108
Device not selected - printer, 103
Dialogue boxes, 41
    cancel button, 41
    choosing from, 42-44
    hidden lists, 43
    lists, 42
    selecting filenames, 57-58
    selection sliders, 43-44
Directories, 21-22
    deleting, 74
    selecting, 73
    windows, 72-73, 83-84
Directories within directories, 22
Disaster recovery, 265-267
Disk - emergency restart, 248-249
Disk - hard, 247, 249-250, 269-270
Disk compacting, 273-274
Disk drives
    description, 6
    names, 24
    primary, 251
    secondary, 251
    selecting, 70-71
Disk partition table, 249-250
Disk space - reclaiming, 69-270
Disks
    floppy, 86-87, 246
    formatting, 88-89
    hard, 246
    labelling, 71
    labelling internally, 88
    repairing - hard, 247-248
Display - not working, 260
Display formats - clipboard, 166
Displaying files - file manager, 84
Dithered colours, 111, 120
DOS - description, 12
DOS prompt, 252
Double click rate, 100
Double clicking the mouse - arrow, 30-31
Double clicking the mouse - I bar, 31
Downside of Windows, 15-16
Dragging the mouse - arrow, 30
Dragging the mouse - I bar, 31
Drive not ready message, 105

E-mail, 201
Edit colours - paintbrush, 129
Editing - cardfile, 178-179
Editing highlighted text, 31
Editing pictures, 120
Editing text in write, 145-146
Editing text in paintbrush, 123
Emergency restart disk, 248 249, 266 267
End task button - task list, 68
Enhanced settings, 107-108
    device contention options, 108
    scheduling options, 108
Eraser tool, 126
Eraser tools - general, 125
Error - unrecoverable application, 44
Example of a path name, 24-25
.Exe files, 58
Expand branch option - file manager, 73
Extended memory, 272
Extensions for filenames, 20-21

FDISK, 250
Fields -databases, 176-177
File
    looking for a, 82-83
    printing to a, 102-103

iii

Index

    selecting one, 74
File attributes, 77
    archive, 77
    hidden, 77
    read only, 77
    system, 77
File compression, 208
File conversions - write, 139
File formats - wordprocessor, 139-140
File manager, 69-89
    associate option, 82
    change attributes option, 76
    confirm on delete, 74, 86
    confirm on mouse operation, 86
    confirm on replace, 86
    confirm on subtree delete, 86
    confirmation option, 85
    copy disk option, 87-88
    copy option, 75
    create directory option, 73
    delete option, 75
    deselect all option, 79-80
    expand branch option, 73
    files displayed by details, 84
    files displayed by name, 84
    files sorted by date, 85
    files sorted by name, 84
    files sorted by size, 84
    files sorted by type, 84
    format diskette option, 88-89
    include option, 84
    label diskette option, 88
    make system diskette option, 89
    minimise on use option, 70
    move option, 75
    open option, 75, 81
    print option, 75
    rename option, 76
    replace on open, 83
    run option, 82
    saving the changes, 89
    search option, 82-83
    select all option, 79-80
    status bar, 70
    tree display, 72
File selection - problems, 80
File size - notepad, 173
File transfer - terminal, 201-202, 208
File transfer protocols, 202,204-205
Filename extensions, 20-21
Filename extensions for back up files, 141-142
Filename selection box, 57-58
Filenames, 20, 59

Files, 20
    adding to program manager, 59-60
    archiving, 269
    deselecting all, 79-80
    displayed by detail - file manager, 84
    displayed by name - file manager, 84
    pif, 253-254
    printing, 93
    recorder, 221-223
    selecting all, 79-80
    selectinglists of, 78
    selecting scattered, 79
    sorted by date - file manager, 85
    sorted by name - file manager, 84
    sorted by size - file manager, 84
    sorted by type - file manager, 84
    text only, 139-140, 169
    Word, 139-140
    working with selected, 81
Find option - write, 151-153
First aid kit, 258-275
Flash option - print manager, 92
Floppy disk capacity, 246
    sizes, 246
Flow control - terminal communication settings, 205
Flow control methods, 210
Font
    courier, 123
    helv, 123
    modern, 123
    roman, 123
    script, 123
    symbol, 123
    system, 123
    terminal, 123
    tms rmn, 123
Fonts, 44
    adding, 105-106
    attributes, 45
    bitmap, 47-48, 156
    changing - paintbrush, 123
    changing - write,155
    in notepad, 171
    outline, 46,48
    printer, 48-49
    removing,105-106
    settings - control panel,105-106
    setup - printers, 49
    Windows, 48
    write, 154-157
Foreground colour, 118
Foreground colours,126

Index

FORMAT, 249
Format diskette option - file manager, 88-89
Formatting disks, 88-89
Function keys - terminal settings, 204

Get colours - paintbrush, 130
Getting on line - terminal, 206
Goto page - write, 154
Graphical environment, 11
Greyed out menu options, 35
Group windows - program manager, 63

Hard disk, 264, 265, 266, 267, 269, 270
    back-up, 246-247
    compacting, 273-274
    repair, 247-248
    checking, 247
    partition table, 249-250
Hardware - changing, 243-244
Headers footers - paintbrush, 133
Headers footers - write, 161-162
Help
    bookmarks, 52
    crossreferences, 51
    files, 50
    key - F1, 50
    making notes, 52
    marking your place, 52
    printer driver, 105
    user guide, 50
Help topic - copying, 52
Help topic - printing, 52
Help window, 51-52
Help window menu, 52
Helvfont, 123
Hidden attribute, 77
Hidden files, 77
Hidden lists in dialogue boxes, 43
Highlighted text, 31
    cancel, 32
    deleting, 31
    editing, 31
    replacing, 31
Holding the mouse - arrow, 30
Housekeeping for Windows, 245-247
How to use tips, 3
Hue/sat/lum boxes - colour settings, 110
Hyphens - optional, 159

I bar, 30-31
Icon spacing - desktop, 113
Image attributes, 116-117
Image attributes - applying changes, 118 I

mage size, 116
Image view, 119-120
    colours, 120
    menu options, 120
    tools, 120
Inactive printer, 102
Include - file manager, 84
Indents - write, 160-161
Index line - cardfile, 175-176
Info button - paintbrush, 131
Information area - cardfile, 175
Installing a printer, 104
Installing another version of Windows, 242-243
Installing printers, 239
Installing Windows, 5, 227-230
    preparation, 228-229
    screens, 231-236, 239-241
    setup, 230-231
International settings - control panel, 95
    country, 95
    currency format, 98
    date format, 97
    keyboard, 96
    language, 96
    list separator, 96
    measurement, 96
    number format, 98
    time format, 98
Interpolating, 117
Invisible characters -searching for, 152

Justified text - write, 160

Keyboard - international, 96
Keyboard commands bypass the menus, 36
Keyboard selection mode, 79
Keyboard settings - control panel, 99
Keyboard shortcuts to selecting menu options, 36
Keywords- database, 176

Label diskette option - file manager, 88
Labelling disks, 71
Language - international, 96
Leaving Windows, 7
Left aligning - write, 159
LHARC, 208
Line spacing - write, 160
Line tools - general, 128
List separator - control panel, 96
Lists in dialogue boxes, 42
Loading Windows disks, 230
Lockups, 7
.Log in notepad, 172

Index

Lost icons - tip, 34

Macro - recorder, 220-223
Make backup - write, 141-142
Make system diskette option - filemanager, 89
Manual page breaks, 144
Markercard - cardfile, 177
Marking text - see Highlighting Marking your place in help, 52
Measurement - international, 96
Memory -calculator, 188-189
Memory - types of, 6
Memory availability, 268-269
Menus
    closing, 36
    definition of, 33
    selecting a, 35
    selecting an option, 35
    Menu options, 35
    greyed out, 35
    calendar, 185-186
    clock, 182
    direct from keyboard, 36
    keyboard shortcuts to selecting, 36
    on/off switches, 36
Merging - cardfiles, 180
Minimise on use option - file manager, 70
Minimise on use option - program manager, 65
Minimised - clock, 182-183
Minimising windows, 34-35
Minimum timeslice, 108
Mixing colours, 110-111
Modems, 202-203
    cardfile, 180
    commands - terminal settings, 205
Modern font, 123
Monthview - calendar, 184
Mouse
    buttons, 29
    click - arrow, 30
    click - I bar, 31
    controls - changing, 32
    double click -arrow, 30-31
    double click - Ibar, 31
    double click rate, 100
    drag - arrow, 30
    drag - I bar, 31
    hold - arrow, 30
    left right buttons swapping, 100
    not working, 260
    shift click - arrow, 31
    tracking speed, 100
    using the, 28-29

Mouse settings - control panel, 100
Move option - file manager, 75
Moving around
    calendar, 186
    cardfile, 178
    files with the mouse, 37-38
    write files, 145-146
Moving between windows, 38
Moving pictures in write, 150
Moving windows, 33-34
MS-DOS, 69, 76, 227, 236, 247, 248, 262, 263
MS-DOS and Windows, 19-20
MS-DOS path, 258
.Mspfiles, 130
Multitasking, 14, 90, 107-108

Naming files, 20
New option - program manager, 56
New option - paintbrush, 130
Nightmare scenario, 265-267
Non-Windows applications, 107-108, 252-257
    clipboard, 257
    running, 252-253
    window controls, 257
Normal in character menu - write, 157
Normal option - paintbrush, 124
Notepad, 169-174
    change, 171
    datestamp, 172
    file size, 173
    fonts, 171
    page setup, 171-172
    search options, 170
Notepad files - write, 169-170
Notes in help files, 52
Null modem cable, 202, 210
Number format - control panel, 98

.Old files, 238
On line help - using, 50-52
On-line services - using, 206-207
Open info button - paintbrush, 131
Open option - filemanager, 75, 81
Open option - paintbrush, 130-131
Opening - write files, 139-140
Opening a dialogue box by mistake - tip, 41
Opening a file with no extension - tip, 76
Opening a window, 75
Operator precedence, 189-190
Optional hyphens in write - tip, 159
Out of disk space sickness, 269-270
Outof memory - system resources, 269
Out of memory disorder, 268-269

Index

Outline fonts, 46,48
Outline option - paintbrush, 124

Page breaks -
    writeautomatic, 144
    manual, 144
    markers, 143
Page layout options
    paintbrush, 133
    write, 163
Page setup
    calendar, 171-172
    cardfile, 171-172
    codes,171-172
    notepad, 171-172
    paintbrush, 133, 171-172
Page size - write, 143
Paintbrush, 116-136
    character attributes, 124
    cut and paste, 120
    display, 116, 118
    edit colours, 129
    exit, 135,136
    file menu, 130-136
    fonts, 123
    get colours,130
    new option, 130
    normal option, 124
    open info button, 131
    open option,130-131
    outline option,124
    page layout, 133
    page setup option, 133
    print option, 133-134
    printer setup option, 135
    save as option, 131-132
    save colours, 130
    save option,131
    scaling printouts,133-134
    shadow option, 124
    text editing, 123
    undo option, 121
    zooming in,118-119
    zooming out, 119
Paintbrush colours in write, 148
Paintbrush cutouts
    in cardfile, 167
    in write, 167
Paintbrush file types, 132
Paintbrush files in write, 148-150
Paintbrush page layout
    headers and footers, 133
    margins, 133

.Pal files, 130
Palette - choosing a, 117
Paper size - see Image size Parameters - communication, 101
Parity - terminal communication settings, 205
Paste -clipboard, 164
Pasting pictures - cardfile,179
Pasting text - cardfile, 179
Path, 258,275
Path names, 23, 57-59, 83
    example, 24-25
Pattern desktop option, 112
Pause - print manager, 91
Pausing a printer, 91
.Pcx files,130, 132
Permanent swap file, 274-275
Phone number - terminal settings, 203
Pick menu - paintbrush, 122
Picktool, 121
Picture - viewing a, 118
Picture slots - write, 149
Pictures - cardfile, 179
Pif editor, 254-256
Pif editor options
    386 enhanced, 255-256
    advanced - 386
    enhanced, 255-256
    standard mode, 254-255
.Pif files, 253-254
Pixel view, 119, 127
    colours, 119
    menu options, 119
    tools, 119
Point size, 45
Polygon tool, 129
Port settings - control panel, 101
Ports - selecting for printers, 102
Ports - serial, 101
Primary disk drive, 251
Print file size - print manager, 93
Print files, 91, 93
Print manager, 90-93
    buttons, 91
    date time sent, 93
    disadvantages, 93
    flash option, 92
    print file size, 93
    priority option, 92
Print option - file manager, 75
Print option - paintbrush, 133-134
Print queues, 90-91
Print screen key,167-168
Printed picture problems, 117,124-125
Printer

vii

Index

active, 102
adding a,103, 104
configuring a,102
default, 102
device not selected, 103
fonts, 48-49
inactive, 102
installing a, 104, 239
ports, 102
removing a,103
setup, 103
timeouts,102
transmission retry, 103
unlisted, 104
Printer driver, 104
Printer driver helpfiles, 105
Printer settings - control panel, 102-105
Printer setup option - paintbrush, 135
Printer setup option - write, 143
Printing - cardfile, 179-180
Printing - write, 142-143
Printing a file- file manager, 75
Printing a help topic, 52
Printing to a file, 102-103
Priority option - print manager, 92
Program description - file manager, 60-62
Program icons, 60, 62
Program manager, 54-66, 252-253
    adding programs to, 56, 58-59
    arrange icon option, 65
    auto arrange option, 64
    changing groups, 63
    creating groups, 63
    delete option, 60
    deleting groups, 63
    group windows, 63
    minimise on use option, 65
    new option, 56
    properties option, 61-62
    recorder macros, 223-224
    saving changes to, 66
    selecting a group, 65-66
    Windows setup, 58-59
Program manager and files, 59-60
Programming functions - calculator, 192-195
Programs - running, 55-56
Properties option- program manager, 61, 62

Queues for printing, 90-91

RAM, 6
RAM - CMOS, 249-250
Ramdrv.sys, 273

Read only file attribute, 77
Reboot, 240-241
Reclaiming disk space, 269-270
Recorder, 218-225
    files, 221-223
    macros, 220-223
    macros - program manager, 223-224
    problems, 225
    shortcut keys, 224
Records - databases, 175-177
Recovering from a disaster, 265-267
Recovering from crashes, 263-264
Red/green/blue boxes - colour settings, 110
Removed printer - reinstalling a, 105
Removing a printer, 103
Removing fonts, 105-106
Rename option - file manager, 76
Repaginate option - write,143-145
Repairing damage to hard disks, 247-248
Repeat last find option - write,153-154
Replace on open option - file manager, 83
Replacing highlighted text, 31
Reset, 7, 8, 240-241, 264
Restore option - cardfile, 179
Resume button - print manager, 91
Right aligning - write, 159
Roller tool, 126-127
Roman font, 123
Root directory, 23
RS-232, 202- 203
Ruler - write, 158
Run option - file manager, 82
Running non-Windows applications, 252-253
Running programs, 55-56
Running Windows, 241, 258-259

Save as option - paintbrush, 131-132
Save colours - paintbrush, 130
Save option - paintbrush, 131
Saving - clipboard files, 165
Saving - write files, 140
Saving changes to program manager, 66
Saving settings - terminal, 206
Saving the changes - file manager, 89
Scaling printouts - paintbrush, 133-134
Scheduling options - 386
    enhanced, 108
Scientific calculator, 189-197
Scientific functions - calculator, 191-192
Scissor tool, 121
Screen - copying the, 168
Screen view - paintbrush, 120-121
Scriptfont, 123

Index

Scroll bars, 36-38
Search option - cardfile, 178
Search for upper lower case - write, 153
Search for whole words - write, 153
Search guidelines - write, 151
Search menu - write, 151-153
Search option - file manager, 82-83
Search options - notepad, 170
Searching for invisible characters - write, 152
Searching with wildcards - write,152
Secondary disk drive, 251
Select all option - filemanager, 79-80
Selected files - working with, 81
Selecting a group - program manager, 65-66
Selecting a menu, 35
Selecting a menu option, 35
Selecting all files - filemanager, 79-80
Selecting blocks of text with the mouse - tip, 146
Selecting directories, 73
Selecting disk drives, 70-71
Selecting file/path names from dialogue boxes - tip, 57-58
Selecting files - problems, 80
Selecting files with keyboard, 79
Selecting fonts in notepad calendar and cardfile, 171
Selecting lists of files, 78
Selecting one file, 74
Selecting pictures - write, 149-150
Selecting scattered files, 79
Selecting text - highlighting, 31
Selecting text from the margin - write, 146
Selection mode- keyboard, 79
Selection sliders in dialogue boxes, 43-44
Send option - terminal, 209
Serial ports, 101
Set up applications option - Windows setup, 58-59
Setting up a printer, 103
Setting up printer fonts, 49
Settings - terminal, 203-205
Setup
    modifications to autoexec.bat, 237-238
    modifications to config.sys, 237-238
    Windows installation by, 230-231
Shadow option - paintbrush, 124
Shapetool, 129
Shift clicking the mouse -arrow, 31
Shift F1, 50
Shortcut keys -recorder, 224
Size menu - paintbrush,124
Sizing grid - desktop, 113
Slowness syndrome, 272
Smartdrv.sys, 272-273
Sorting files - file manager, 84-85
Sound settings - control panel, 99

Standard calculator, 189
Statistical functions - calculator, 197
Statistics box
    calculator, 195-197
    other uses for, 198
Status bar - file manager, 70
Stop bits - terminal communication settings, 205
Style menu - paintbrush, 123-124
Sub directories, 22
Subtrees, 22
Swap file - permanent, 274-275
Swapping left right mouse buttons, 100
Sweeping cutouts, 121
Switch menu options, 36
Switch to button - task list, 68
.Syd files, 174
Symbol font, 123
System attribute, 77
System configuration editor, 174
System directory contents, 271
System font, 123
System.ini, 174
System resources - running out of, 269

Tabs - write, 162-163
Task list, 67-68
    arrange icon button, 68
    cancel button, 68
    end task button, 68
    switch to button, 68
Terminal, 200-217
    advantages, 201
    disadvantages, 201
    filetransfer, 201-202, 208
    getting on line, 206
    on-line services, 207
    saving settings, 206
    send option, 209
    testing strategy, 212-216
    ills -cures, 217
Terminal font, 123
Terminal settings, 203-205
    binary transfer, 205
    function keys, 204
    modem commands, 205
    phone number, 203
    terminal emulation, 204
    terminal preferences, 204
    text transfer, 204
Testing communication links, 209-211
Testing strategy - terminal, 212-216
Text editing, 145-146
Text editor, 137

Index

Text only files,139-140, 169
Text sizes in paintbrush printouts - tip, 124-125
Text tool, 122-123
Text transfer - terminal settings, 204
Tilingwindows, 39
Time format - international, 98
Timeouts - printer, 102
Tip - before running non-Windows programs, 253
Tip - check tosee what additional software needs, 98
Tip - converting files to a WP not compatible with write, 140-141
Tip - copying cutouts, 122
Tip - creating a log, 172
Tip - creating a RAM disk may rename drives, 24
Tip - cures for nibbled paintbrush printouts, 135
Tip -dealing with the unexpected, 80-81
Tip - don't get confusedbetween buttons, 40
Tip - don't get trigger happy with OK buttons, 42
Tip - don't hide an inner window's title bar, 40
Tip - don't tabulate text already in paragraphs, 163
Tip - don't use filemanager options on open files, 78
Tip - how to find which drive is which, 24
Tip - how to leave Windows using the keyboard, 7
Tip - if a file appears to be empty, 37
Tip - if you lose the programmanager, 54
Tip - if you open a dialogue box by mistake, 41
Tip -limits of using calculator with clipboard, 190-191
Tip - lost icons, 34
Tip - lots of unrecoverable application errors, 263
Tip - not sure where a file is, 27
Tip - opening a file/running a program without program manager, 60
Tip - opening a file with no extension, 76
Tip - opening a window, 75
Tip - optional hyphens inwrite, 159
Tip - page setup codes in notepad calendar and cardfile, 171-172
Tip - paragraphs that should follow one another,160
Tip - putting in manual page breaks without repaginate, 144
Tip - recovering from Windows induced amnesia, 238-239
Tip - running CHKDSK from within Windows, 248
Tip - selecting blocks oftext with the mouse, 146
Tip - selecting different trees, 71
Tip - selecting file path names from dialogue boxes, 57-58
Tip - selecting fonts in notepad calendar and cardfile, 171
Tip - shift F1, 50 Tip - size of printed image, 134-135
Tip - spend time arranging your screen, 38-39
Tip - text sizes in paintbrush printouts, 124-125
Tip - to edit a highlighted area of text, 31-32
Tip - to print all available fonts, 155
Tip - two cursors, 30
Tip- using setup from MS-DOS, 261
Tip - what is a point, 45

Tip - what's virtual memory, 260
Tip - X and Y co-ordinates, 120
Tips - how to use them, 3
Tms rmn font, 123
Tool box, 227=257
Tools - paintbrush
    airbrush, 122
    brush,127-128
    colour eraser, 126
    curve,128
    cutout, 121
    eraser, 126
    erasers general, 125
    line general, 128
    pick,121
    polygon, 129
    roller, 126 -127
    scissor, 121
    shape,129
    text, 122-123
Transmission retry - printer, 103
Tree display - file manager, 72
Trees, 22-23
TSR programs,236-237, 259
.Txt files, 170
Types of memory, 6

UAE, 261-263
UAE - after a, 262
Undo option - paintbrush, 121
Undo options - write,147-148
    editing - write, 147
    formatting - write, 147-148
    typing - write, 147
Unlisted printer, 104
Unrecoverable application error (UAE), 44, 261-263
Use printer resolution,117, 134
User guide as a source of help, 50

Vector fonts - see Outline fonts
Viewing a picture, 118

Wallpaper - desktop option, 112-113
Wallpaper and memory, 268
Wildcards,25-26, 57, 80, 82-83
Wildcards as search aids - write, 152-153
Win, 227, 258-259
Win.ini, 94, 173, 182-183
Window
    active, 38
    altering the size of, 34
    border width, 113
    control button, 33

Index

control menu, 33
controls - non-Windows applications, 257
Windows - working with
    cascading, 39
    minimised, 34-35
    moving, 33-34
    moving between, 38
    tiling,39
    within windows,39-40
Windows and MS-DOS, 19-20
    benefits of,13-15
    directory contents, 271
    disks- loading, 230
    downside, 15-16
    housekeeping, 245-247
    installation, 227-241
    installation - preparation, 228-229
    installing another version, 242-243
    odes, 259
    performance - improving, 272
    running, 241,258-259
Windows setup, 58-59, 241-245
    adding applications, 244-245
    changing hardware, 243, 244
Word files, 139-140
Wordprocessor, 137-138
Working with cutouts, 121
Write, 137-163
    aligning text, 158-160
    altering picture size, 150-151
    centred text, 159
    change all button, 154
    change option, 154
    change selection button, 154
    changing case, 146
    changing fonts, 155-157
    character attributes, 155, 157
    file conversions, 139
    find option, 151-153
    fonts, 154-157
    go to page, 154
    headers/footers, 161-162
    indents,160 - 161
    justified text, 160
    leftaligning, 159
    line spacing, 160
    makebackup, 141-142
    moving pictures, 150
    normal option - character menu, 157
    page break markers, 143
    page layout options, 163
    page size, 143
    paintbrushcolours, 148

paintbrush cutouts, 167
paintbrush files, 148-150
pictureslots, 149
printer setup, 143
repaginate, 143-145
repeat last findoption, 153-154
ight aligning, 159
ruler, 158
search for upper lower case,153
search for whole words, 153
search guidelines, 151
search menu, 151-153
searching for invisible characters, 152
searching with wildcards, 152
selecting pictures, 149-150
selecting text from the margin, 146
tabs, 162-163 text only files, 139-140
undo, 148
undo editing,147
undo formatting, 147-148
undo option, 147
undo typing, 147
wildcards as search aids, 152-153
Write file format converting from, 140
    converting to, 140
Write files, 139
    opening, 139-140
    printing, 142-143
    saving, 140
Wysiwyg, 45-46

X and Y co-ordinates - tip, 120
Xon Xoff, 210

Zooming in - paintbrush, 118-119
Zooming out - paintbrush, 119

Index